Opera Seria and the
Evolution of Classical Style
1755–1772

Studies in Musicology, No. 78

George Buelow, Series Editor

Professor of Music
Indiana University

Other Titles in This Series

Opera Seria and the
Evolution of Classical Style
1755–1772

by
Eric Weimer

UMI RESEARCH PRESS
Ann Arbor, Michigan

Produced and distributed by
UMI Research Press
an imprint of
University Microfilms International
A Xerox Information Resources Company
Ann Arbor, Michigan 48106

Library of Congress Cataloging in Publication Data

Weimer, Eric.
  Opera seria and the evolution of classical style,
1775-1772.

  (Studies in musicology ; no. 78)
  Revision of thesis (doctoral)—University of Chicago,
1982.
  Bibliography: p.
  Includes index.
  1. Opera—18th century—History and criticism.
I. Title. II. Series.
ML1704.W44 1984   782.1'09'033   84-2699
ISBN 0-8357-1581-7

To JPV

Contents

List of Tables

List of Figures

Preface

I am most grateful to those publishers who kindly gave permission to reprint material as musical examples. The excerpt from Jommelli's *Fetonte* is taken from the Denkmäler deutscher Tonkunst edition (published by Breitkopf & Härtel, Wiesbaden); the passages from Hasse's *Ruggiero* derive from Klaus Hortschansky's edition (published by Arno Volk, Cologne); all the Haydn examples are taken from the Diletto musicale edition of the symphonies, copyright © 1966 by Ludwig Doblinger, Vienna, reprinted courtesy of Associated Music Publishers, Inc., U.S. agents.

* * *

My interest in the music of eighteenth-century opera seria was sparked in the Spring of 1976, when Professor Howard Mayer Brown conducted a graduate seminar at the University of Chicago on opera seria. Professor Brown then asked me to assist him in the preparation of what was to become the first series of *Italian Opera, 1640-1770* (New York: Garland Publishing, 1978), a sixty-volume set of facsimiles of manuscript scores and printed librettos. As I perused more and more operas, I was surprised by the high quality of the arias—many of them reveal considerable depth, ingenuity, and dynamism. As I read the secondary literature on the forty-five composers represented in the first series of *Italian Opera,* however, I was struck by the lack of scholarly attention to and understanding of this music. Most important, I realized that opera seria arias, most of which can be dated quite precisely, offer a superb context in which to investigate the evolution of musical style.

I decided to focus on the arias in the opere serie composed between 1755 and 1772 by Johann Adolf Hasse, Niccolò Jommelli, and Johann Christian Bach, these composers having already been the subject of rigorous biographical and bibliographical investigation. The resulting study concerns not only these three men, however, but also the stylistic milieu in which they worked. After an introduction to the composers and their operas (chapter 1), each chapter treats a separate aspect of style and/or style change in the third quarter of the eighteenth century. And several chapters introduce evidence from the operas of composers other than Hasse, Jommelli, and J.C. Bach.

Chapter 2 traces harmonic expansion, one of the key ingredients in the evolution of the preclassical and early classical styles. This chapter considers harmonic rhythm in the operas not only of Hasse, Jommelli, and J.C. Bach but also of twenty-nine other composers of the period 1716-84. Chapter 3, the core of the book, examines the nature of "classical counterpoint" in the mature works of Haydn and Mozart and traces its development in the late operas of Jommelli and the early symphonies of Haydn. Chapter 4, the first of three chapters devoted to orchestration, sets forth standard patterns of combining wind instruments and compares the wind instrumentations prescribed by Hasse, Jommelli, and J.C. Bach (and, to a lesser extent, Gluck and Traetta) with the size and make-up of the particular orchestras for which they composed their operas. Chapters 5 and 6 trace, respectively, the evolution of Hasse's oboe parts from baroque to classical style and the growth in size and independence of the woodwind component of the orchestra.

To complete this project, I have benefitted from the kind assistance of many people. Howard Brown generously put his large collection of microfilms at my disposal and offered advice at every step of the way. Marita McClymonds presented me with a substantial amount of material pertaining to Jommelli's operas, and Frederick Millner frequently advised me about the reliability of certain Hasse manuscripts. Without their help, I would doubtless have made many fundamental bibliographical errors. Robert Sullivan and Patrick Gallagher offered many invaluable suggestions regarding writing style and the organization of material. Professor Robert Morgan of the University of Chicago also read the entire text, offering valuable suggestions, and Lenna Strompolos assembled and typed the bibliography. The Visiting Committee to the Department of Music, University of Chicago, made funds available for the purchasing of some sixty microfilms. Without their generous support, this undertaking would have been impossible. The librarians and staffs of the library of the Conservatorio di musica "Giuseppe Verdi" in Milan, the Österreichische Nationalbibliothek in Vienna, the British Library in London, and the Biblioteca Ajuda in Lisbon cheerfully helped in ways too many to enumerate here. Finally, I would like to thank my parents, whose encouragement and financial assistance were crucial to the completion of this study.

1

Opera Seria as the Subject of Style Analysis

Opera Seria and Classical Style

In the 1760s and 1770s, Metastasian opera seria gradually but inexorably declined in popularity, giving way largely to lighter forms such as opera buffa and Singspiel. The reasons were many. The inevitable alternation of weighty da capo aria and secco recitative, the unrelieved earnestness and high moral tone assumed by all characters, the conventions of the exit aria and *lieto fine*—all contributed to a slowness of pacing and a plot which seemed increasingly artificial and stilted to an audience seeking greater vivacity, naturalness of expression, and variety of subject matter. Also, the vast expenditures required to erect elaborate stage sets and machinery and to support large numbers of virtuoso singers, dancers, and instrumentalists became increasingly difficult to meet. Particularly in the German and Austrian cities that at various times had boasted regular and lavish productions—Vienna, Berlin, Dresden, and Stuttgart—the number of opera seria productions decreased sharply.[1]

But the extent and consequences of this decline should not be exaggerated. In Italy, composers continued to set Metastasio's beloved texts well into the 1780s and 1790s. Elsewhere, productions were fewer but nonetheless consequential for dramatists, composers, and singers alike. Even Mozart, whose present reputation as an opera composer rests primarily on his opere buffe and Singspiel, at least in the late 1770s desired nothing more than to compose a grand opera seria,[2] both to express his own taste in opera and to secure a permanent position. More important, while the text and large-scale musical organization of opera seria retained much that seems archaic, the music itself—the arias first and foremost, but also the sinfonias, accompanied recitatives, and occasional ensembles—continued to evolve stylistically. This book will document such development in the opere serie of three leading composers of the 1760s and early 1770s. In the absence of any proof to the contrary, in fact, one can assume that such style change paralleled and kept pace with that of the younger, ultimately more popular genres, such as opera buffa, string quartet, and symphony. The music of Mozart's great opera seria *Idomeneo* (Munich, 1781)—its textures, counterpoint, phrase rhythm, intricate wind writing, and so on—is no less "modern" than the Haffner Symphony or the first of the six "Haydn Quartets" (K. 387), both of which he composed within the following two years. By the same token, as we shall see, remarkably similar stylistic innovations pervade Niccolò Jommelli's opere serie of 1770-71 and Joseph Haydn's symphonies of 1770-72. The setting of old-fashioned texts simply did not necessitate the composition of old-fashioned music.

In recognition of the importance of opera seria in the musical life of the eighteenth century, research into the genre has burgeoned recently. Curiously, however, we have learned little about the music itself: the circumstances of performance and their effect on the music, the styles of individual composers, and the relation of these styles to general currents of style change. For one thing, most studies focus on one composer, or on one period of a composer's life, or on just one opera.[3] Such exclusive focus precludes a rigorous assessment of a composer's importance or the delineation of overall style and style change. Second, the chaotic state in which many of the manuscript sources survive has forced scholars to concentrate on basic biographical and bibliographical problems: comparing manuscript scores with printed librettos, identifying different versions of the same opera and determining their dates and places of performance, ferreting out misattributed manuscripts and substitute arias, and so on. This work is indeed essential, and much more remains to be done. At the same time, however, such concerns should not monopolize our research. We do not need to examine every manuscript copy of an opera before evaluating the music itself, nor do we need to investigate every composer of the time— major and minor alike—before drawing conclusions about the period in general.

Third, analysis of opera seria arias generally deals with the music chiefly in terms of the text. Those formal, melodic, harmonic, and orchestral effects that seem to serve dramatic ends thus receive the most attention. But an investigation of such links between drama and music, though essential to our understanding of a composer as dramatist, necessitates a case-by-case approach that rarely does justice to all aspects of the music, most of which bears only a loose relation to the text. Such obviously unrelated aspects of the music include the length and structure of the orchestral ritornellos, the manner in which the composer modulates to a secondary key, the type of sequences and other conventional harmonic progressions used for extended melismas, the structural function of wind instruments, and the general rate of harmonic change. Such matters had little to do with either the text or other circumstances of an opera's first performance, such as the singer for whom the aria was written, the orchestra that was to accompany the singer, or the impresario or aristocratic patron who engaged the composer. Rather, they were bound inextricably with, and should be considered in the context of, larger issues of style in the eighteenth century: the polarization of tonic and dominant tonalities, the decrease in the rate of harmonic change, the evolution of a more subtle relation between melody and accompaniment, the emergence of more articulated harmonic and phrase structures, and a gradual redefinition of the orchestral function of woodwinds.

When analyzed in these terms, the massive repertoire of opera seria arias, duets, and sinfonias has much to tell us about style and style change, and in the context not only of opera seria but of all genres. Meriting particular attention is the decade of the 1760s and the first years of the 1770s, certainly one of the critical periods of Western music. It was then that the young Mozart traveled to the leading music centers of Europe—Vienna, Mannheim, Paris, London, Rome, Naples, and Venice—absorbing all that the best composers of the day had to offer. It was then also that Haydn, twenty-four years Mozart's senior, began composing symphonies and chamber works in such great numbers and made his most profound stylistic advances: whereas his symphonies and string quartets of the early 1760s are short, light, and showy, those of the early 1770s are longer, more intense and dramatic, and more complex and contrapuntal.

Despite the obvious importance of this period, we have too little precise information about the elements comprising Haydn's stylistic growth, the manner and time in which they appeared, and the extent to which other composers shared in the process. More generally, we know too little about the relation of Haydn's and Mozart's early music to that of their contemporaries. Partly responsible is the bewildering array of composers and the mountains of surviving operas, chamber works, symphonies, etc., many of which defy exact dating. The sheer numbers of sources render it difficult to define the period at all.

Also responsible for the lack of research into the musical styles of the 1760s is the point of view that Haydn and Mozart developed what we call "classical style" entirely on their own. Charles Rosen, whose book *The Classical Style: Haydn, Mozart, Beethoven*[4] has in only a few years become a standard text on the subject, asserts that the classical style *is* the music of Haydn, Mozart, and Beethoven:

> It is only in the works of Haydn, Mozart, and Beethoven that all the contemporary elements of musical style—rhythmic, harmonic, and melodic—work coherently together, or that the ideals of the period are realized on a level of any complexity...the work of Haydn and Mozart cannot be understood against the background of their contemporaries.[5]

As far as Rosen is concerned, these three giants single-handedly welded the new style out of the disparate, imperfect, and often contradictory ingredients already present in the music of the 1750s and 1760s. The mature classical period therefore began c. 1775, the preceding two decades possessing no style of its own:

But a style of such power or integration did not exist before the work of Mozart and Haydn in the late 1770s. Before then the scene was more chaotic with many seemingly equal rival forces; for this reason the period from the death of Handel to Haydn's *Scherzi* (or *Russian*) Quartets, op. 33, is difficult to describe.

It is the lack of any integrated style... between 1755 and 1775 that makes it tempting to call this period "mannerist."[6]

While Rosen's analyses of Mozart's and Haydn's works of the late 1770s and 1780s are perceptive and well reasoned, his account of the composers and music of the 1760s and early 1770s is cursory and misleading. Figures such as Johann Christian Bach, Karl Ditters von Dittersdorf, and Luigi Boccherini are dismissed with a few generalizations (mostly pejorative). Even Haydn's earlier works, such as the monumental string quartets and symphonies of 1770-74, receive scant attention. The chapter entitled "String Quartet" proceeds immediately to Haydn's op. 33 of 1781; the following chapter, "Symphony," when briefly treating the works of the early 1770s, devotes too much space to criticisms of Symphony no. 43 ("Merkur"), arguably one of the weakest of these works, and to contrapuntal and motivic techniques used in several passages of the Symphonies nos. 46 and 47. Only the music of Carl Philipp Emanual Bach and Christoph Willibald Gluck is discussed at any length, and it must be due largely to Bach's music—"violent, expressive, brilliant, continuously surprising, and often incoherent"[7]—as well as Gluck's—with its "pages of incoherence, harmonically and in particular rhythmically"[8]—that Rosen labels the period 1755-75 "mannerist."

While C.P.E. Bach and Gluck were unquestionably two of the leading composers of the mid-century, their music does not necessarily speak for the period as a whole. Both were aggressively individualistic, their careers shaped by unusual events or circumstances. Bach's training at the hands of his father Johann Sebastian in Leipzig differed substantially from the first-hand Italian training that so many of his contemporaries shared. Moreover, he traveled little, living his entire adult life in the relative isolation of Berlin and Hamburg. Gluck's experience was more cosmopolitan but nonetheless unique. Essentially self-taught as a composer, he traveled extensively, encountering Handel's oratorios during a stay in England in 1745-46. Most important, through his work revising and preparing French ballets and opéras comiques for performance in Vienna in the 1750s, Gluck acquired an intimate knowledge of French literary and operatic styles and traditions. Crucial factors such as these could not help but bring about rather idiosyncratic music. Our opinion of the relation of Haydn and Mozart to their contemporaries should therefore not rest solely upon a comparison of the styles of Haydn and Mozart with those of Gluck and C.P.E. Bach. We need instead to look at composers closer geographically, culturally, and to some extent chronologically. (C.P.E. Bach and Gluck, both born in 1714, were one generation removed from Haydn and two generations removed from Mozart.)

One direction in which to look for a compositional "mainstream," or at least a style that more directly and intimately influenced Haydn and Mozart, is the school of Italian or Italian-trained composers active in Italy and in the more cosmopolitan German and Austrian outposts of Italian culture, such as Vienna, Dresden, Stuttgart, Mannheim, and Munich. Mozart, after all, spent fifteen months of his childhood in London, where he came into contact with the thoroughly Italianized J.C. Bach; he heard performances of Italian opera throughout his European travels; and he spent a total of almost two years of his adolescence studying in Italy itself. Haydn lacked first-hand Italian experience but admitted to having learned the "true fundamentals of composition" from the Italian opera composer Nicola Porpora in the mid-1750s. While his isolation at Eszterháza and Eisenstadt from 1761 and the lack of imported operas in the Eszterháza repertoire before 1776 argues against further Italian influence in the period 1761-76, Haydn did visit Vienna periodically, and the stylistic parallels found in his symphonies of 1770-72 and Jommelli's operas of the same period (see chapter 3) strongly suggest that he was by no means cut off entirely from the music of the outside world.

To explore major issues of style and style change in the 1760s and early 1770s, this book will investigate the opere serie of such Italian or Italian-trained composers. The primary focus of the study will consist of the 641 arias belonging to the thirty-five fully extant opere serie composed in 1755-72 by three leading figures in that genre: Johann Adolf Hasse, Niccolò Jommelli, and Johann Christian Bach. Some of the results of this study will be compared with style change in two secondary repertoires: (1) the fifty-seven symphonies composed by Haydn from the beginning of his career as a symphonist in the late 1750s to 1772 and (2) a broad spectrum of fifty-five other opere serie by thirty-two composers from 1716 to 1784. In the course of developing methods to monitor style change in this period, we will find that certain standard accounts of the stylistic evolution of Hasse, Jommelli, J.C. Bach, and even Haydn are quite imprecise if not fundamentally in error. Further, we shall see that some theories concerning the evolution of classical style itself—the role played by composers other than Haydn and Mozart, and the time and context in which various elements of the style first appeared—deserve serious rethinking.

Hasse, Jommelli, J.C. Bach, and their Operas

Hasse, Jommelli, and J.C. Bach, the composers of the 641 arias forming the primary repertoire under investigation, deserve study on three counts. First, their operas have already been the object of fairly thorough bibliographical investigation and source criticism. In particular, the lists of manuscript sources compiled by Frederick Millner for the operas of Hasse,[9] by Marita McClymonds for the operas of Jommelli,[10] and by Edward Downes for the operas of J.C. Bach[11] allow one to proceed directly to considerations of style. Second, their careers varied enormously, each composer representing a different generation. Considered together, they worked in all the major centers of Italian opera—Naples, Rome, Venice, Milan, Vienna, Mannheim, Stuttgart, Dresden, and London—and thus encountered various traditions as well as different concepts of opera "reform." It is scarcely an exaggeration to claim that their music presents us with a cross-section of European style currents. Third, each composer was a major figure in his own right.

Johann Adolf Hasse (1699-1783), the oldest of the three composers, began his career as a singer in Hamburg and Brunswick. In 1722, he set off for Italy, where he traveled extensively, studied with Nicolà Porpora and Alessandro Scarlatti, and eventually composed numerous operas for Naples, Venice, and Milan. In 1731, he inaugurated what was to become a long and brilliant career as maestro di capella to the Saxon Electoral court at Dresden. The fame of his Dresden opera performances traveled far and wide, and he continued to receive commissions elsewhere: Turin, Rome, Naples, Bologna, Pesaro, Vienna, and especially Venice.

The year 1755—the beginning of the seventeen-year period under investigation here—thus found Hasse in Dresden, where he still reigned over the operatic establishment. One year later, however, the Seven Years' War broke out, Frederick the Great of Prussia invaded Saxony, and Hasse's patron, Elector Friedrich August II, fled to Warsaw. Hasse eventually returned to Italy where in 1758-60 he composed five more operas for Naples and Venice. Soon the Imperial family in Vienna began awarding him commissions for both feste teatrale and an opera seria *(Il trionfo di Clelia),* and in autumn 1760 Hasse and his family settled in Vienna where he would remain a court favorite of the Empress Maria Theresia. At the same time, Hasse continued to compose operas (*Zenobia* and *Siroe*) for the Electoral court still in exile in Warsaw, and he may also have directed revivals of his earlier works there. Upon conclusion of the war in 1763, Hasse even resumed his old post in Dresden. After the performance of only one opera *(Siroe),* however, the Elector died and the new ruler dismissed Hasse unceremoniously. The composer returned to Vienna, received an Imperial commission *(Romolo ed Ersilia)* for the wedding of Archduke Leopold (later Emperor Leopold II) to Maria Luisa of Bourbon, and then resolved to retire from the operatic stage. Eventually the Imperial family intervened, prevailing upon him to compose an opera seria to celebrate the wedding of Archduke Ferdinand and Maria Beatrice d'Este in Milan in 1771. This work, *Ruggiero,* was Hasse's last opera seria.

During the period 1755-72, Hasse composed at least fourteen opere serie.[12] For two of these he mostly borrowed music from his earlier operas.[13] This study will consider only the remaining twelve opere serie, each of which contains mostly new music and survives complete:

1. *Ezio,* second version (Dresden, January 20, 1755)
2. *Il re pastore* (Dresden,[14] October 7, 1755)
3. *Olimpiade* (Dresden, February 16, 1756)
4. *Nitteti* (Venice, Carnival of 1758)
5. *Demofoonte,* second version (Naples, November 4, 1758)
6. *Achille in Sciro* (Naples, November 4, 1759)
7. *Artaserse,* second version (Naples, January 20, 1760)
8. *Zenobia* (Warsaw, October 7, 1761)
9. *Il trionfo di Clelia* (Vienna, April 27, 1762)
10. *Siroe* (Warsaw,[15] Carnival of 1763)
11. *Romolo ed Ersilia* (Innsbruck, August 6, 1765)
12. *Ruggiero* (Milan, October 16, 1771).

Niccolò Jommelli (1714-74) also received his training in Naples but made his debut as a composer of opere serie in 1740 with his *Ricimero, re de'Goti* (produced in Rome). Over the next thirteen years, he composed no less than thirty more such works, most for Italy—Rome, Venice, Turin, Naples, and Parma, among others—but a few for Vienna. In 1754, Jommelli became "Musikdirektor und Oberkapellmeister" at Stuttgart, a position he would maintain for fifteen years, and the year 1755 saw the production of *Pelope,* Jommelli's first Stuttgart opera to survive. His patron, Duke Carl Eugen, wanting to transform his opera house into the showcase of the realm, made Jommelli supreme head of his musical establishment and rewarded him with every conceivable amenity. Jommelli, for his part, molded the orchestra into one of the best disciplined ensembles in Europe and composed opera after opera into which he frequently incorporated unusually large numbers of ensembles and accompanied recitatives as well as certain French elements: programmatic orchestral music, choruses, spectacle, and long scene complexes. Soon he acquired a reputation as one of the most original opera composers of the day. By the late 1760s, however, the Duke faced his subjects' growing resentment over oppressive fiscal policies and so in sweeping dismissals began to release dancers, singers, and instrumentalists. Jommelli, fearing for his wife's deteriorating health, returned to Italy in 1769. (Since 1754, he had journeyed to Italy only once, producing two operas in Naples and Rome in 1757.) After his return to Italy, Jommelli composed another spate of operas, most for Naples and Rome but one for a patron who now became Jommelli's staunchest supporter: King José I of Portugal. After 1772, Jommelli composed but one more opera seria, *Il trionfo di Clelia* (Lisbon, 1774), not included in this study.

All told, Jommelli composed twenty-five opere serie during the period 1755-72.[16] Only sixteen survive:

1. *Pelope* (Stuttgart, February 11, 1755)
2. *Artaserse,* second version (Stuttgart, August 30, 1756)
3. *Creso* (Rome, February 5, 1757)

 4. *Temistocle* (Naples, December 18, 1757)
 5. *Olimpiade* (Stuttgart, February 11, 1761)
 6. *Semiramide riconosciuta,* third version (Stuttgart, February 11, 1762)
 7. *Didone abbandonata,* third version (Stuttgart, February 11, 1763)
 8. *Demofoonte,* third version (Stuttgart, February 11, 1764)
 9. *Enea nel Lazio,* second version (Stuttgart,[17] January 6, 1766)
10. *Vologeso* (Stuttgart, February 11, 1766)
11. *Fetonte,* second version (Stuttgart, February 11, 1768)
12. *Armida abbandonata* (Naples, May 30, 1770)
13. *Demofoonte,* fourth version[18] (Naples, November 4, 1770)

Johann Christian Bach (1735-82), the youngest of the three composers, was the youngest son of Johann Sebastian Bach. In 1754 he left the care of his brother Carl Philipp Emanuel in Berlin and journeyed to Italy where he studied with the famed Padre Martini in Bologna and became organist at the Cathedral in Milan. He wrote his first opera in 1761 for Turin but was soon lured to Naples, where he enjoyed great acclaim, composing two operas for the same season. In spite of these initial Italian successes—his *Catone in Utica* (Naples, 1761) was revived no less than five times within three years of its premiere[19]—in 1762 Bach went to London where he became music master to Queen Sophie Charlotte and came into frequent contact with the young W.A. Mozart (who lived in England from April 1764 to July 1765). During the remainder of the period under consideration, Bach left England only once; he returned to Germany in 1772 for the performance of *Temistocle,* the first of two operas he was to write for Mannheim.

In all, Bach composed eight opere serie during the period 1755-72, of which seven survive nearly complete:[20]

 1. *Artaserse* (Turin, Carnival of 1761)
 2. *Catone in Utica* (Naples, November 4, 1761)
 3. *Alessandro nell'Indie* (Naples, January 20, 1762)
 4. *Orione* (London, February 19, 1763)
 5. *Adriano in Siria* (London, January 26, 1765)
 6. *Carattaco* (London, February 14, 1767)
 7. *Temistocle* (Mannheim, November 5, 1772)

In all, the thirty-five operas forming the primary repertoire of this study offer a rich and varied sample of mid-eighteenth-century Italian opera. Nine of the operas were written for Naples, the city which served as the training ground for most Italian opera composers and which set standards for the genre through much of the century. Near the opposite end of the spectrum, nine other operas were composed for Stuttgart, where Jommelli, Duke Carl Eugen, and the celebrated French dancing master Jean Georges Noverre strove to fuse the best of Italian and French operatic traditions. One opera was composed for Mannheim, the city whose orchestra thrilled so many with its technical prowess and unusually wide range of dynamics. At least three operas were witnessed in performance by the young Mozart during his travels through Europe: Bach's *Adriano in Siria* (London, 1765), Jommelli's *Armida abbandonata* (Naples, 1770), and Hasse's *Ruggiero* (Milan, 1771).[21] Most important, these operas as a whole were written by some of the best composers of the 1760s and early 1770s. Bach fashioned some of the most forward-looking opera orchestrations of his day (see below, chapters 4 and 6). Moreover, he probably influenced the young Mozart profoundly.[22] Jommelli does not seem to have influenced Mozart or Haydn, yet changes in his textures, accompanimental patterns, and counterpoint c. 1770 bear an uncanny resemblance, even in many minute details, to fundamental changes which revolutionized Haydn's symphonic style at about the same time (see chapter 3).

The Manuscript Sources

A chief factor which has no doubt discouraged scholars from investigating the music of opera seria is the present state of the manuscript sources: their overwhelming numbers and frequent unreliability. For each of countless operas, various manuscript copies can be found in European libraries, each copy differing from the others in many significant details. Such diversity, of course, reflects the conditions under which operas were composed and performed in the eighteenth century. As Donald Grout writes:

> The arias were like Leibniz's monads, each closed off from the others, and all held together only by the "preestablished harmony" of the libretto. Thus their order could be changed, new numbers added, or others taken away, without really doing violence to the musical plan of the opera as a whole—though, needless to say, the drama might suffer. Composers therefore freely substituted new arias for old in revivals of their works, or for performances with a different cast. A composer at Rome, for example, who had orders to revise a Venetian opera to suit the taste of the Roman singers and public, would have no compunction about replacing some of the original composer's arias with some of his own, perhaps taken from an earlier work where they had been sung to different words. Indeed, it was exceptional for an opera to be given in exactly the same form in two different cities.[23]

This process of revision sometimes resulted in a kind of pasticcio, where "an opera...migrated from city to city, undergoing patching and alteration at every stage...."[24] As a result, the modern scholar often faces a plethora of manuscript scores for any one opera. Each of these scores may represent a different stage in this ongoing process of revision and thus differ from the others in a sometimes thoroughly bewildering manner. One might assume that it is practically impossible to identify a composer's original contribution.

While such a bleak assessment of the reliability of the sources may serve as a useful generalization, it does not apply to all operas, at least not to most of those composed by Hasse, Jommelli, and J.C. Bach during the period 1755-72. For one thing, substitutions and revisions that were added to a score are often recognizable as such. Sometimes a copyist added the substitute arias as an appendix; or, he inserted them immediately before or after each of the corresponding original arias. In either case, the older arias remain in the score, and differences in paper size, number of staves per page, or handwriting betray the existence of the new arias.[25]

More significant, many opere serie were performed at only one opera house and during only one season. Such was particularly the case in Germany and Austria, where the production of opera seria was largely a state enterprise, the genre lacking the popular appeal that it enjoyed in Italy. A local ruler subsidized and frequently oversaw many aspects of a work's preparation— musical, dramatic, scenic, and balletic. In mid-century Stuttgart, for example, a significant operatic establishment arose only because of the personal taste, vanity, and extravagance of Duke Carl Eugen, who squandered the resources of both his private funds and the state treasury on lavish opera productions. Further, when a ruler faced a hopeless financial situation or was succeeded by someone with different tastes, the production of serious operas ground to a halt almost immediately.[26] In a climate where the production of opera was so dependent upon the initiative, taste, and financial resources of one ruler, operas were not likely to be exported to other cities; consequently, they were not revised.

Many of the operas which Jommelli and J.C. Bach composed between 1755 and 1772 were in fact produced only once.[27] Although Jommelli had acquired an international reputation by the early 1750s, the operas he composed for Stuttgart between 1754 and 1768—and these account for most of his operatic output of the late 1750s and the 1760s—largely remained in Stuttgart. A few of these works were performed again in Stuttgart in the 1770s and 1780s[28] (after Jommelli had returned to Italy); those that were exported went to one city only: Lisbon.[29] Even most of the seven operas Jommelli composed for Italy between 1755 and 1772 were performed in only one city and during one season. As with some of the Stuttgart operas, one of these Italian operas was revived in the city which saw its premiere;[30] those that were exported went only to Lisbon.

Similarly, Johann Christian Bach enjoyed great success, yet only his *Catone in Utica* (Naples, 1761) and *Alessandro nell'Indie* (Naples, 1762) traveled to other cities. His first opera, *Artaserse* (Turin, 1761), three of his four London operas, and his *Temistocle* (Mannheim, 1772) were performed in only one city and during only one season. (The remaining London opera, *Orione,* was later revived in London.) With most of the operas of Jommelli and Bach having seen such a limited number of performances, the extant manuscript scores do not vary significantly. Those that do have been carefully examined by

Edward Downes and Marita McClymonds so that we know which scores best present the original versions.

The situation with Hasse's operas is more complex; all of the operas he composed during the period under discussion were revived, some fairly frequently. Fortunately, we can consult Hasse's own autograph scores for all but two of his fourteen opere serie dating from this period.[31] The disadvantage of relying on these sources, however, lies in the fact that Hasse prepared some of his own operas for later revivals; most of the operas he composed in 1755-62 for Dresden, Venice, Naples, and Vienna he brought or sent to Warsaw where they were performed for the exiled Electoral court.[32] In addition, seeking to put his manuscripts in order during the last years of his life, Hasse may have further altered and added certain details.[33] The autograph scores thus do not preserve the original versions of Hasse's operas in all respects, although there is little evidence of substantial or crucial alterations other than the addition of oboe and horn parts in ritornellos.

Another problem that must be faced is Hasse's penchant for borrowing music from his earlier arias and fitting them with new words, a practice Jommelli and J.C. Bach rarely followed. By 1755, after all, Hasse had been composing operas for some thirty years, and he sometimes turned to his previous creations for inspiration. Arias of 1755-72 based on earlier arias of the same period are so designated in appendix B. Future research will doubtless identify arias borrowed as well from works predating 1755. Nonetheless, a style analysis of the music contained in the Hasse autographs reveals gradual and consistent stylistic evolution, thus arguing that borrowed arias make up but a tiny minority of the 235 Hasse arias investigated here and that the autographs constitute a reliable source for studying Hasse's development as a composer.

Method

The primary repertoire under consideration—641 arias, each comparable in length to a movement from a classical symphony—is quite extensive. To isolate elements of style and monitor their chronological development, one must investigate a massive amount of music—works representing several composers, different cities, and a period of at least ten or fifteen years. Such a great number and variety of arias could prove unwieldy, and an investigation into their style could easily yield a series of vague and superficial generalizations. To prevent such an outcome and to organize both the investigation of the material and the subsequent presentation of the results, this study has frequently limited the repertoire in one of two ways. Each not only reduces the amount of music to be analyzed but also allows one to arrive at more specific conclusions.

First, chapters 2 and 5 will focus exclusively on one part of each aria: the "first vocal section." This segment constitutes a significant element in the "five-part da capo" construction, a scheme which governed the large-scale structure of arias throughout the second quarter of the eighteenth century. Frederick Millner describes the "five-part da capo" form as follows:

> The text was composed of two stanzas, A and B, each usually of four lines, though three-, five-, and eight-line stanzas also exist. The typical aria opens with an instrumental ritornello (the A ritornello), which stays in the tonic. The soloist then sings the first stanza of text (A_1), using the theme introduced in the ritornello, but adding sections of coloratura or fioritura, and the aria modulates to the dominant, if in major, or to the relative major, if in minor. At the close of the first stanza, a very short ritornello (the A_1 ritornello), often employing a motive from the theme, is heard. The first stanza is then sung again (A_2), usually modulating quite quickly back to the tonic, and occasionally even opening in the tonic. This makes use of the main theme, newly composed and not simply repeated. Often, there are brief digressions to other keys during this stanza, which is always longer than A_1. It can include a fermata near the final cadence, at which point the singer adds a cadenza. A closing ritornello (the A_2 ritornello) then confirms the tonic.
>
> The second stanza (B) follows. It is often sung to material related to the melody of the first stanza, though it can also be completely new, going so far as to have a different meter and tempo. It begins in a new key, most commonly the submediant, but also the tonic minor or subdominant, and usually modulates to still another key, usually the minor mediant, or minor dominant. At this point, the simplest procedure is the sign "da capo," or "D.C.," which indicates that the singer and orchestra are to return to the very beginning of the aria.[34]

Schematically, this form can be diagrammed as follows (for an aria in a major key):

A rit.	A_1 stanza	A_1 rit.	A_2 stanza	A_2 rit.	*Fine*	B stanza	D.C.
I--I	I-------V	V----V	V(I)----I	I----I		vi---iii	

In the context of Millner's description, the first vocal section can be described as the first complete setting of the first stanza of text.[35] More specifically, it can also be defined as that part of the aria which begins with the first entrance of the voice, modulates to a secondary key, and concludes with a perfect cadence leading to an orchestral passage in the new key. (During the third quarter of the eighteenth century, two new aria constructions gained popularity and eventually replaced the five-part da capo scheme entirely: the "half da capo" and the "simple ternary" or "modified da capo."[36] Since these modifications did not affect the first vocal section, the definition remains the same, regardless of the large-scale construction of the aria.)

The first vocal section deserves special scrutiny first of all because it resembles the exposition in sonata form. Both first vocal section and exposition contain a first theme, a modulation usually to the dominant key, some sort of second theme, and an emphatic cadence or series of cadences in the new key. A study of the first vocal section should therefore reveal much about certain issues that are normally considered in the context of instrumental music: the historical development of the "second theme," the expansion of the exposition, and so on. The first vocal section also merits special attention because its structure is more consistent from aria to aria than that of the second vocal section. While the first vocal section always begins in the primary key and ends in the secondary key (usually the dominant), the second vocal section may begin in the primary key, the secondary key, or even a third key. While the first vocal section always contains a modulation, the second vocal section does not necessarily do so. The first vocal section therefore provides a better framework in which to compare a large number of arias.

The second means of limiting the repertoire arises in the chapters devoted primarily to rhythm: chapter 2, which traces the gradual decrease in the rate of harmonic change and the resultant expansion of themes and cadences, and chapter 3, which examines rhythmic patterns used in both melodies and accompaniment and thereby traces the development of "classical counterpoint." Since one can arrive at specific conclusions concerning such matters only after eliminating the variables of tempo and meter, both chapters will focus on arias of the same, or equivalent, tempo and meter. One cannot learn anything by comparing, for example, a $\frac{3}{4}$ "Andante" aria with a $\frac{2}{4}$ "Allegro" one. This book will not present a thoroughgoing categorization of arias according to tempo and meter but will isolate for special consideration "fast arias in duple meter." "Duple meter" refers of course to C, $\mathbb{C}$, or $\frac{2}{4}$. "Fast" refers primarily to tempo designations containing the word "Allegro": "Allegro con brio," "Allegro con spirito," "Allegro di molto," "Allegro moderato," and so on. The only pertinent designations which do not contain the word "Allegro" are "Presto" and "Spiritoso."

The vast majority of "fast" arias (of all meters) have remarkably similar rhythmic qualities. The shortest note value to pervade the bass line is the eighth, and the shortest note value to pervade the violin parts is the sixteenth. Sixteenth-note triplets and "Lombardic" alterations of sixteenth notes (such as ♫. ♫.), on the other hand, are virtually nonexistent. It is important to note that arias with the designation "Allegretto" are not considered "fast," for most of these arias feature far more sixteenth notes in the bass line, sixteenth-note triplets, and various Lombardic rhythms, all of which tend to induce a more moderate tempo as well as a gentle lyricism usually absent from the more energetic and martial "Allegro" arias.[37] Fast arias in duple meter usually account for 25 to 45 percent of the arias in any opera and constitute the largest aria species with similar rhythmic characteristics. ("Fast arias" are so designated in the incipit lists of appendixes A, B, and C.)[38]

By thus concentrating on specific portions of arias as well as certain types of arias, we will be able to identify many compositional formulas: harmonic progressions used in the "first theme," cadential progressions, standard melodic and accompanimental rhythms, melodic contours, and so on. After identifying such formulas, we can then trace their use by various composers over the course of time—some of the formulas which will be examined were popular for half a century—and thus chart the evolution of musical style in the third quarter of the eighteenth century with a degree of precision that would otherwise be impossible.

The Role of the Aria Text

The ensuing study of classical style as it evolved in opera seria arias will not take into account any aspect of an aria's text, such as the number of syllables per line, number of lines per strophe, rhyme scheme, syntax, affect and imagery, context in the plot, or motivation or even identity of the dramatic character who delivers the text. For the sake of brevity, in fact, the 641 arias of Hasse, Jommelli, and J.C. Bach will be referred to not by text incipit but by numbers indicating their order in the operas in which they appear. Bach's *Artaserse* 12 is thus the twelfth aria in that work. (Text and melodic incipits as well as enumerations of wind instrumentations for all 641 arias are furnished in appendixes A, B, and C.)

Such wholesale disregard for the text in the context of style analysis does not imply that the text did not affect the music. Such was hardly the case. The composer, after all, occupied a rather subservient position among those involved in the creation, production, and performance of opera seria and had to answer to a variety of forces largely beyond his control. A royal patron, for example, might select the libretto.,[39] A singer, in addition to specifying range and tessitura, might demand or refuse opportunities for virtuosos display.[40] The strengths and weaknesses of a particular orchestra could encourage the composer to fashion relatively exposed or difficult parts for some instruments but to neglect others.[41] The impresario or the general audience might favor shorter arias, less recitative, more virtuosic arias, and so on, and oblige the composer to conform to their wishes. Of all such forces, the aria text , with its given number of syllables per line, given location of accented syllables, punctuation, and images virtually demanding word painting, must have imposed the most specific and stringent requirements.

One obvious example of such influence is that of imagery and emotional content—"affect," in other words—on tempo. Direct, "first-person" expressions of action or violent feeling (such as anger, vengeance, or fear) thus inspired "Allegro" settings, as did metaphors involving storms, the sea, or wild animals, images abounding in Metastasio's verse. More tender or painful sentiments (such as those of love or sorrow), on the other hand, suggested moderate or slow tempos. Another example of text influence is that of affect on wind instrumentation. Amorous or pastoral texts prompted (but did not absolutely require) flutes; martial texts, trumpets and drums. There are, of course, many such examples of text influence. All had limited impact, however, affecting only surface detail, such as the choice between syllabic and melismatic declamation, and the use of relatively "exotic" wind instruments, melodic chromaticism, sudden dynamic shifts and rests, and so on. The text, in other words, did not affect the underlying musical style. Consequently, analysis in terms of text goes only so far, as is the case in the above two examples involving tempo and wind instrumentation. The recognition that affect influences tempo illuminates nothing else in the music. Similarly, dwelling upon the mere choice of wind instruments ignores far more intriguing and significant matters of orchestration: where in an aria the instruments sound and how they relate melodically and rhythmically to each other and to the strings.

The limits of text influence derive from the compositional process, which particularly for the eighteenth-century Italian opera composer entailed numerous complex assumptions and technical procedures, most so habital and ingrained as to become virtually subconscious. Such habits do not change as a composer sets a new text, confronts a new orchestra, or appeases a demanding singer.[42] Rather, they give rise to a virtual infinity of musical detail, much of it quite diverse. Contrasting texts can therefore elicit contrasting music, but the style—such matters as harmonic vocabulary and rhythm, degree of melodic and rhythmic independence in accompanimental lines, phrase structure and manner of phrase articulation, tonal and motivic organization—remains the same. Such is the case in fact with the elements of style investigated in this book: harmonic rhythm (chapter 2), texture and accompanimental rhythms and contours (chapter 3), structural functions of oboes and horns (chapter 5), and the composition of the independent melodic woodwind ensemble (chapter 6). They permeate most or all arias of a particular opera, regardless of text, singer, or orchestra, and change only gradually and for reasons which one cannot readily attribute to any immediate circumstance of an opera's composition or performance.

There is a second reason why considerations of text need not enter into a style analysis of eighteenth-century arias. Not only did text influence only surface detail, but it did so in a manner quite haphazard and limited in extent. To understand this aspect of the relation of text and music, it is useful to consider the structure of the "A section" of the da capo aria and its association with the first strophe of a two-strophe aria text.

Most aria texts of the mid-century were brief, supplying the composer with few words. In a letter of November 14, 1769, Jommelli expressed his frustration:

> Quegli eterni 4 versetti per parte, in ogni Aria, e sempre per lo più di 7 o 8 piedi l'uno; e peggio poi, quel replicarci di più, in così picciol numero di versi, l'istesse parole, quasi dovesse il Poeta comprarle al Mercato, e pagarle a caro prezzo.[43]

Jommelli had reason to complain. Metastasio's librettos, which Jommelli set throughout his life and which virtually all composers of opera seria set again and again from the late 1720s to the 1770s, 1780s, and even beyond, contain short aria strophes. Most comprise but four lines; such strophes (quatrains) utilize all verse types, but particularly the most common: *settenario* and *ottonario* (seven and eight syllables), respectively, per line). Other arrangements appear mostly in conjunction with particular verse types and characterize, in all, one to ten arias per drama. In general, the fewer lines per strophe, the more syllables per line. Three-line strophes (tercets), the most common alternative, thus typically employ *ottonario* and *decasillabo* (ten syllables per line); six-line strophes (sexains), only slightly less frequent, employ *quinario* and *senario* (five and six syllables, respectively, per line). Further deviations—strophes of two, five, or seven or more lines—are rare; most of these Metastasio penned early in his career.[44]

For much of the century, the typical aria strophe therefore comprised four lines of seven or eight syllables apiece. At the same time, however, the typical musical setting of that text gradually increased in size. This expansion derived not from the text but from forces that were simultaneously shaping instrumental music as well. One of these was harmonic expansion, a process which lasted at least fifty years, retarding harmonic change and elongating phrases (see chapter 2). Another was the gradual polarization of tonic and dominant tonalities. What began at the turn of the century as a rather fleeting modulation to the dominant grew by 1720 to include a more emphatic cadence and a subsequent repetition of part of the opening ritornello in the new key (the medial ritornello). This dominant key area increased in length and independence to encompass perhaps some sort of "second theme," often introduced by a dramatic half cadence and followed in turn by a cadential progression where virtuosic vocal display could intensify the drive to the medial ritornello. Afterwards, the second vocal section could begin in the dominant key or in a new key, thus prolonging or even increasing the instability brought about by the initial modulation. A third force was the sense for resolution and symmetry. The second vocal section ends by resolving tonal instability; most of the material introduced in the dominant key during the first vocal section reappears in the second vocal section but in the tonic key. To provide balance, the second vocal section generally repeats the first theme (although not always in the first key) as well as any thematic material heard before only in the first ritornello.

The elements of long-range tonal instability, resolution, and symmetry that shaped the structure of the A section of the da capo aria, of course, constitute much of "sonata form." In addition, the ternary factor in sonata form appeared, as composers in the 1760s and 1770s adopted an abbreviated version of the da capo format, the "modified da capo," whereby the B section immediately follows the first vocal section and medial ritornello, the aria concluding with the subsequent second vocal section. This condensation not only removed the unwieldy repetition of an increasingly lengthy A section but also imparted the equivalent of a clearly demarcated development and recapitulation. After the modulation to and establishment of a secondary key in the first vocal section and medial ritornello, there now followed the B section, which almost always began and concluded in separate keys, modulating freely between—thus a development. The B section, moreover, with new and contrasting music (perhaps with different meter, tempo, and instrumentation) virtually required that the second vocal section commence with an emphatic and simultaneous reaffirmation of the original tonality and the "first theme"—thus a recapitulation.

Taken together, the first and second vocal sections, whether heard twice (as in full da capo) or once (as in modified da capo), dwarfed the text. In fashioning a first theme, the composer would often use two lines of text—half the first strophe, in many cases. He would then set the remaining words, usually a couplet, to the next phrase which might begin the modulation to the dominant, the last word of the strophe frequently coinciding with a crucial V/V chord.

While J.C. Bach followed this model quite consistently, Hasse and Jommelli occasionally departed from the norm, although in opposite directions. Hasse did not hesitate to use the entire strophe for his first theme. Accordingly, he sometimes fashioned a long, arching theme cadencing in the tonic key at the end of the strophe[45] or composed an "AA theme" where both couplets of a quatrain underlie identical phrases remaining squarely in the tonic key. In either case, he exhausted the text before modulating. Jommelli, on the other hand, tried to introduce words more sparingly. Word repetition and the insertion of brief melismas enabled him to reserve part of his text for the subsequent modulation. He sometimes managed in fact to compose a first theme to only one line of text, almost invariably in the case of tercets (and concomitant *decasillabo* or *ottonario*) but occasionally with quatrains (and shorter verse types, such as *settenario*). Many of his "AA themes" simply repeat the first line or the first couplet, a practice foreign to Hasse and J.C. Bach, who always assigned new words to the second half of such themes.[46] Nonetheless, even Jommelli never managed to withhold any words for the secondary key area.

By the time a composer set the first strophe in its entirety, he had reached only the conclusion of the first theme, the beginning of the modulatory phrase, or the V/V chord. For the remainder of the first vocal section, as well as for all of the second vocal section, he could only reuse the same words. Less concerned with presenting complete sentences in a time sufficiently short for their comprehension, the composer manipulated the words to suit the music. He could insert extensive melismas (often prolonging a word to unintelligible lengths), fashion some sort of contrasting "second theme" (using words that also underlie the first theme), insert extraneous interjections, such as "ah," "si," or "no," and repeat or even scramble fragments of text. Particularly near the end of each vocal section, the composer could repeat the final words of the strophe again and again to fill out extended, and perhaps repeated, cadential phrases.

With the text receiving such free treatment throughout the second half of the first vocal section and most of the second vocal section, one must assume that the text made its greatest impact on the music at the outset of the first vocal section, i.e., during the first theme and following phrase(s). We cannot hope to trace this influence exhaustively but will consider two important issues: (1) the textual basis of the ABB theme, and (2) the affect of syllable count and word accentuation on the melodic rhythms of the first theme.

The Textual Basis of the ABB Theme

The ABB format reigned as the most popular opening phrase structure of Italian vocal music throughout the mid-eighteenth century. In terms of the text, it usually comprises the first two verses with a restatement of the second (or, rarely, of only the end of the second verse). If, however, a strophe includes only three verses or a relatively large number of syllables per line—*ottonario* or *decasillabo*—the theme may set only the first verse, the second half of that line being repeated. Musically, the ABB pattern comprises three segments, the last two of which are cadential and not necessarily identical. The first cadence is usually perfect, imperfect, or deceptive, and rarely half or plagal; the second, more emphatic, is almost always perfect, rarely half or plagal, and never deceptive. The length, melodic shape, rhythm, and harmonic structure of the two B segments are usually, but not necessarily, alike (see chapter 2 for numerous examples of ABB themes).

J.C. Bach composed ABB themes quite frequently. They begin most of his arias—35 to 85 percent of the arias in each opera.[47] Hasse constructed similar themes rather less often, in 25 to 65 percent of the arias in each opera.[48] Jommelli alternately favored or else virtually ignored the ABB format. In *Semiramide riconosciuta* (Stuttgart, 1762), for example, he constructed such themes for ten of eighteen arias. In the following year, in *Didone* (Stuttgart, 1763), he did so for only two of eighteen arias. Similarly, he composed eight ABB themes of a possible sixteen in *Enea nel Lazio* (Stuttgart, 1766), but only two of a possible fourteen two years later in *Fetonte* (Stuttgart, 1768).

The ABB theme does not seem to have arisen to serve the text, i.e., to emphasize an important second verse by repeating it. If composers had so wanted to highlight any individual text line by repeating it at the outset of an aria, they would also have fashioned "AAB themes" or "ABCC" themes. Such constructions are, practically speaking, nonexistent. Rather, the explanation for the genesis of the ABB theme is musical; the ABB theme, as we shall see in chapter 2, evolved in the 1720s as the long-breathed, continuous phrasing of the late baroque was giving way to shorter, more clearly delineated and obviously balanced units. The ABB theme, with its clear divisibility and repeated cadential segments, epitomizes the new phraseology. The double cadence, moreover, helps articulate the theme as a whole from the remainder of the first vocal section.

While the structure of the ABB theme did not serve the text, its use by some composers depended on syntax. Hasse, for example, fashioned an ABB theme only when the opening couplet presents one complete sentence or main clause. When the couplet forms a dependent clause or only part of a clause, he instead set the first lines to a simpler phrase concluding with a short, unobtrusive cadence or else incorporated them into a longer, relatively seamless phrase encompassing the third or even the fourth verse. Such care derives from the fact that the ABB theme almost inevitably constitutes a distinct musical statement and may also lead immediately to a sonorous orchestral interjection of tonic chords. The text repetition, emphatic cadences, and orchestral interruption halts the word flow and virtually demands that the preceding words form a complete thought.

J.C. Bach, on the other hand, generally ignored syntax. ABB themes begin most of his arias, as we have seen, even if the entire strophe contains but one sentence, as in the first strophe of Alessandro 9:

> Non sarei sì sventurata,
> Se, nascendo infra le schiere
> Delle amazzoni guerriere
> Apprendevo a guerreggiar.[49]

In Bach's setting, an ABB phrase ending with a two-bar caesura interrupts a participial phrase and separates a noun ("schiere") from a modifying prepositional phrase ("delle amazzoni guerrier"):

Example 1

(Bach: Alessandro 9)

In his response to syntax, Jommelli alternately resembles Hasse or J.C. Bach. On one hand, he often demonstrated a concern that his phrase structures mirror the syntax. If a strophe comprises but one complete sentence, he might, like Hasse, allow the music to proceed directly to the modulation without phrase repetition, definitive tonic cadence, or long caesura. On the other hand, it is not difficult to find ABB themes or long vocal caesuras that work at cross purposes with the text.

The ABB theme thus rarely enhanced the text. Its structure served a musical purpose and could in fact distort the text. Such frequent contradictions between phrase structure and syntax in the arias of Bach, the youngest of the three composers under consideration, suggests that the "modern" sense for well-delineated phrases encouraged these clashes. To produce his high degree of phrase articulation and tonal stability, Bach often repeated phrases and separated them with long caesuras that usually contain wind interjections. At the opening of the first vocal section, consequently, he utilized the ABB construction and also extended and orchestrally reinforced the following caesura far more frequently than Hasse or Jommelli did. He did so almost automatically, with little regard for syntax. It would be worthwhile to determine whether other composers of Bach's generation made a similar choice in favor of musical clarity.

The Impact of Syllable Count and Accentuation

If the text controlled any aspect of an aria, one might suppose it to be the rhythm of the first theme. The text, after all, bound the composer to a given number of syllables with a given number and placement of accented syllables which he would place on relatively important beats, particularly the first beat in $\frac{2}{4}$, $\frac{3}{4}$, and $\frac{3}{8}$ meters, or the first and middle beats of $\frac{4}{4}$ and $\frac{6}{8}$ meters.

Despite these constraints, there were myriad possibilities for translating the text elements of syllable count and word accent into specific musical rhythms. The composer, first of all, could select any time signature. Second, the time intervening between accented syllables he could apportion to unaccented syllables in a great variety of ways. Third, he could vary the time span between those accented syllables. In the following *settenario* setting, for example, four beats separate the first accented syllable ("Caro") from the second ("ben"), but only two beats separate the second accented syllable from the third ("addio"):

Example 2

Ca - ro mio ben addio   (Hasse: Ezio 16)

When Hasse extended the first syllables, the ratio between the length of the first foot and that of each succeeding foot was, as here, 2:1. Jommelli, and J.C. Bach, among others, carried the practice a step further, frequently prolonging the first syllables so that the ratio becomes 4:1:

Example 3

È fol·lia se nascon-dete   (Bach: Catone 7)

Ottonario lines in particular received varied treatment. With its four accents placed on even-numbered syllables, *ottonario* could elicit declamatory rhythms with the four accented syllables posited equidistantly (figure 1a); or, the end or beginning could be contracted (figure 1b, c) or the beginning expanded (figure 1d).

Figure 1.   Ottonario Incipits

a) O nel sen di qualche stella   (Bach: Catone 4)

b) No non chiedo amate stelle   (Hasse: Demofoonte 13)

c) Disperato in mar turba - (to)   (Bach: Adriano 2)

d) Finchè un zefiro soave   (Hasse: Ezio 9)

Varying the meter, the length of time separating accented syllables, and the division of that time among unaccented syllables made possible an almost infinite number of declamatory rhythms. Other techniques allowed a composer to circumvent the given number of syllables and, in effect, create a syllable count of his own choosing. For one thing, he could disregard the poetic convention of elision, whereby a vowel ending a word and a vowel beginning the next word are reckoned as one syllable, and set such contiguous vowels to separate notes. In the following example, Hasse treated a *settenario* line as if it contained nine syllables:

Example 4

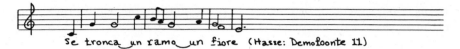

Se tronca un ramo un fiore (Hasse: Demofoonte 11)

Second, a composer could repeat single words or brief phrases. This practice, not to be confused with the repetition of the entire second line of text in an ABB theme, normally begins after the presentation of the entire strophe. Hasse thus never repeated single words or brief phrases during the first theme. Jommelli and J.C. Bach at first followed suit but then allowed themselves to reuse text fragments at the very outset of the aria, doubtless to enable them to fashion longer melodies. In Bach's early operas, only two or three arias per work contain repeated words or phrases during the initial presentation of the first two verses. By the time of *Carattaco* (1767), however, such arias number nine of twenty; in *Temistocle* (1772), twelve of nineteen. Jommelli made the transition earlier, motivated perhaps by his move to Stuttgart in 1754. For his second setting of *Demofoonte* (Milan, 1753), composed only months before he set out for Germany, Jommelli rarely permitted such repetition. Yet it abounds in the first of his extant Stuttgart operas, *Pelope* (1755).

The third and most radical technique was to allot portions of the opening phrase to the orchestra. This practice was uncommon—only Jommelli utilized it consistently—but resulted in the virtual emancipation of the musical line from the original syllable count. In an aria from *Olimpiade* (Stuttgart, 1761), for example, Jommelli fashioned an extended eight-bar phrase out of a mere four short words:

Example 5

Caro   caro   son tua così

son tua   son tua così   (Jommelli: Olimpiade 12)

Taken together, these techniques lent considerable flexibility to a composer's response to syllable count. Another convention allowed the composer to circumvent even the original accentuation. He did not invariably have to place every accented syllable on a beat stronger than those occupied by the preceding and following unaccented syllables. Specifically, he could suppress the first accent in an iambic *quinario* or *settenario* line[50] by placing the first (unaccented) syllable on the first beat in triple meter, the second (accented) syllable following on the second beat:[51]

Example 6

Se tutti mali   miei   (Hasse: Demofoonte 12)

Similarly, he could transfer the third musical accent in *ottonario*[52] from the fifth back to the fourth syllable:

Example 7

Non temer   ch'io mai ti dica   (Bach: Artaserse 12)

Such accent transfer frequently, but not necessarily, arose when a series of adjacent monosyllabic words produces a rather ambiguous accentuation in the first place.[53]

The enormous range of techniques by which a composer could respond to syllable count and accent placement ensured that a given text could elicit a multitude of possible musical rhythms. The particular rhythm selected by a composer thus reflects not so much the text but other, more personal factors: the composer's melodic and orchestral styles and the degree to which he was willing to repeat single words or to separate successive accented syllables. While this investigation of the impact of two particular text elements on the music at the very beginning of the first vocal section cannot speak conclusively for the relation of text and music in all its aspects, we should consider three significant implications. First, the fact that the beginning of the first vocal section was frequently the only place where the text was presented more or less intact suggests that the influence of syllable count and accent placement on the subsequent course of the music was even weaker than it had been initially. Second, the impact of other text elements, such as number of lines per strophe or rhyme scheme, on the compositional process doubtless was similarly loose and indirect, if not even more so. Third, the investigation of the interrelationship of text and music should be undertaken not in the isolation of single arias but in the context of many arias by the same composer as well as by other composers. Such a perspective frequently reveals that a musical event that seems inspired by the text in one aria actually arises in many, or most, arias regardless of text or that the particular event in question is but one of a great variety of ways the composer has responded to the same text stimulus. The impact of text should therefore be assessed only after a musical style is understood in considerable scope and detail. Until that point is reached, the arias of opera seria deserve to be studied from other viewpoints.

Harmonic Expansion from 1716 to 1784

The course of eighteenth-century musical life, with its plethora of unresearched or partially researched composers and its many national and even civic styles and traditions, presents several basic, but still largely unanswered, questions: how, when, where, and because of whom did general styles of composition change? More specifically, where are the roots of what we call "classical style?" Having discarded the once popular notion of 1750 as a watershed in eighteenth-century music history, scholars now point to two other years, both approximations for what were doubtless gradual metamorphoses. The first year, 1720, saw the rise of a new generation of Neapolitan opera composers—Hasse, Leo, Pergolesi, and Vinci, to name but a few of the most successful—and their perfection and subsequent dissemination of a new style wherein the characteristically late-baroque irregular phrase lengths, hyperactive bass line, and competing instrumental and vocal parts gave way to a more orderly and balanced series of short, clearly delineated phrases, with the bass line and other accompanimental layers supporting a prominent vocal line.[1] The second time of change, 1780, saw the transformation of the relation of melody to accompaniment, at least in the works of Haydn and Mozart. At this time, according to Charles Rosen,[2] the rigid distinction between melody and accompaniment gave way to a more fluid texture in which all musical layers are more motivic and thus better integrated and virtually interchangeable. As a result, each phrase flows naturally into the next, allowing composers to achieve greater drama and sometimes even surprise within a tightly organized and logical framework.

But what transpired during the sixty years from 1720 to 1780? Chapter 3 will challenge some of Rosen's conclusions and present evidence that the profound stylistic changes which he describes actually took place ten years earlier, around 1770. Still, this process occurred relatively rapidly, so that any stylistic evolution of the preceding fifty years remains unaccounted for.

Another direction in which to look for style change during this period, at least within the context of opera seria, is the "reform" which arose in the late 1750s and early 1760s and centered around the litterati Francesco Algarotti, Ranieri de'Calzabigi, Niccolò Jommelli, and Tommaso Traetta. This chapter of eighteenth-century operatic history has always attracted the attention of scholars, but the innovations associated with the reform concerned not so much the music itself as the text and large-scale organization: the use of more direct and emotional language, a return to spectacle and mythological subject matter, the linking of the overture to the drama which follows, and the inclusion of more dances, accompanied recitatives, ensembles, and choruses.

Some scholars have nevertheless ascribed significant developments of a purely musical nature to composers involved in the reform. Donald Grout, for example, writes in the standard textbook on the history of opera:

> The German influence on Jommelli and Traetta is seen in their treatment of the orchestra, in a greater complexity of texture and increased attention to idiomatic use of the instruments.... Likewise due to German influence is the greater richness and variety of the harmonies in both Jommelli and Traetta, as compared with their Italian contemporaries.[3]

Such assertions, none of which have been proven, seem to reflect a long standing prejudice that most of the crucial stylistic evolution of the second half of the eighteenth century took place exclusively on German or Austrian soil; consequently, Italians who composed operas, particularly "reform operas," in Germany or Austria wrote more complex and "advanced" music. Much of this book will challenge this Germanocentric thesis. Chapter 3 will demonstrate that Jommelli fashioned his most subtle and complex textures not in the reform operas he composed for Stuttgart, but in the late, dramatically more old-fashioned operas he composed for Naples and Rome. Similarly, chapters 4 and 6 will show that both Jommelli and Gluck designed wind parts that retain more conservative features than those of J.C. Bach, a composer who virtually ignored the reform and wrote most of his operas for Italy and London. In the context of at least two important elements of music—texture and wind instrumentation—it therefore seems that the operatic reform of the late 1750s and early 1760s occasioned no significant changes in style and that, consequently, the "reform" had little to do with the development of the classicism of Haydn and Mozart.

Probably there was no single year or even group of years between 1720 and 1770 when musical style underwent a general and profound change. Charles Burney, writing in the 1780s, attests to the idea that a single style was developed in the 1720s and 1730s and then maintained until his own day:

> Vinci...was the first among his countrymen, who since...1600, seems to have occasioned any considerable revolution in the musical drama.... Vinci seems to have been the first opera composer...who rendered...[his music] the friend, though not the slave to the poetry, by simplifying and polishing melody, and calling the attention of the audience chiefly to the voice part, by disentangling it from fugue, complication, and laboured contrivance.[4]

> Pergolesi...[was] if not the founder, the principal polisher of a style of composition both for the church and stage which has been constantly cultivated by his successors and which at the distance of half a century...still reigns throughout Europe.[5]

Burney maintains, in other words, that Vinci was the first opera composer to write in what we call a "preclassical style," that Pergolesi perfected this style, and that composers of the 1770s and 1780s still followed suit.

It is not difficult to marshall evidence both to support and to refute Burney's statement. On one hand, the arias of the 1770s and 1780s do share certain traits with those of the 1730s. Even Mozart's *Idomeneo* (Munich, 1780), stamped with the composer's genius in every bar, conforms in certain ways: the tonal and ritornello structure of many arias, first vocal sections commencing with ABB themes,[6] and identical harmonic formulas used for melismas and cadences. At the same time, the arias of the 1770s and 1780s differ profoundly from those of the 1730s. The later ones, longer and grander, feature a more fully developed secondary key area; greater contrasts of dynamics, texture, and orchestration; and more widely spaced yet more compelling climaxes.

One underlying phenomenon fostered this simultaneous continuity and diversity of style during the sixty years from 1720 to 1780: gradual harmonic expansion. In the 1720s, the phrase rhythm of the Neapolitans anticipated that of the mid-century; phrases are short and often repeated, with cadences occurring at fairly regular intervals. The harmonic rhythm, on the other hand, remained essentially baroque, featuring what Manfred Bukofzer terms "continuo homophony";[7] chords change in such rapid succession that the bass line, though subordinate to the melody, changes pitches quickly and in more or less equal step with the melody. Over the course of the next four decades, the harmonic rhythm gradually decreased. Chords changed more slowly, and phrases consequently grew in length. At the same time, however, composers retained a great number of melodic, harmonic, and structural formulas, thus maintaining a stylistic continuity.

Harmonic expansion set in motion or at least contributed significantly to many of the crucial stylistic developments of the mid-eighteenth century. First, the character of melodies and bass lines changed. In fast works, the melody could employ increasingly longer note values, thus the "singing Allegro;" the bass line, if it were to remain fast, repeated the same pitch, thus the "Trommelbass." Second, the secondary key area grew little by little in length and independence, its arrival frequently heralded by a dramatic half cadence and caesura. Third, the relation of woodwinds to strings changed profoundly. As chords changed less and less frequently in relation to the notes of the melody, winds no longer had to serve as ripieno instruments but could now sustain a harmonic background. As phrases became more distinct, moreover, the winds, either singly or in ensembles, could lend their various timbres to articulate phrase beginnings, cadences, or whole phrases (see chapters 5 and 6). Fourth, arias steadily increased in size. It is scarcely an oversimplification to explain the history of large-scale aria forms in mid-eighteenth-century opera seria in terms of an ongoing attempt to prune dead wood from an inexorably expanding organism: first by repeating only half of the A section (the "half da capo" aria), then by inserting the B section in the middle of the A section (the "modified da capo" aria), and finally by dispensing with a repeated A section altogether (the "two tempo" aria).

To gain a better understanding of the course and scope of eighteenth-century harmonic expansion, we will trace some basic elements of harmonic rhythm in ninety opere serie composed between 1716 and 1784. These works consist of the thirty-five opere serie composed by Hasse, Jommelli, and J.C. Bach from 1755 to 1772, six other opere serie written by the same three composers at other times in their careers, and forty-nine opere serie composed by twenty-nine other composers between 1716 and 1784.[8] While comprising but a tiny sampling of the thousands of operas produced in Italy, England, Germany, and Austria during this period, these ninety works nonetheless run the gamut from the late baroque style of Alessandro Scarlatti to the mature classicism of Haydn and Mozart and thus should provide us with some idea of the harmonic trends of the settecento.

While treating a great number of operas, the following study will limit its focus by examining only fast arias in duple meter and by comparing harmonic rhythms in the context of two specific events: (1) the ABB theme that opens the first vocal section[9] and (2) the cadence or cadential phrase that concludes the first vocal section.[10] Based on the harmonic rhythm of these two events, the ninety operas of 1716-84 fall into four chronological periods: 1716-30, 1730-40, 1741-60, and 1761-84.

1716-30

This fifteen-year period is represented by fifteen operas of ten composers, most of whom were born between 1660 and 1690:

1. Attilio Ariosti (1666-1729): *Vespasiano* (London, 1724)
2. Antonio Maria Bononcini (1666-1726): *Griselda* (Milan, 1718)[11]
3. Francesco Gasparini (1668-1727): *Il Bajazet,* second version (Reggio, 1719)[12]
4. Geminiano Giacomelli (1686-1743): *Lucio Papirio Dittatore* (Parma, 1729)
5. Antonio Lotti (1667-1740): *Alessandro Severo* (Venice, 1716)[13]
6. Giuseppe Porsile (1672-1758): *Spartaco* (Vienna, 1726)
7. Domenico Sarri (1679-1744): *Arsace* (Naples, 1718)
8. Alessandro Scarlatti (1660-1725): *Telemaco* (Rome, 1718), *Marco Attilio Regolo* (Rome, 1719), and *La Griselda* (Rome, 1721)[14]
9. Leonardo Vinci (1696?-1730): *Didone abbandonata* (Rome, 1726), *Catone in Utica* (Rome, 1728), and *Artaserse* (Rome, 1729)[15]
10. Antonio Vivaldi (1678-1741): *Tito Manlio* (Mantua, 1719) and *Orlando,* second version (Venice, 1727)

According to the evidence of the fifteen operas listed above, composers of the 1710s and 1720s wrote brief first vocal sections and extended the lengths of phrases by means of sequences, not outright repetition. They thus composed few ABB themes. Although they occasionally set a second verse line twice in succession, they even then did not necessarily fashion true ABB themes, for the second setting of the second verse would greatly exceed the first in length and modulate, leading directly to the second ritornello (in the secondary key). In such cases, the setting of the first two verses constitutes the entire first vocal section, the first strophe containing only two verses (see example 8). Real ABB themes, on the other hand, appear rarely and almost invariably in slow or triple-meter arias.[16] In all fifteen operas investigated here, only three fast arias in duple meter begin in this manner.[17] The end of the first vocal section, much like the beginning, rarely contains repetition or attains any degree of independence. Chords change every eighth note or quarter note:

Example 8

(Bononcini: <u>Griselda</u>, "Cara sposa")

Example 9

(Sarri: <u>Arsace</u>, "Torno a i ceppi")

1730-40

This second period is represented by eleven operas of seven composers, including Johann Adolf Hasse at the beginning of his career. All seven composers were born between 1670 and 1710:

1. Antonio Caldara (c. 1670-1736): *Olimpiade* (Vienna, 1733). By far the oldest of the seven composers represented here, Caldara served at the Imperial court in Vienna from 1716 until his death in 1736
2. Francesco Feo (1691-1761): *Andromaca* (Rome, 1730)[18]
3. Johann Adolf Hasse (1699-1783): *Cleofide* (Dresden, 1731) and *Siroe,* first version (Bologna, 1733)[19]
4. Leonardo Leo (1694-1744): *Farnace* (Naples, 1736), *Demetrio* (Naples, 1741), *Demofoonte,* second version (Naples, 1741), and *Andromaca* (Naples, 1743)[20]
5. Giovanni Battista Pergolesi (1710-36): *Olimpiade* (Rome, 1735)[21]
6. Rinaldo di Capua (?-?): *Vologeso* (Rome, 1739)[22]
7. Antonio Vivaldi (1678-1741): *Griselda* (Venice, 1735)

By 1730, the ABB format had become a virtual mannerism of younger, Neapolitan-trained composers, such as Francesco Feo, Johann Adolf Hasse, Leonardo Leo, and Giovanni Battista Pergolesi. As evidence of this trend, ten of the eleven operas listed above contain ABB themes in profusion. In four these works, moreover, all but one or two fast arias in duple meter (from a total of ten or twelve such arias per opera) begin in this fashion: Feo's *Andromaca,* Pergolesi's *Olimpiade,* and Leo's *Farnace* and *Andromaca.* Only Caldara's *Olimpiade* (Vienna, 1733) contains no ABB themes. Living in Vienna, Caldara evidently lost contact with Italian style trends.

The ABB themes of the 1730s share many features. The A segment usually lasts half a bar, although it sometimes attains a length of as much as two bars.[23] Each B segment lasts one bar.[24] Together they often utilize a harmonic formula: $V - I - V - I$ (figure 2). Chords change rapidly, usually on every half note or quarter note. While the great majority of ABB themes in the operas of the 1730s thus conform to the dimensions $(\frac{1}{2}\text{-}2) + 1 + 1,$[25] a few additional ABB themes of that time surpass the rest in length and thus anticipate the themes of later decades. Leo's *Andromaca* (Naples, 1743), the composer's last opera, contains three ABB themes with the dimensions $(1\text{-}2) + 2 + 2$ (for examples of such themes, see figure 4).[26] This work, which at any rate dates from the 1740s, shows that Leo began to extend his phrase lengths and decrease the rate of harmonic change, but only at the very end of his career. Pergolesi's *Olimpiade* (Rome, 1735) likewise contains three ABB themes with similar dimensions.[27] More important, this popular opera boasts an even longer ABB theme with the dimensions $5 + 3 + 3$. The text of this aria, "Gemo in un punto e

Figure 2.   ABB Themes of the 1730s

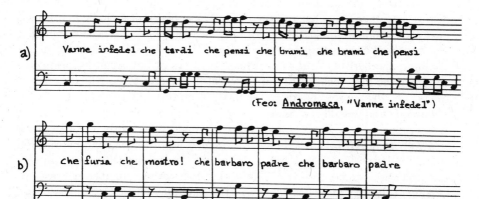

a) Vanne infedel che tardi che pensi che brami che brami che pensi

(Feo: <u>Andromaca</u>, "Vanne infedel")

b) che furia che mostro! che barbaro padre che barbaro padre

(Hasse: <u>Siroe</u>, "Che furia che mostro")

Figure 3.   Cadences of the 1730s

a) è   sua   calma   non è

(Hasse: <u>Siroe</u>, "O placido il mar")

b) con la ca-nuta età con la ca-nuta età

(Pergolesi: <u>Olimpiade</u>, "So ch'è fanciullo Amore")

fremo," elicited unusually long themes from other composers as well, as we shall see. Finally, one ABB theme in Vivaldi's *Griselda* (Venice, 1735) also shares the dimensions $1 + 2 + 2$.[28]

The end of the first vocal section, like the beginning, had evolved by 1730 into something of a separate entity. One can usually speak of a "cadential phrase."[29] Like each B segment of the great majority of ABB themes composed at this time, almost all cadential phrases last one bar; moreover, they frequently appear twice in succession and conclude with chords—usually I_4^6 and V—each lasting one beat (figure 3b). One particular type of one-bar cadential phrase gained remarkably wide currency: the "ascending bass cadence." Here the bass line begins on the tonic of the secondary key, ascends stepwise to the fifth degree, and then skips back to the tonic. The concurrent melodic line almost always descends stepwise (figure 3a). The "ascending bass cadence," although it had appeared occasionally in operas of the 1710s and 1720s, became an all too common mannerism of the 1730s. Hasse, for example, utilized this formula to conclude the first vocal section in seven of his nine fast duple-meter arias in *Siroe*. Of the eleven operas examined from this period, only Caldara's *Olimpiade* and Vivaldi's *Griselda* ignore this device.

Longer cadences occur mostly in the operas that also feature several relatively long ABB themes. Leo's *Andromaca*, accordingly, contains one aria where the I_4^6 and V chords each last two beats.[31] Pergolesi's *Olimpiade* contains one aria with similar chords[32] and another aria with an augmented, two-bar version of the ascending bass cadence[33] (for examples of such longer cadences, see figure 5). In addition, Rinaldo's *Vologeso* (Rome, 1739) contains two arias where the I_4^6 and V chords each last two beats,[34] and Leo's *Demofoonte* (Naples, 1741) contains two more such arias.[35]

1741-60

This twenty-year period is represented by the eleven operas composed by Hasse and Jommelli from 1755 to 1760[36] and by thirteen other operas written by eight composers, including Jommelli at the beginning of his career. All eight composers were born between 1700 and 1720:

1. Baldassare Galuppi (1706-85): *Olimpiade* (Milan, 1747)
2. Christoph Willibald Gluck (1714-87): *Semiramide riconosciuta* (Vienna, 1748) and *Il re pastore* (Vienna, 1756)[37]
3. Carl Heinrich Graun (1703-59): *Artaserse* (Berlin, 1743) and *Montezuma* (Berlin, 1755). The oldest of the eight composers listed here, Graun, like Caldara before him, spent most of his operatic career in the relative isolation of a German court
4. Ignaz Holzbauer (1711-83): *Alessandro nell'Indie* (Milan, 1759)
5. Niccolò Jommelli (1714-74): *Ezio,* first version (Bologna, 1741), *Semiramide riconosciuta,* first version (Turin, 1741), and *Demofoonte,* second version (Milan, 1753)[38]
6. Gaetano Latilla (1711-88): *Ezio* (Naples, 1758)
7. Domingo Terradellas (1713-51): *Merope* (Rome, 1743) and *Sesostri* (Rome, 1751)[39]
8. Georg Christoph Wagenseil (1715-77): *Ariodante* (Venice, 1745). Born and educated in Vienna, Wagenseil first went to Italy for the production of *Ariodante,* his first opera seria[40]

ABB themes enjoyed as much popularity in the 1740s and 1750s as they had in the 1730s. Of the twenty-four operas listed above, only one, Wagenseil's *Ariodante* (Venice, 1745), contains no such themes. (Wagenseil, who journeyed to Italy only immediately before the production of his *Ariodante,* perhaps had little exposure to current Italian compositional trends.) The other operas of this period all contain ABB themes, and in five of these works, all but one or two of the fast arias in duple meter begin in this fashion: Jommelli's *Ezio,* Terradellas's *Merope* and *Sesostri,* Galuppi's *Olimpiade,* and Hasse's *Ezio.*

In fourteen of the twenty-four operas comprising this third group—the two by Gluck, Hasse's *Nitteti* and *Demofoonte,* the seven operas by Jommelli, and the three by Galuppi, Holzbauer, and Latilla—ABB themes conforming to the scale so common in the 1730s do not exist. Instead, most ABB themes are twice as long: the A segment extends for one or two bars, although it sometimes attains a length of as much as four bars, and each B segment extends for two bars. As before, the B segments often utilize harmonic formulas, both the one so common in the 1730s and a new one: $I - I^6 - IV(ii^6) - V - I$ (or vi) $- I^6$ (or vi) $- IV(ii^6) - V - I$. In the latter case, the concurrent melodic line often descends stepwise. So common are all these attributes that many ABB themes of the period sound very similar, their bass lines being virtually identical (see figure 4).

Figure 4.   ABB Themes of the 1740s and 1750s

a) La figlia m'of-fende m'ol-traggia la-mante m'ol-traggia la-mante

(Jommelli: Pelope 15)

b) Va tra le selve incane barbaro geni-tore barbaro geni-tore

(Hasse: Artaserse 15)

Smaller, 1730s-size ABB themes still occur in some operas of the 1740s and 1750s, but only in those composed either in the very early 1740s or in northern Germany. Terradellas's *Merope* (Rome, 1743) thus contains themes of different sizes. Of ten ABB themes that open fast arias in duple meter, four have the dimensions (1-4) $+ 2 + 2$, but six have the smaller, more old-fashioned dimensions (½-2) $+ 1 + 1$.[41] More significant, the operas that Graun composed

for Berlin and that Hasse composed for Dresden contain more short ABB
themes than long ones. Graun had visited Italy in 1740-41, so it seems that his
operas of the next two decades simply preserved the style common in Italy c.
1740. Hasse composed six small ABB themes and only three longer ones for his
three Dresden operas of 1755-56: *Ezio, Il re pastore,* and *Olimpiade.*[42] After he
left Dresden and returned to Italy in 1757, however, he continued to construct
themes of both varieties, but with the numbers reversed. His *Nitteti* (Venice,
1758), *Demofoonte* (Naples, 1758), *Achille in Sciro* (Naples, 1759), and
Artaserse (Naples, 1760) together contain three short ABB themes but six
longer ones.[43]

At the other end of the spectrum, some composers occasionally fashioned
ABB themes longer than any we have discussed so far. Terradellas did so for six
of his fast duple-meter arias in *Sesostri* (Rome, 1751). In five of these arias, at
least one of the B segments extends three bars (for examples of such extended
themes, see figure 6); in the other aria, the A segment extends six bars.[44] Why
Terradellas composed such long themes in 1751 remains a mystery, for the
other composers examined here ventured beyond the standard dimensions ([1-
4] + 2 + 2) only rarely, and never for more than one aria per opera. In the
twenty-three remaining operas belonging to this period, in fact, only four arias
begin with themes comparable in length to those Terradellas composed. Two of
these four arias set the same text that elicited Pergolesi's longest ABB theme
(see p. 30), a startling fact indeed. The text is "Gemo in un punto e fremo"; the
operas, Galuppi's and Hasse's settings of *Olimpiade.*[45] The other two themes in
question occur in Jommelli's *Ezio* and *Semiramide riconosciuta,* both of
1741.[46]

As with the ABB themes, most cadences of the 1740s and 1750s are twice
as long as their counterparts of the 1730s. The "ascending bass cadence" again
appears in most operas,[47] but the phrase now lasts two bars instead of one
(figure 5a):

Figure 5.   Cadences of the 1740s and 1750s

(Hasse: Olimpiade 1)

(Galuppi: Olimpiade "Gemo in un punto")

Other cadential phrases, usually repeated twice in succession, also extend for two bars, the final two chords—usually I_4^6 and V—each now lasting two beats instead of one (figure 5b). The shorter original version of the ascending bass cadence still makes an occasional appearance, but only, as one might expect, in relatively early operas or in operas produced in northern Germany. Terradellas thus composed a few one-bar ascending bass cadences for *Merope* (Rome, 1743)[48] but none for *Sesostri* (Rome, 1751). Jommelli composed such cadences for *Semiramide* (Turin, 1741)[49] but none for any of his later operas examined here. And the relatively isolated Graun and Hasse fashioned such cadences for virtually all their operas examined from this period. In Hasse's seven operas of 1755-60, for example, the first vocal section of only three fast duple-meter arias concludes with a two-bar ascending bass cadence,[50] whereas the first vocal section of eleven other fast duple-meter arias concludes with the original, one-bar version of that cadence.[51] The other composers listed here occasionally utilized one-bar cadences (almost always repeated), but they never reverted to the one-bar ascending bass formula.

Of the composers of the 1740s and 1750s, only Jommelli wrote cadences in which the final I_4^6 and V chords each last more than two beats. In some arias of the 1750s, he thus fashioned relatively climactic cadences that feature four-beat I_4^6 and V chords. In one such case he incorporated these chords into the ascending bass formula, thus producing a three bar version of that cadence:[52]

Example 10

(Jommelli: Demofoonte [1753]. "O più tremar")

1761-84

This twenty-two year period is represented by the twenty-four operas composed by Hasse, Jommelli, and Bach between 1761 and 1772 and by sixteen other operas written by eight composers, including Bach later in his career. Most of these eight composers were born between 1720 and 1740:

1. Johann Christian Bach (1735-82): *La clemenza di Scipione* (London, 1778)[53]
2. Andrea Bernasconi (1706-84): *La clemenza di Tito* (Munich, 1768). Bernasconi began his career in Italy but worked from 1753 as Vizekapellmeister and then as Hofkapellmeister in Munich
3. Joseph Haydn (1732-1809): *Armida* (Eszterháza, 1784)[54]

4. Gian Francesco di Maio (1732-70): *Demofoonte* (Rome, 1764) and *Adriano in Sciro* (Rome, 1769)[55]
5. Wolfgang Amadeus Mozart (1756-91): *Mitridate, re di Ponto* (Milan, 1770), *Lucio Silla* (Milan, 1772), *Il re pastore* (Salzburg, 1775), and *Idomeneo, re di Creta* (Munich, 1781)[56]
6. Nicola Piccinni (1728-1800): *Catone in Utica* (Mannheim, 1770)
7. Giuseppe Sarti (1729-1802): *Didone abbandonata* (Copenhagen, 1762). In 1752, Sarti left Italy for Copenhagen, where he held a variety of posts from 1755 to 1765 (and again from 1768 to 1775)
8. Tommaso Traetta (1727-79): *Armida* (Vienna, 1761), *Sofonisba* (Mannheim, 1762), *Ifigenia in Tauride* (Vienna, 1763), *Siroe* (Munich, 1767), and *Antigone* (St. Petersburg, 1772)[57]

The thirty-nine operas examined from this period fall into three categories.[58] First, eleven of the operas, most notably the five composed by Hasse, contain ABB themes no different from most of those of the 1740s and 1750s: their dimensions are (1-4) + 2 + 2.[59] Even though Hasse spent most of the years 1757-60 in Italy and wrote his last opera, *Ruggiero,* for Milan, he in fact never fashioned longer ABB themes during this period. On two occasions, he even composed miniature ABB themes that resemble those of the 1730s: their dimensions are (½-2) + 1 + 1.[60] By the 1760s, the sexagenarian Hasse had evidently become too set in his ways to fashion themes much different from those he had been composing for the previous thirty years.

Six other operas belong to this first category: Bach's *Adriano in Siria* (London, 1765), Sarti's *Didone abbandonata* (Copenhagen, 1762), Jommelli's *Demofoonte* III (Stuttgart, 1764), *Fetonte* (Stuttgart, 1768), and *Demofoonte* IV (Naples, 1770), and Traetta's *Antigone* (St. Petersburg, 1772). The lack of longer ABB themes in the Bach and Jommelli operas is hardly significant, however, since each work contains only one or two fast duple-meter arias with ABB themes. Traetta, as we shall see, composed other operas with longer ABB themes. The lack of such themes in Sarti's *Didone abbandonata,* on the other hand, seems to be more telling, since the work contains four fast duplemeter arias with ABB themes. Sarti left Italy for Copenhagen in 1753, so he probably composed operas there that simply preserved the style popular in Italy in the early 1750s.

The second category, by far the largest, comprises Bach's remaining operas of 1761-72 plus his *La clemenza di Scipione,* Bernasconi's *La clemenza di Tito,* Jommelli's *Olimpiade, Semiramide riconosciuta, Enea nel Lazio, Vologeso, Achille in Sciro,* and *Ifigenia in Tauride,* the two operas by di Maio, Mozart's *Mitridate,* Piccinni's *Catone in Utica,* and Traetta's *Armida, Sofonisba, Ifigenia in Tauride,* and *Siroe.* In each work, although at least one ABB theme preserves the dimensions standard in the 1740s and 1750s, at least one other theme—and usually three or four other themes—introduces a more

Example 11

O nel sen di qualche stella O sul margi- ne di Lete O sul

margi- ne di Lete

(Bach: Catone 4)

extended version of the ABB principle. Sometimes such a longer theme represents a further augmentation of the standard theme size of the 1740s and 1750s: each B segment lasts four bars and the chords change once per bar (see example 11, which again utilizes the formula $I - I^6 - IV[ii^6] - V - I[or vi] - I^6 - IV[ii^6] - V - I$). Themes such as these account for only a small proportion of the longer themes, however, for the ABB themes of the 1760s and 1770s in fact feature a far greater variety of dimensions and proportions than those of the 1730s, 1740s, and 1750s. First, the A segment may last two, three, or four bars, although it occasionally attains a length of up to six bars. Second, at least one B segment may last three or four bars, although it occasionally attains a length of up to eight bars.[61] Third, the lengths of the two B segments of any one theme may differ. Di Maio's *Adriano in Siria* (Rome, 1769) illustrates the variety of ABB themes present in so many operas of the 1760s and 1770s. In this work, eleven fast duple-meter arias begin with ABB themes. As Table 1 shows, di Maio composed only three themes according to the same dimensions: "Chi s'espone a grande impresa," "Leon piagato a morte," and "Piange l'amato bene." Otherwise, by composing B segments of two, three, and four bars and combining B segments of different lengths, the composer managed to fashion a great variety of ABB themes.

The third and last group consists of operas in which *all* ABB themes are longer than those standard in the 1740s and 1750s. In other words, there are no themes of dimensions (1-4) + 2 + 2, all themes resembling the longer ones found in the operas of the second category. The operas of this third group date from the 1770s and 1780s: Haydn's *Armida*, Jommelli's *Armida abbandonata* and *Ifigenia in Tauride*, and Mozart's *Lucio Silla*, *Il re pastore*, and *Idomeneo*.

For additional examples of the longer ABB themes of the 1760s and 1770s, we turn to the operas of Jommelli. From 1761, the year of his *Olimpiade*,

Table 1.   Dimensions of ABB Themes in di Maio's *Adriano in Siria*

Aria	Length of ABB theme
"Dal labbro, che t'accende"	2 + 4 + 3
"Sprezza il furor del vento"	3 + 4 + 4
"Dopo un tuo sguardo, ingrata!"	7 + 2 + 2
"Prigioniera abbandonata"	3 + 4 + 3
"Qual nocchier, se in mar turbato"	3 + 3 + 4
"Chi s'espone a grande impresa"	2 + 4 + 4
"Mi chiama a bel contento"	1 + 2 + 4
"Più non temo avverso il Fato"	3 + 2 + 4
"Leon piagato a morte"	2 + 4 + 4
"Barbaro, non comprendo"	4 + 2 + 2
"Piange l'amato bene"	2 + 4 + 4

Jommelli consistently began to experiment with elongated ABB themes. A theme with the dimensions 4 + 3 + 3 thus appears in *Olimpiade* (figure 6a); a theme with the dimensions 2 + 4 + 4, in *Semiramide* (1762).[62] The dimensions 3 + 4 + 4 occur first in *Enea nel Lazio* (1766, figure 6b) and then in several subsequent operas.[63] In the late operas Jommelli composed for Italy, the dimensions 4 + 4 + 4, 6 + 6 + 3, 5 + 3 + 3, and 7 + 3 + 3 occur respectively in *Armida abbandonata* (1770, figure 6c), *Achille in Sciro* (1771), and *Ifigenia in Tauride* (1771).[64] A somewhat smaller format, which nevertheless employs relatively long B segments, is 2 + 3 + 3, found in *Armida abbandonata* (1770).[65] All told, Jommelli constructed approximately 50 percent of his ABB themes of the 1760s and 1770s with such extended dimensions. It is important to note the means he often used to build and unify these themes. First, he frequently utilized long note values in the melody, repeated single words or pairs of words, and joined two cadences to form each B segment (figure 6b).[66] Regardless of the number of cadences, however, Jommelli sometimes quickened the harmonic rhythm toward the end of each B segment, thus creating greater rhythmic drive (figure 6b, c).[67]

The cadences of the 1760s and 1770s, much like the ABB themes of the same period, are varied, representing a mixture of the old and the new. Composers still utilized the ascending bass formula and fashioned paired, two-bar cadential phrases. At the same time, however, the period saw two significant changes regarding cadences. First, composers gradually abandoned the ascending bass formula, doubtless because its use precludes any substantial harmonic suspense. A phrase utilizing this formula not only ends on I but also begins on I and emphasizes other forms of tonic harmony: I^6 and I_4^6. Among the first composers studied here to change were Jommelli and J.C. Bach. Jommelli used the formula frequently in his operas of the 1740s, occasionally in those of the 1750s, but extremely rarely after 1760, the cadence concluding the first

Figure 6. Jommelli's Longer ABB Themes

(Jommelli: Olimpiade 15)

(Jommelli: Enea 10)

(Jommelli: Armida 1)

vocal section of only one aria in all his twelve operas of the 1760s and early 1770s.[68] Similarly, Bach employed the cadence once in his first opera, *Artaserse* (Turin, 1761), and resorted to it only once again in all of his subsequent operas.[69] All of the other composers investigated here continued to use the ascending bass formula, but only in the 1760s and early 1770s and usually in its three-bar version (see example 10). Mozart thus used it frequently in *Mitridate* (1770) and *Lucio Silla* (1772) but not at all in *Il re pastore* (1775) or *Idomeneo* (1781). None of the other operas of the late 1770s or early 1780s feature this once ubiquitous cadence.

Second, composers frequently wrote cadences with final I_4^6 and V chords that each last a full bar (often the preceding IV or ii^6 chord lasts one bar as well). While Traetta almost never composed such cadences, J.C. Bach, di Maio, and Mozart did for approximately half of the arias in each of their operas examined here (figure 7a). Some composers occasionally prolonged the I_4^6 chord even further. Di Maio, for example, fashioned a climactic cadence with a three-bar I_4^6 chord for "Più non temo avverso il Fato" in his *Adriano in Siria* (figure 7b).[70] By the 1770s, therefore, the cadence of the first vocal section had changed profoundly. Instead of a rather hasty, matter-of-fact phrase ending, we often find great harmonic suspense, as deceptive cadences and prolonged I^6, IV, and I_4^6 chords delay the final tonic chord (and beginning of the medial ritornello).

Figure 7.   Cadences of the 1760s

Hasse stands somewhat apart, having composed no cadences with whole-note I_4^6 and V chords until the very end of his operatic career, in *Ruggiero* (Milan, 1771).[71] Hasse had in fact become an anomaly on several counts by the 1760s and 1770s. He retained a fast harmonic rhythm, composing themes and cadences scarcely different from those of the 1750s, 1740s, and sometimes even the 1730s. Such compositional conservatism parallels his relative constancy in matters of drama and orchestration. As Charles Burney wrote when traveling through Vienna in 1772:

> Metastasio and Hasse, may be said, to be at the head of one of the sects; and Calsabigi and Gluck of another. The first, regarding all innovations as quackery, adhere to the ancient form of the musical drama, in which the poet and musician claim equal attention from an audience;...The second party depend more on theatrical effects, propriety of character, simplicity of diction, and of musical execution, than on, what *they* style, flowery descriptions, superfluous similies, sententious and cold morality, on one side, with tiresome symphonies, and long divisions, on the other.[72]

By the end of his operatic career, Hasse was probably the most reactionary composer of opera seria. As chapter 5 will demonstrate, however, Hasse finally adopted relatively "modern" techniques of orchestration, but at a very slow pace.

This survey of the harmonic rhythm of thirty-two composers of 1716-84 suggests a reason for Hasse's musical conservatism: through most of the 1730s, 1740s, 1750s, and in part of the early 1760s, Hasse worked primarily in Dresden and Warsaw. Again and again, we have seen evidence linking Germany—particularly northern Germany—with a conservative musical style. First, those composers who left Italy before 1730 or learned their craft outside Italy did not utilize the ABB theme and ascending bass cadence. Such was the case with Caldara and Wagenseil.[73] Second, those composers who gained some significant exposure to Italian opera in Italy but then left for parts far north utilized the standard formulas but preserved, sometimes for decades, the harmonic rhythm prevalent in Italy at the time they departed. Such was the case with Graun and Sarti.[74] Hasse cultivated closer ties with Italy and visited there periodically in the 1740s and 1750s. Nevertheless, he composed most of his operas for Dresden and Warsaw. Relatively isolated and virtually free of competition, Hasse did not have to emulate the younger composers active in Italy and southern Germany.

Just as composers with the least exposure to opera in Italy maintained a more "baroque" harmonic rhythm, all composers who received their training in Italy and worked primarily in Italy or southern Germany shared in the evolution of a slower, more "classical" harmonic rhythm. All utilized the ABB and ascending bass formulas and gradually decreased the rate of harmonic change in more or less equal increments and with similar effects on their arias. The slow pace and continuity of this development argues strongly that the mid-eighteenth century was not a time of stylistic chaos. As far as the composers

investigated here are concerned, we see a fairly linear progression from the
brief, clipped ABB themes and hasty cadences composed by Feo, Hasse, Leo,
and others in the 1730s to the longer, more lyrical ABB themes and more
monumental cadences composed by Bach, Jommelli, di Maio, and others in
the 1760s and early 1770s. No doubt other aspects of style—melodic style and
woodwind orchestration—which seem to have arisen as natural outgrowths of
harmonic expansion saw similarly gradual and consistent development.

What makes the simultaneous retardation of harmonic rhythm and
retention of various phrase and cadential formulas so intriguing is its
continuation into mature works that Mozart and Haydn composed in the early
1780s. For the fast duple-meter arias of *Idomeneo* (Munich, 1781), for
example, Mozart composed two ABB themes, of which the longer has the
dimensions 2:5:5:

Example 12

(Mozart: *Idomeneo*, "Se il tuo duol")

The melody opens with a triadic ascent so typical of the period (see figure 6a,b and example 11), and the first B segment concludes with the more or less standard deceptive cadence. This ABB theme thus shows how one small section of a Mozart aria can be understood in terms of a gradual evolution of style over a period of sixty years. The bass line of example 12 largely follows the "Trommelbass" pattern, although the alternating quarter notes and quarter rests in the second B segment testify to Mozart's high degree of textural and rhythmic variegation. Chapter 3 will investigate such bass lines but demonstrate that many of the rhythmic and textural characteristics of Mozart's and Haydn's mature styles arose rather early, around 1770, and in the music of other composers, including Jommelli and J.C. Bach.

3

Texture: The Development of "Classical Counterpoint" in Jommelli, J.C. Bach, and Haydn

Introduction

Around 1770, the dramatic music of Niccolò Jommelli underwent a profound transformation, a new style revealing itself at the beginning of *Armida abbandonata* (Naples, 1770), the first of his late operas for Italy, and pervading his subsequent works for the Italian stage. The style of Johann Christian Bach changed at about the same time and with similar results: his *Temistocle* (Mannheim, 1772), though composed and performed north of the Alps, exhibits for the first time many of the traits new as well to Jommelli's operas of the same period.

This style shift, like the fifty-year-long process of harmonic expansion, principally affected rhythmic organization. The new style associated with the year 1770 developed far more rapidly, however, at least in the works of Jommelli and Bach, and shaped smaller-scale rhythmic and, secondarily, melodic details, indeed the tiniest, bar-by-bar nuances of stress and contour. New groupings of eighth notes and quarter notes gained currency, permeating most layers of the musical fabric—principally the bass line, but other instrumental parts as well, and, in the case of Jommelli, even the vocal line. While enlivening the rhythmic and melodic surface, these new patterns had far-reaching effects: melodies are more supple, the texture breathes a new vitality, and important chords stand out in sharper relief.

Apparently the change was neither local nor short-lived. Jommelli and Bach, after all, worked in entirely different circles: Jommelli, in Stuttgart (1754-69), then Naples and Rome (from 1769 until his death in 1774); Bach, in London (1762-72), then Mannheim (1772). The changes they incorporated into their serious operas of the early '70s resonate, moreover, in another repertoire far removed both geographically and generically: the symphonies of Joseph Haydn. The year 1771, according to H.C. Robbins Landon, saw the advent of the composer's "full maturity."[1] At that time, Haydn wrote a series of symphonies—including the still-popular nos. 44 ("Trauer"), 45 ("Abschied"), and 48 ("Maria Theresa")—in which "the increased breadth and scope of a new style, often reaching true monumentality in the quick movements"[2] reveals astonishing similarities, often in the minutest details, to the innovations adopted virtually simultaneously by Jommelli and J.C. Bach. A detailed analysis of the late opere serie of Bach and Jommelli should therefore isolate specific aspects of what was apparently a general change in melodic rhythms and contours, in accompanimental patterns, and in the resultant textures. Such a study will also demonstrate the rhythmic power inherent in opera seria and provide a context in which to evaluate the early styles of Haydn and Mozart.

Texture in the 1770s and 1780s is generally studied in the context of the string quartet, particularly those of Haydn's first four collections: op. 9 (1769 or 1770), op. 17 (1771), op. 20 (1772), and op. 33 ("Gli scherzi," 1781).[3] Of these, the fourth has stirred the most controversy. Haydn himself, in a now famous letter of December 3, 1781, boasted that the new works contained therein "sind auf eine gantz neue besondere art, denn zeit 10 Jahren habe Keine geschrieben."[4] Ever since Adolf Sandberger brought these words to light in 1900,[5] scholars have engaged in argument and counterargument as to Haydn's intent. This ongoing debate in fact provides the most direct access to current interpretations and theories regarding the evolution of classical texture in general.

Sandberger, first of all, takes Haydn at his word and proclaims that it was in the quartets of op. 33 that the composer first perfected the technique of "motivische Arbeit": fragments, variants, and recombinations of motives saturate the texture particularly in the development section. Other scholars suggest that Haydn made his bold statement merely to promote sales of what was actually the first collection of quartets he composed directly for publication and dissemination outside Eszterháza.[6] Still others argue that another collection, either op. 17 or op. 20, saw *the* breakthrough to the classical style.[7] All agree, however, on one point: between the quartets of "op. 1" and those of op. 33, Haydn's texture changed radically and with profound consequences for classical style. Their writings abound with general terms to describe the new relationship of parts: "polyphonic," "equal-voiced," based on "thematic development," etc.

Charles Rosen also states emphatically that op. 33 played a crucial and unique role in the historical development of Haydn and Mozart's mature styles. Of greater interest, however, he offers a refreshing and perceptive reinterpretation of the behavior of texture in the classical string quartet and, by extension, in other classical genres as well. To start, he singles out the opening of the B minor quartet of op. 33 (example 13) for special praise:

> The opening bars . . . are revolutionary. . . . this page represents a fundamental revolution in style, and its most original aspect, the handling of the interaction of principal part and accompaniment, can be observed throughout the set. The relation between principal voice

and accompanying voices is transformed before our eyes. In measure 3, the melody is given to the cello and the other instruments take up the little accompanying figure. In measure 4, this accompanying figure has become the principal voice—it now carries the melody. No one can say just at what point in measures 3 and 4 the violin must be judged the principal melodic voice, and where the cello shifts to a subordinate position, as the passage is not divisible. All that one knows is that the violin starts measure 3 as accompaniment and ends measure 4 as melody.

This is the true invention of classical counterpoint. It does not in any way represent a revival of Baroque technique, where the ideal...was equality and independence of the voices.... The opening page of this quartet, for example, affirms the distinction between melody and accompaniment. But it then transforms one into the other.[8]

Example 13

(Haydn: Op. 33, no. 1, first mov't)

Rosen's treatment of classical counterpoint is significant on five counts, each with significant implications.

First, he does not explain the new texture in terms of equality of voices or baroque technique. The new texture, accordingly, is not "equal-voiced" at all. Over the course of a movement, Haydn gives each line equal opportunity to carry melodies, motives, or purely accompanimental figures; at any one moment, however, he distinguishes melody from accompaniment. Also, specific contrapuntal techniques alone—imitation, canon, inversion, diminution, and so on—cannot make a texture "classical." Second, Rosen does not explain classical counterpoint primarily in terms of motivic technique. In fact, he resorts to the term "motive" only after he has defined his basic concepts, thus implying that motivic techniques alone, like the contrapuntal devices enumerated above, do not account for all of the new style. Third, Rosen does not draw his musical examples from the development section or from the modulatory area of the exposition—precisely where one would expect to find the greatest concentration of motives or imitation. Instead, he focuses on the opening of the exposition and the beginning of the recapitulation. The new texture may appear anywhere, it would seem, and thus affects the interaction of virtually all melody and accompaniment, whether or not the latter imitates the former or utilizes motives. Fourth, Rosen correlates the rise of classical counterpoint to the evolution of new types of individual lines, particularly those of the melody and the bass. Such new accompaniment, for example, is "at once . . . thematic and . . . subordinate."[9] "Thematic elements," on the other hand, " . . . often became very short since they were to be used as accompanying figures."[10] The search for the roots of classical counterpoint must therefore account for changing melodic and accompanimental styles. Fifth, Rosen treats the components of the new style not as a series of isolated events, but in terms of large-scale function, process, and rhythm. Classical counterpoint, accordingly, involves continual change, growth, and sometimes surprise. Melodic and accompanimental roles pass almost imperceptibly from one line to another as smooth and logical transitions connect rhythmically disparate phrases. The relation of texture to structure thus constitutes a significant subject of research.

The present investigation of the operas of Jommelli and J.C. Bach and of the early symphonies of Joseph Haydn supports Rosen's interpretation of classical counterpoint. Example after example in these works shows that the mere presence or absence of imitation or of motivic techniques tells us little about texture and that the real components of the new style—melodically conceived accompaniment, lines beginning as accompaniment and ending as melody, convincing transitions from one phrase to the next—are more subtle, although virtually omnipresent. At the same time, however, this study disagrees with Rosen's portrayal of the historical context of the new style. Briefly, Rosen assumes that classical counterpoint first appeared in its most perfected form in 1781, that it remained more or less the exclusive property of Haydn, Mozart, and Beethoven, and that it grew out of Haydn's experience composing opere buffe in the 1770s. Each of these assumptions lacks hard evidence, however. Too little is known about Haydn's own stylistic development in the 1760s and 1770s, about the styles of his contemporaries, and particularly about comic opera. While most of Haydn's opere buffe have at last appeared in modern edition, Rosen nowhere examines them closely. And the operas of Haydn's contemporaries—Guglielmi, Gassmann, Piccinni, Galuppi, Paisiello, to mention only a few—have largely escaped even thorough bibliographical investigation; comprehensive style analysis is practically nonexistent.

On the basis of the repertoires examined here, the following alternatives to each of Rosen's three points can be formulated:

1. 1770, not 1781, marked a watershed in the development of classical counterpoint, most of the traits Rosen identifies appearing at this time in the operas of Jommelli and J.C. Bach, as well as in the symphonies of Haydn.

2. Jommelli and Bach handled the new style with the same consistency and skill that Haydn did in the early 1770s.
3. The fundamental changes which brought forth the classical style of the 1770s affected all genres simultaneously and in more or less equal measure.

This last issue deserves further comment. To evaluate the roles played by serious and comic opera in the evolution of classical counterpoint, one must avoid confounding two levels of rhythm: the small-scale rhythm and pacing exemplified by Haydn's op. 33 and the large-scale organization and flow of an entire opera. In this latter respect, it is simple to find most eighteenth-century opere serie wanting. Even Mozart's *Idomeneo,* with its magnificent choruses, colorful orchestration, and ingenious blurring of the boundaries between recitative and aria, cannot captivate a modern audience as can *Figaro, Don Giovanni,* or *Così fan tutte.* There is too little variety among the numbers of *Idomeneo.* Aria follows upon aria; most are long, with serious texts, a modulation to the dominant, a medial ritornello, and a recapitulation. Each number, in short, carries all the weight and intensity of the opening "Allegro" or slow movement in a late Mozart symphony or string quintet but none of the wit or relaxation of the Minuet or Finale. In the comic operas, on the other hand, the musical numbers vary continually in length, tonal structure, number of singers, and emotional content of the text; many are accompanied by lively stage action.

Quite another matter is the pacing within each aria, duet, etc.—the rhythmic elements which in Mozart's mature works enliven the accompaniment, impart a subtle give-and-take to melody and accompaniment, and enable a phrase to stand on its own yet move inexorably both to its cadence and to what lies beyond. On a somewhat larger scale, these same elements organize phrases so that an entire section, such as an exposition or first vocal section, gradually gains momentum. As far as these levels of pacing are concerned, *Idomeneo* is hardly inferior to *Figaro;* its arias and ensembles differ in some respects from those of the late comic operas, but they are no less "classical," no less "Mozartean." The aria texts to *Idomeneo* may not have required Mozart to devise contrasting themes or such clearly delineated, but organically related, phrases; yet he did so anyway.

The same relation between opera seria and opera buffa no doubt existed earlier. In the 1760s and 1770s, accordingly, the overall structure of opera buffa became more variegated and more distinct from that of opera seria. At the same time, the small-scale elements of rhythm, stress, and contour evolved simultaneously in both genres. Composers, in other words, did not begin to fashion a "classical" texture and pacing within an aria only when the text or dramatic situation inspired them to do so. For final proof of these points, we must await stylistic studies of opere buffe of the 1760s and 1770s and comparisons of such works with contemporaneous opere serie. Until such time, the fact that significant classical traits appeared simultaneously in the opere serie of Jommelli and Bach and in the early symphonies of Haydn strongly suggests that classical counterpoint evolved concurrently in most, if not all, genres.

The ensuing comparison of the textures of Jommelli, Bach, and Haydn will investigate music only of the same tempo and meter: fast arias (and movements) in duple meter. Of the various textural layers in such works, the bass line will receive the most attention. Melodic lines, intended usually for the voice in one case but for violins in the other, would doubtless pose special problems for comparison; only those of Jommelli will be analyzed in any detail, to demonstrate how changes in texture often entail a change in melodic style as well.

Jommelli: Stuttgart versus Naples and Rome

Jommelli's orchestration, apparently unique in his day, has always provoked strong reaction. Toward the end of the composer's life, and for a short time following his death, a few critics marvelled at its ingenuity and depth, but most complained bitterly of an accompaniment they found contrived and dense, or too assertive and noisy.[11] Recent musical scholarship, whether focusing on Jommelli or surveying Italian opera in general, maintains a more neutral stance but cites similar qualities, particularly regarding the operas Jommelli composed from 1755 to 1768 for the court of Duke Carl Eugen at Stuttgart. As the following samples testify, such remarks describe Jommelli's textures in general terms and attribute their novelty to German taste and orchestral practice:

> The German influence on Jommelli...is seen in...[his] treatment of the orchestra, in a greater complexity of texture and increased attention to idiomatic use of the instruments.... Likewise due to German influence is the greater richness and variety of the harmonies in...Jommelli...as compared with [his] Italian contemporaries.[12]

> The growing independence and refinement of the orchestra in [Jommelli's] arias, *accompagnati,* and purely instrumental movements reflected...the flourishing state of German instrumental music of the time.[13]

> The instrumental texture [in Jommelli's Stuttgart operas] is frequently thick and contrapuntal.[14]

Jommelli's later operas—the works he composed for Rome, Naples, and Lisbon between 1770 and 1772—have received less attention than the Stuttgart operas. Hermann Abert[15] concentrates on the Vienna and Stuttgart operas; Audrey Lynn Tolkoff, on the Stuttgart operas alone. Writing two hundred years ago, Charles Burney offered this account of Jommelli's stylistic progress after Stuttgart:

When he was in the service of the Duke of Württemburg, finding the Germans were fond of learning and complication, he changed his style in compliance with the taste and expectations of his audience; and on his return to Italy [in 1769], he tried to thin and simplify his dramatic Music, which, however, was still so much too operose for Italian ears.[16]

A comparison of Jommelli's Stuttgart operas with the late ones for Italy confirms that Jommelli's style indeed changed, though not quite as Burney saw it. First, while textures in the late operas are thinner, lighter, and more transparent than those in the Stuttgart operas, the later textures are by no means simpler but actually more complex and contrapuntal. The evolution of Jommelli's style demonstrates that lightness does not necessarily entail simplicity and that words commonly used to describe texture—"light," "heavy," "complex," and so on—can easily mislead and confuse. Second, Jommelli did not change his colors merely to suit a different operatic climate. Although the new style discerned by Burney first appeared in its perfected and most consistent form in *Armida abbandonata* (Naples, 1770), also the first of Jommelli's late operas for Italy, the composer had begun moving in this direction before leaving Stuttgart. In fact, changes in melodic and textural styles in Jommelli's operas of 1755-72 suggest a threefold division of the composer's post-1755 career:

1. 1755-63: During his first nine years at Stuttgart—he became "Musikdirektor und Oberkapellmeister" on January 1, 1754— Jommelli maintained one textural style associated largely with the "Trommelbass." Seven operas survive: *Pelope* (Stuttgart, 1755), *Artaserse* (Stuttgart, 1755), *Creso* (Rome, 1757), *Temistocle* (Naples, 1757), *Olimpiade* (Stuttgart, 1761), *Semiramide riconosciuta* (Stuttgart, 1762), and *Didone abbandonata* (Stuttgart, 1763)

2. 1764-68: During his last five years at Stuttgart—he left the Württemberg court on March 29, 1769—Jommelli retained much from the first period yet began tentatively to adopt new techniques that would reach fruition only later. Four operas survive from this period of transition: *Demofoonte* III (Stuttgart, 1764), *Enea nel Lazio* (Stuttgart, 1766), *Vologeso* (Stuttgart, 1766), and *Fetonte* (Stuttgart, 1768)

3. 1770-72: Jommelli demonstrated a new style based on more fragmented lines and structural articulation in *Armida abbandonata* (Naples, 1770) and maintained it fairly consistently through *Demofoonte* IV (Naples, 1770), *Achille in Sciro* (Rome, 1771), and *Ifigenia in Tauride* (Naples, 1771)[17]

During the first period, the composer was already cramming his arias with all the orchestrational "extras" for which he became famous: independent and sometimes even *divisi* viola parts, hyperactive second violin parts, and rapid passagework—particularly sweeping scales and arpeggios—for all violins. The resulting texture in no way approaches classical counterpoint, however, for each line preserves its own melodic and, particularly, rhythmic profile throughout an aria. The bass line, first of all, conforms to the standard preclassical Trommelbass: an ongoing series of eighth notes, or sometimes quarter notes, repeats pitches in groups usually of two, four, or eight. In example 14, therefore, rests are rare; ties or any other form of syncopation, nonexistent. Rhythmic accents, falling always on strong beats, are regular and incessant. Even the passages containing more melodic variety (see mm. 10-13, 22-24, and 30-32) still emphasize notes falling on the beat, never those of the intervening half beats. In measures 10-13 and 23-24, for example, the first of every pair of eighth notes always carries the higher pitch.

Example 14

(Jommelli: Didone 7)

Violins infrequently double the voice and thus constitute an independent layer. If they seem to compete with the singer, it is due not to any comparable lyrical qualities, however, but to their great velocity or sheer mass of sound. In example 15, sixteenth notes abound in the violin parts, the seconds imitating the firsts. This imitation is far removed from either Baroque polyphony or classical counterpoint, however; the notes rush by too quickly and have the effect of a shimmering accompaniment to the more substantial bass line with its customary repeated eighth notes:

Example 15

(Jommelli: Pelope. 1)

A third layer, the vocal line, features a wider variety of note values, particularly quarter, half, dotted half, and whole notes. The rhythm, nevertheless regular and ponderous like that of the strings, always emphasizes first and third beats (example 16):

Example 16

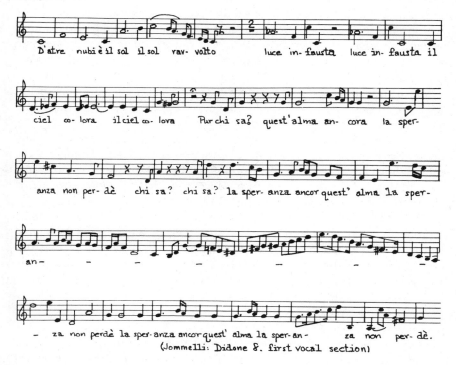

D'atre nubi è il sol il sol rav-volto   luce in-fausta luce in-fausta il

ciel co-lora il ciel co-lora Pur chi sa? quest'alma an- cora la sper-

anza non per-dè chi sa? chi sa? la sper-anza ancor quest' alma la sper-

an — — — — —

— za non perdè la sper-anza ancor quest' alma la sper-an- za non per-dè.

(Jommelli: Didone 8. first vocal section)

Bass instruments in eighths, violins in sixteenths and sometimes thirty-seconds, the voice in eighths, quarters, and halves—all add up to a stratified, heterogeneous texture remaining more or less intact from beginning to end of each aria. Where these layers occasionally share similar rhythms, they then preserve distinct melodic qualities. For example, if the voice, like the violins, executes sixteenth notes—particularly in melismas—the notes are apt to be scalar, whereas those of the violins are more repetitive and disjunct. Or, if the voice, like the bass instruments, articulates a series of eighth notes, they will again be more conjunct. In short, during the period 1755-63, Jommelli hardly transformed the relationship between melody and accompaniment. On the contrary, he rigidly retained the distinction and, inasmuch as he fashioned unusually rapid and independent violin and viola parts, simply added more layers.

In the second period, Jommelli preserved much of the stratified texture of the first period yet began to adopt techniques that would become a truly integral part of his style only in the third period. The very existence of this transition lends a new dimension to our understanding of Jommelli's development and of his relation to supposedly divergent German and Italian operatic traditions and orchestral practices. That it occurred at all argues against the idea of a single Stuttgart style of orchestration. That it occurred so late in Jommelli's tenure there suggests that the composer was not simply conforming to different, more advanced German techniques—he would presumably have adopted such procedures at an earlier date. At the same time, the stylistic proximity of the second period to the third period counters the notion of a uniquely Italian, or Neapolitan, style of orchestration. In positive terms, the transition serves as yet more evidence that the change in Jommelli's style was no isolated or local event, but part of a general shift affecting many composers—including J.C. Bach and Haydn—at about the same time.

In his third period, Jommelli created a texture far more complex than any we have seen so far. Each line features a wider variety of note values, and the entire fabric changes continually, working jointly with phrase structure, tonal organization, and orchestration to produce arias that are better articulated texturally and more dramatic. In light of this greater fluidity and complexity, texture will be analyzed according to three criteria: (1) the rhythms and melodic contours of individual lines, (2) the short-term vertical alignment of these lines, that is, their interaction at any given moment, and (3) the behavior of this vertical alignment over the course of an aria. In each category, texture in Jommelli's third period will be compared directly with that in his first period.

Individual Lines

The most obvious and fundamental innovation of Jommelli's late arias concerns the bass line. Instead of a Trommelbass, we find a more fragmented and variegated line. Upper accompanimental parts changed as well and to similar effect. As a result, greater variety in the intensity and placement of rhythmic and melodic stress enlivens all parts: stresses fall frequently on offbeats, particularly the second beat but also the second and sixth half beats. To produce such accentuation, five specific rhythmic patterns serve as virtually ubiquitous earmarks of the new style:

Pattern 1: 𝅘𝅥x=(○) or 𝅘𝅥x 𝅘𝅥x (𝅗𝅥 𝅗𝅥) *(in the bass line).* Shorn of many of the repeated notes which necessarily comprise a Trommelbass, the bass line is here confined to one or two strong beats per bar. Significantly, the bass line thus gains melodic interest, for changes of pitch formerly obscured in an unarticulated stream of eighths or quarters now devolve upon isolated notes and, as a result, project more clearly.

Pattern 2: 𝄾 𝅘𝅥𝅘𝅥𝅘𝅥 *(in any string part).* Such patterns occur in three rhythmic contexts: arrayed side-by-side (pattern 2a: 𝄾 𝅘𝅥𝅘𝅥𝅘𝅥 𝄾 𝅘𝅥𝅘𝅥𝅘𝅥), introducing a steady succession of eighths (pattern 2b: 𝄾 𝅘𝅥𝅘𝅥𝅘𝅥 𝅘𝅥), or preceding a longer note (pattern 2c: 𝄾 𝅘𝅥𝅘𝅥𝅘𝅥 𝅗𝅥 , 𝄾 𝅘𝅥𝅘𝅥𝅘𝅥 𝅗𝅥 𝅗𝅥). In each case, the first note falls on the second or sixth half beat, thus producing a gentle syncopation. Any upper accompanimental line beginning in this fashion will project more clearly than one starting flush on the downbeat. If the second or fourth beat or the second or sixth half beat carries the highest pitch, moreover, the line, now with "melodic syncopation,"[18] will gain a subtle lyrical distinction as well (figure 8).

Figure 8.   Melodic Syncopation in Pattern 2

(Jommelli: Achille 1)   (Jommelli: Armida 1)

Jommelli used pattern 2 also to enliven the bass line, and he did so far more frequently in the third period than he had in the first. Of the thirty fast duple-meter arias of the later period, twenty-one—or 70 percent—contain this rhythm; in many of these arias, the pattern appears again and again.[19] Of the forty-six fast duple-meter arias of the earlier period, however, only eleven—or 24 percent—utilize pattern 2.[20]

Pattern 3: 𝄾 𝅗𝅥 𝅗𝅥 𝅗𝅥 𝅘𝅥 *(in an upper accompanimental line).* This syncopated pattern avoids not only the first and third beats, but the second and fourth as well.

Pattern 4: (a) ♩♩♪♪♪♪ (b) ♩♪♪♪♪ (c) 𝅗𝅥♪♪♪♪ *(in the vocal lines and occasionally in instrumental parts).* While string parts of the third period often employ patterns 1 and 2 and thus become quite fragmented, the vocal line had to remain more sustained, unless of course it set a chain of epithets or other brief outbursts. Jommelli avoided strong beats just the same, here by means of a tie over the first or third beat, the rhythmic momentum resuming on the second or sixth half beat.[21] Such rhythms behave much like pattern 2: they produce a slight syncopation, intensified further if the second or fourth beat or the second or sixth half beat carries the highest pitch ("melodic syncopation," see figure 9).

Figure 9.   Melodic Syncopation in Pattern 4

By and large, each of the three versions of this pattern appears only slightly more frequently—whether in the bass line or in the vocal part—in the arias of Jommelli's third period than in those of his first. More important, however, melodic syncopation[22] further intensifies this rhythm far more often in the later arias. In the vocal line, such melodic syncopation occurs in eight late arias[23]— or 27 percent of all late fast duple-meter arias—but in only two early ones[24]—or 4 percent of all early fast duple-meter arias. In the bass line, it occurs in twelve late arias[25]—or 40 percent of all late fast duple-meter arias—but in only seven early ones[26]—or 15 percent of all early fast duple-meter arias. This contrast becomes even more acute when one considers only those instances where pattern 4 contains two kinds of syncopation: melodic syncopation after the tie and a syncopated tied note (pattern 4a). Such passages occur in late arias only.[27] In the early operas, in short, pattern 4 hardly detracts from the regular emphasis on first and third beats.

Pattern 5: x ♩ x ♩ *(in the bass).* Jommelli used this pattern only in the 1770s. It deserves mention not because it arises frequently—Jommelli utilized it only in *Achille* 14—but because it appears also in Haydn's symphonies of the same years (see p. 81).

Short-Term Vertical Alignment

In addition to lending greater rhythmic flexibility and accentual variety to individual lines, patterns 1-5 create a more transparent blend of all string parts. Bass instruments, often retreating to one or two notes per bar, allow violins and violas to come to the fore, as for example in a "bass pedal for upper strings."[28] In example 17, the viola pedal resembles a Trommelbass but has a far lighter effect, for only violas execute the pedal. Continuo instruments—cellos, double basses, bassoons, and cembalo—enter only to buttress the first chord in measures 1 and 3, thereby articulating the phrase structure:

Example 17

Fa   che si   spieghi   che si spieghi al- meno

(Jommelli: Achille 10)

By the same token, violins and violas sometimes allow bass instruments to come to the fore. In general—and this is the crux of the textural change—the ongoing stream of eighth notes (or sometimes sixteenth notes) which had formerly permeated all string parts appears in the arias of the 1770s now in one voice, now in another. Those accompanying lines momentarily without this rhythmic momentum separate their notes with rests or sustain them, whole notes, dotted half notes, and ties becoming much more common. The resultant vertical alignment of motion and repose, of kinetic and potential energy, comes in several specific guises. The most common combines patterns 1 and 2 to form an "interlocking bass and upper accompaniment:"[29]

1. [musical notation]

2. [musical notation]

3. [musical notation]

4. [musical notation]

Such formulas, rare in the earlier operas,[30] appear regularly from 1770 on, particularly accompanying melismas in the A section[31] and anywhere in the B section.[32] In several other arias, moreover, these rhythms extend as an ostinato through most or all of both vocal sections, producing an accompaniment which could be termed "motivic," although the motive in question never strays from the first violin part (example 18):[33]

Example 18

(Jommelli: *Achille* 14)

Whether in the context of "interlocking bass and upper accompaniment" or other innumerable patterns which also combine eighth notes with sustained or fragmented lines, the active part did not have to confine itself, as before, to repeating one note of a chord. If it were the only moving part or one of two moving parts, it could achieve a certain lyricism by either arpeggiating the chord or, more significant, mixing nonharmonic tones with the chord tone(s) (example 19):

Example 19

Figure 10. Jommelli's Early Usage of Pattern 2

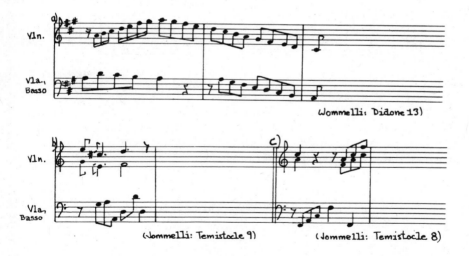

The increased use of such accompanimental nonharmonic tones—usually passing tones or oscillating auxiliary tones—against a sustained or fragmented background provided by other strings counts in fact as one of the most significant developments of the 1770s.

This innovation becomes more obvious when we reexamine those arias with pattern 2 or 4 in the bass line. In a majority of the eleven early arias with pattern 2, the accompanying violins and violas simultaneously play eighth notes or sixteenth notes as well; the bass instruments either double them in octaves or thirds[34] (figure 10a) or else serve as the foundations of rapidly changing chords[35] (figure 10b). In either case, the bass line, with the exception of its eighth-note rest on the downbeat, follows the rhythm of the upper strings and has no opportunity to introduce nonharmonic tones. In other instances of pattern 2, the upper strings may utilize longer note values or rests, but the bass instruments still avoid nonharmonic tones and rely on chordal formations[36] (figure 10c). Nonharmonic tones set against a more sustained violin line appear in only three early arias, and only once in each.[37] In the case of pattern 4 in the bass line, the rhythm in question occurs in a greater variety of textural contexts. Nonetheless, in six of the seven arias where melodic syncopation enlivens pattern 4 (see p. 56), the bass line completely avoids nonharmonic tones[38] (example 20):

Example 20

(Jommelli: Temistocle 9)

In the late arias, quite simply, patterns 2 and 4 occur in the context of slower harmonic motion and of a vertical alignment where all or most of the upper string parts are sustained. The bass therefore can—and usually does—introduce nonharmonic tones[39] (example 21):

Example 21

(Jommelli: Armida 1)

Long-Term Behavior

In the 1770s, by using a wider variety of note values and stressing offbeats more frequently, Jommelli created an accompanimental fabric which sounds more contrapuntal than that of his earlier music. Real imitation or motivic work is rare, however. Rather, different rhythmic patterns—most based on patterns 1-5—follow one another closely, appearing now in one voice, now in another. All express various degrees of forward motion. In the bass line, pattern 1 (♩𝄾 ♩ or ♩𝄾♩𝄾) is relatively stable; pattern 4 (♩ ♪♪♪) is more lyrical and moving; quarter notes repeating the same pitch are more insistent; and eighth notes repeating the same pitch (Trommelbass) are driving and relentless. In the upper string parts, pattern 2b (𝄾 ♪♪ ♩) is relatively placid; pattern 2a (𝄾♪♪♪ 𝄾♪♪♪), breathless and agitated; pattern 2c (𝄾 ♪♪♪ ♩), impulsive; and pattern 3 (𝄾 ♪♪♪ ♪), more urgent. Jommelli seems to have understood the various degrees of stability and instability inherent in each of these patterns, for he used them with a new awareness of their effect on the overall pacing. By judiciously arranging them one after another, he could increase the drive to cadences, particularly those concluding the first theme and the second phrase, as well as the arrival at the dominant chord of the secondary key and the conclusion of each vocal section. Texture, in other words, articulates structure.

The first half of the first vocal section of "Fra l'ombre un lampo solo" from Jommelli's *Achille in Sciro* (Rome, 1771) exemplifies many aspects of the new style: rests on, or ties over, strong beats; melodic syncopation; melodically conceived accompanimental fragments with nonharmonic tones; and the interaction of all these elements to build momentum towards specific harmonic goals (example 22). The passage opens with an ABB theme of considerable length. The "A" segment extends for six bars; each "B" segment, for three bars. The accompaniment, with a four-bar Trommelbass and violin figures regularly emphasizing first and third beats, at first resembles that of the composer's earlier style. The vocal line, on the other hand, molds the first five bars into one gesture of gradually mounting intensity. As key ingredients of this process, two ties lead to melodic syncopations. The first tied note (mm. 1-2) arches toward a series of quarter notes which peak on G; the second (mm. 4-5), toward eighth notes which ascend to B-flat. The vocal line then descends, at which point the bass line takes over the eighth-note momentum with a sinuous fragment containing nonharmonic tones and melodic syncopation (m. 6). During the remainder of the first theme, Jommelli highlights the dominant triads (mm. 9 and 12) that begin the cadence of each B segment. In the bass and second violin parts, each V chord is preceded by a half note, then pattern 2c—relative calm, then a sudden impetus to the following downbeat with its dominant chord.

The ensuing orchestral affirmation of tonic harmony (m. 13) consists not of blunt chords but of arpeggiations which emphasize the second and fourth beats. During the modulation (mm. 14-18), most lines aim toward the V^6_5/ii

Example 22

sagace basta bas- ta al nocchier sa-gace che già ri-

trova il polo già riconosce il mar Basta al noc-

(Jommelli: Achille 3)

chord (m. 17), the first to introduce a pitch (E-natural) outside the original key of E-flat. In measure 16, for example, the syncopation of the first violin part and the tie in the vocal line generate momentum; the first violins do not attack a strong beat until they arrive at this chord. The V/V chord (m. 18) then inaugurates a dominant prolongation in the new key of B-flat and the texture changes immediately, all four groups of strings playing very different parts: violas, a sixteenth-note trill on the dominant; second violins, virtually uninterrupted eighth notes; first violins, rapid flourishes; cellos and double basses, quarter notes in contrary motion to the second violins. As the harmony oscillates between tonic and dominant triads, the rhythm becomes more syncopated and restless. First violins stress offbeats (mm. 24-25), and second violins execute a broken series of notes on even-numbered half beats (mm. 24-25, a variant of pattern 3). Finally, all parts converge on a unison arpeggio in measure 26, as if to announce that the secondary key area—and a new theme—is about to begin.

In "Fra l'ombre un lampo solo," Jommelli achieved great rhythmic momentum and textural variety largely by utilizing the rhythmic formulas enumerated above, melodic syncopation, and nonharmonic tones. Patterns 2, 3, or 4, first of all, appear in twelve of the twenty-seven measures duplicated above.[40] Melodic syncopation arises frequently, not only in the contexts of pattern 2 and 4, but elsewhere as well,[41] thus suggesting a theory that would be difficult to prove: that the melodic and accompanimental lines of the 1770s, at least in the operas of Jommelli but perhaps everywhere, contain more melodic syncopation than those of the 1750s and 1760s. Nonharmonic tones, finally, lend even more melodic interest to certain accompanimental lines.[42]

While tabulations and comparisons of certain rhythmic and melodic patterns in Jommelli's arias illuminate the new style of the 1770s, an equally vivid and even more immediate glimpse of the same change is afforded by examining the revisions Jommelli made in 1770-72 whenever he borrowed material from his earlier operas. After returning to Italy in 1769, Jommelli resumed the composition of new operas at a hectic pace. In little more than a year, five opere serie and two other stage works—*Le avventure di Cleomide* and *L'amante cacciatore*—issued from his pen. Perhaps because he was so pressed for time, Jommelli occasionally looked back to his operas of 1755-68 for inspiration (table 2). In most cases, Jommelli retained only the first theme or the first few phrases and then set out on a new course. He did not, after all, possess scores of most of his own Stuttgart operas.[43]

The revisions which transform the opening phrase of "Non curo l'affetto" are particularly revealing (figure 11). Here Jommelli changed the bass line entirely. In the first two bars, instead of a Trommelbass, we find a fragmented line, each bar quoting Pattern 2c with its subtle melodic syncopation and

Table 2.   Sources for Jommelli's Borrowed Arias of 1770-71

Aria	1770-71 Version	Source
O più tremar non voglio	*Demofoonte* IV	*Demofoonte* III
Per lei fra l'armi	*Demofoonte* IV	*Demofoonte* III
Non curo l'affetto	*Demofoonte* IV	*Demofoonte* III
Prudente mi chiedi?	*Demofoonte* IV	*Demofoonte* III
Perfidi, già che in vita	*Demofoonte* IV	*Demofoonte* III
Che mai risponderti?	*Demofoonte* IV	*Demofoonte* III
Passagier che su la sponda	*Achille in Sciro*	*Semiramide*

impetus to the following downbeat. (Compare the same pattern in measures 8 and 11 of "Fra l'ombre un lampo solo,"example 22). He altered the violin parts less, substituting a flowing pattern (♪♫ ♫♪ ♪ ✗) for a more halting one (♫♩. ♫♪ ♩ ✗). In the vocal part, Jommelli left the first two measures intact but fashioned a more definitive climax. In the 1764 version, the melodic climax precedes that of the harmony and of the bass line: the vocal d" at the beginning of measure 3 occurs as the harmony returns to a tonic triad in root position and before the bass leaves its initial pitch. In the 1770 version, the melodic line does not drop in pitch after the initial d" of measure 3 but rises to an e" on the fourth half beat—thus melodic syncopation—and then returns to d" on the third beat. This third note, the new melodic climax, occurs in the context of a I_4^6 chord—the harmonic climax—and accompanies the highest pitch of the bass line. Melody, harmony, and bass line thus work together to impart a surer direction to the phrase. Curiously, only the earlier version includes an independent viola part, thus illustrating how little the mere presence or absence of independent violas tells us about texture.

Jommelli made revisions of a slightly different sort for "Prudente mi chiedi?" When setting the second stanza of text, he retained the key (D Minor), the meter ($\frac{3}{4}$), a syncopated violin part, and, at one point, a descent through a perfect fourth from d to A in the bass line (figure 12). The second version differs nonetheless in its independent viola part and greater chromaticism. Other, more subtle modifications have the same effect as those of "Non curo l'affetto": the regular "oom-pah" accompaniment of bass and violins gives way to a more rhythmically complex texture where, in each bar, a slur in the bass stresses the second beat and an octave leap in the first violins creates a jagged melodic syncopation on the fourth half beat.

This last example suggests that the transformation of Jommelli's rhythmic style affected arias other than those in fast duple-meter. While a full account of his other arias is not necessary here, it must be pointed out that his slow duple-meter arias of the 1760s had exhibited more rhythmic variety than their fast counterparts. Yet by 1770, they, too, underwent a change and, as a matter of course, came to utilize patterns much like those so abundant in the

Figure 11. Two Versions of Jommelli's "Non Curo l'Affetto"

(Jommelli: Demofoonte III 5,
Demofoonte IV 5)

Figure 12. Two Versions of Jommelli's "Prudente mi Chiedi?"

fast arias in duple meter. Arias in triple or compound triple meter, both fast and slow, manifest a similar change, featuring patterns such as the following:

1. $(\frac{6}{8})$

2. $(\frac{3}{4})$

This new rhythmic complexity which pervades most, if not all, of Jommelli's late arias forces us to reassess the general course of the composer's career. *Fetonte* (Stuttgart, 1768), his last opera for Stuttgart and the only one available to generations of music students, was not the composer's last word. Instead, his subsequent operas for Italy constitute the crowning achievements of his career. In these works, Jommelli had to forego choruses and ensembles; yet in purely musical terms, he achieved a mastery of his materials that makes the Stuttgart arias, particularly the early ones, seem turbid and clumsy in comparison. Although this new style had its beginnings before Jommelli left Stuttgart, the fact that it matured in Italy challenges general assumptions to the effect that Italian composers who sojourned in Germany wrote works more complex than those they intended for the home audience and that the classical style, at least in the second half of the century, evolved primarily in Germany and Austria. In the case of Jommelli, we see quite the opposite; the operas composed for Rome and Naples feature a texture lighter and more transparent but at the same time more subtle, more complex, and more "classical" than operas composed for Stuttgart. This reversal in the case of one mid-century composer should warn us that the search for developments relevant to the emergence of classical style must reach not only beyond a few composers and a few genres but also beyond one geographical area.

J.C. Bach's Texture

Having explained the consistency and behavior of Jommelli's new texture of the 1770s, we can summarize Bach's stylistic progress briefly, paying the greatest attention to those instances in *Temistocle* (Mannheim, 1772) where Bach departed from the letter, but not the spirit, of Jommelli's late style.

In his operas of the 1760s—*Artaserse* (Turin, 1761), *Catone in Utica* (Naples, 1761), *Alessandro nell'Indie* (Naples, 1762), and *Carattaco* (London, 1767)[44]—Bach fashioned a texture much like that of Jommelli's early period (1755-63). In most arias, the Trommelbass extends virtually throughout, and the violin parts, while presenting fewer technical challenges, maintain the same sort of unarticulated momentum.[45] Curiously, most of the few instances of pattern 2 ( ) in the bass line and of interlocking bass and upper accompaniment patterns occur in Bach's first opera, *Artaserse*.[46] More important, those passages utilizing pattern 2 resemble many of those observed in Jommelli's early operas, particularly *Temistocle* (see pp. 59-60 and figure 10): their pitches serve as the foundations of rapidly changing chords—nonharmonic tones are out of the question.

At some point between 1767 (the year of *Carattaco*) and 1772 (the year of *Temistocle*), Bach altered and expanded his textural vocabulary. The results do not agree in every respect with Jommelli's style of 1770-72; it is unlikely, after all, that the two composers had any contact with each other. Bach's melodic style, for instance, changed little, and pattern 4 with melodic syncopation, precisely the element which most readily distinguishes the vocal parts of Jommelli's third period (1770-72) from those of his first (1755-63), thus does not appear more frequently in *Temistocle* than it does in any of the earlier operas.

These differences pale, however, when compared with the ways Bach in 1772 equalled or even excelled Jommelli in creating a texture that is lighter and more fragmented, yet more complex and rhythmically compelling than that of the 1760s. Bach, too, partially dissolved the Trommelbass. In its place, he also frequently confined the bass line to one or two notes per bar, employed interlocking bass and upper accompaniment patterns (in five of the six fast arias of *Temistocle* in duple meter),[47] and devised "bass pedals for upper strings."[48]

Bach also took the new style two steps further. First, he frequently employed another new accompanimental rhythm, pattern 6 (𝄾 ♩♩). An augmentation of pattern 2 and a close ally as well of patterns 3, 4, and 5, pattern 6 likewise avoids the downbeat and enters on an offbeat. The new pattern often accompanies the second theme (see example 24), where it not only helps differentiate that phrase from the preceding material but also lends stability to the new key,[49] since it uses quarter notes rather than the eighths usually found elsewhere. Second, Bach often gave pattern 6 to the instruments on which he had always lavished the most care: woodwinds and horns. Before 1772, Bach, like Jommelli, had required his winds to provide harmonic support generally with sustained chords, usually in half notes or whole notes; they play a harmonic "background," pure and simple. In *Temistocle,* however, Bach wrote fast duple-meter arias in which the accompanimental winds assert a more independent and active identity. They frequently enter not on downbeats, as before, but on the second beat with pattern 6 or a variant thereof, such as 𝄾 ♩♩ . Other patterns which share an attack on a relatively weak beat (𝄾 ♩♩𝄾 or 𝄾 ♩|♩), though present in earlier arias, also appear in *Temistocle* in greater numbers. The move towards melodically interesting and rhythmically enlivened accompaniment thus extended to the winds and, as a result, brought about a new, more integrated relationship of winds and strings.

Passages from three arias of *Temistocle* illustrate how Bach utilized the new techniques of the '70s in various portions of the first vocal section: the first

Example 23

(Bach: Temistocle 1)

theme and second phrase, the second theme, and the final melisma and cadence.

Example 23 comprises a first theme (mm. 1-8) and a second phrase (mm. 8-13) concluding with a half cadence. Each phrase begins calmly and then gains momentum. Bass instruments, for instance, commence with one note per bar, quicken to four, relax to one again (mm. 8-11), and then return to four. Flutes, utilizing a variant of pattern 6, engage in an expansive dialogue with the bass, but only at the beginning of the first phrase. As the first cadence approaches, the violins, which had started out with a great variety of note values, settle on eighth notes exclusively (mm. 6-7). Toward the end of the second phrase, the violins introduce a variant of pattern 3 (m. 12), thus lending urgency as the half cadence approaches.

Example 24 shows the superimposition of several patterns. Only "clarinetti d'amore" maintain a steady flow of eighth notes. Bass instruments retreat to the beginning of each bar (pattern 1); first violins enter on the second half-beat with eighth notes (pattern 2b); second violins enter on the second beat with the equivalent of quarter notes (pattern 6); and oboes interject their harmonic support on the fourth beat. The end result is a second theme at once placid and excited, at once confident and disturbed—the perfect setting for

Example 24

(Bach: Temistocle 18)

Aspasia's indecision ("Ah...si vada; no...si resti"). The first violins, furthermore, illustrate a significant application of the new textural style; a line begins as accompaniment, ends as melody, and serves thereby as a bridge between two rhythmically contrasting passages. In the first four bars of this example where chords change once per bar, the first violins are strictly accompanimental; they quote pattern 2b on one pitch. Much more prominent are the slower parts given to bass instruments, second violins, oboes, and voice. In the last bar, however, the harmonic and declamatory rhythms accelerate, and the first violins and voice now carry a melody in eighths. The transformation comes in measure 5. First violins enter as before as accompaniment but almost immediately become the melody.

Example 25 begins and ends in the dominant key of this E-major aria. The harmonic goals are two: (1) the IV chord (m. 43) that concludes the extensive triplet passage for voice and (2) the final $I_4^6 - V - I$ cadence. Near the first climax, Bach generates momentum by utilizing first a syncopated rhythm

(♪♩ ♪♪♩ ♪) in the second violins and viola (m. 41) and then the related but more urgent pattern 3 in all strings (m. 42). Later, Bach moves toward the second climax by progressing from an interlocking bass and upper accompaniment pattern (mm. 45-46) to driving eighth and sixteenth notes.

Example 25

(Bach: *Temistocle* 5)

Temistocle thus marks the first time that J.C. Bach, at least in his opere serie, utilized several techniques new to, or at least more prevalent in, the contemporary operas of Jommelli: pattern 2 in the bass, "bass pedals for upper strings," "interlocking bass and upper accompaniment," pattern 3 in upper string parts immediately before a cadence, and a wider spectrum of note values in the base line. The resultant texture does not resemble Jommelli's of 1770-71 exactly, but the similarities are striking enough to suggest that Bach, too, participated in a general style shift occurring around 1770.

Haydn: "Sturm und Drang" and Texture

The standard account of Haydn's early development as a symphonic composer derives from theories set forth seventy-five years ago by Théodore de Wyzewa.[50] Arguing for a "crise romantique" in Haydn's personal and artistic life, Wyzewa maintained that the composer, moved by tragic events in his own life as well as by the proto-Romantic literary movement known as "Sturm und Drang," altered his musical style abruptly. His symphonies, now frequently in minor keys, gained in emotional depth and rhythmic drive. Recent scholars, to be sure, have challenged the propriety of applying the term "Sturm und Drang" to Haydn and his music. H.C. Robbins Landon, for example, has demonstrated convincingly that Haydn composed "Sturm und Drang" symphonies several years before the corresponding literary movement, largely of English origin, made its first inroads into Austria.[51] Landon retains some of Wyzewa's terminology, nevertheless: the style change, evident as well in symphonies by Haydn's contemporaries, expressed an "Austrian musical crisis." More important, Landon and other present-day scholars still subscribe to Wyzewa's basic tenets concerning the purely musical manifestations of the change: the new style was bound inextricably with the minor mode and therefore began ca. 1767, when Haydn began employing minor keys frequently. The *MGG* article, "Haydn," written by Landon and Jens Peter Larsen, presents this standard view:

> Aber in einer Reihe von Sinfonien, die der Zeit um 1768/69 angehören dürften (26, 39, 49, 59), findet sich eine so auffallende Intensivierung des Ausdrucks, dass man fast von einem neuen Stil sprechen darf. Was bei diesen Sinfonien als besonders charakteristisch auffällt, ist neben dem starken rhythmischen Impuls, der in den schnellen Hauptsätzen hervortritt, die Wahl der Molltonart.[52]

Landon describes the new style at greater length in his recent *Haydn: Chronicle and Works,* a five-volume work which stands today as the most comprehensive summary of Haydn's life and music. In the chapter entitled "Crisis Years: *Sturm und Drang* and the Austrian Musical Crisis," the author treats the symphonies of 1766-75 as a stylistic unit and lists nine "technical devices which become typical for these years."[53] His list contains serious flaws, however. Most important, in the case of four of the nine items, all musical illustrations and citations of additional exemplary passages refer only to symphonies Haydn composed after 1770; none refers to any he composed between 1766 and 1770. This shortcoming suggests that the symphonies of 1766-75 actually comprise two stylistic groups, and we will see that the symphonies of the early 1770s differ considerably from those of the late 1760s. Landon himself, moreover, in his 1956 monograph *The Symphonies of Joseph Haydn,* treats this repertoire in two separate chapters—"The Symphonies of 1766-1770" and "The Symphonies of 1771-1774"—and lists the same four technical devices, sometimes word for word and accompanied by the same musical examples, in the second chapter only.[54]

To deal with other issues raised by Landon's analysis of Haydn's early symphonic development, the following columns compare two lists of style traits: the first, from Landon's *Haydn: Chronicle and Works,* describes the symphonies of 1766-75; the second, from Landon's earlier *The Symphonies of Joseph Haydn,* describes the symphonies of 1771-74:

1. An increased awareness of contrapuntal forms	The assimilation of contrapuntal devices into Haydn's style
2. An increased use of dynamic marks	The increased dynamic range
3. The use of unison *forte* opening subjects combined	The use of unison *forte* opening subjects combined with sharp

with sharp dynamic contrasts within the main subject	dynamic contrasts within the main theme
4. A new sense of long harmonic line	The increased harmonic breadth
5. Final use of the old *sonata da chiesa* . . . form	
6. Haydn's use of Gregorian plain-chant	
7. Wide "leaps" in the thematic material, longer note values	The wide range of the thematic material
8. Orchestration	Orchestration
9. The use of syncopated patterns	The development of syncopated patterns
10.	The second subject
11.	The double announcement of the main subject
12.	The adoption of the regular period
13.	The use of the *fausse reprise* or sham recapitulation
14.	Slow introduction

On both lists, the first four entries are those attributes which Landon ascribes alternately to 1766-75 or just to 1771-74. The fifth and sixth, relating to use of *sonata da chiesa* format and Gregorian chant, have no place on either list; these techniques appear not only in works of 1766-75 but also in pre-1766 symphonies as well. First, Haydn borrowed the *sonata da chiesa* sequence of movements a total of seven times, in Symphonies 5, 11, 18, 21, 22, 34, and 49.[55] Only the last of these, no. 49, postdates 1765, none of the other twenty-nine symphonies of 1766-75 employing this organization. Second, Haydn incorporated plainchant into a total of three symphonies—30 (1765), 26 (c. 1768/69), and 45 (1772)—and used what seems to be a similar cantus firmus in a fourth, no. 22 (1764), although the source of the melody still eludes identification.[56] Of these four works, two predate 1766. Both sonata da chiesa format and use of cantus firmus therefore hardly deserve to be honored as "technical devices" which became "typical." The situation is slightly more complex with the seventh item, "wide leaps in the thematic material," Landon citing two different factors: increased range and longer note values. A case can be made for the latter, but one must realize that Haydn fashioned themes of comparable range—a thirteenth—in several pre-1766 symphonies as well: 14, 18, 27, 33, and 34.

Of Landon's lists for the symphonies of 1766-75, therefore, four items apply only to symphonies Haydn composed after 1770, and two—and to a certain extent three—other items apply as well to symphonies he wrote before 1766. His other list, accounting as it does for the stylistic gulf separating the 1770s from the 1760s, poses fewer problems but still leaves much unsaid. Concerning "the development of syncopated patterns," Landon perceptively reports the advent of what we have referred to as Pattern 3 and "interlocking bass and upper accompaniment," although he implies that the latter appeared only in slow movements. Concerning "the adoption of the regular period," Landon neither provides examples nor describes its extent or development over time. Concerning the "second subject" and "orchestration," Landon makes little attempt to distinguish a consistent later style from an earlier one. For example, in the case of the second theme, Landon writes: "...during this period [1771-74] he is still uncertain as to how this unwelcome child should be treated."[57] In the case of orchestration, besides remarking that Haydn began to use trumpets and drums in keys other than C Major, Landon merely states, "...it may be said that the type of orchestration developed during the previous decade is now perfected."[58]

In sum, while Landon praises Haydn's quick movements of 1771-74 as "often reaching true monumentality,"[59] he lists only four stylistic elements which arise in these movements with any consistency: "the use of unison *forte* opening subjects combined with sharp dynamic contrasts within the main theme" (in Symphonies 44, 46, 51, 52, and 56), "the double announcement of the main subject" (Symphonies 42, 44, 48, 51, 52, and 56), "the use of the *fausse reprise* or sham recapitulation" in the development section (in Symphonies 41, 42, 43, 46, and 65), and "the increased harmonic breadth" (in Symphonies 42 and 52). These qualities certainly deserve mention but none arises in all the symphonies of 1771-74, and none accounts for more than a few bars of each movement. If Haydn's symphonies of 1771-74 differ fundamentally from those of 1766-70, their distinction must lie elsewhere.

Clearly, Haydn's early symphonies deserve a fresh scrutiny. As Barry Brook complains:

> Why do we seem to be so easily misled by relatively obvious "romantic" style characteristics such as the use of minor keys, dynamic extremes, and sombre moods, while ignoring more fundamental style elements such as phrase structure, tonal motion, and harmonic rhythm?[60]

During the period under consideration, in fact, one very basic element of Haydn's style changed rather suddenly. This development pertains neither to rhythmic drive nor choice of mode, but to texture: around 1770, Haydn adopted many of the same bass patterns and accompanimental rhythms and contours that appeared contemporaneously in the operas of Jommelli and J.C. Bach. Significantly, the new style affected all symphonies of the early 1770s—

major and minor ones alike; shaped melodic and rhythmic details through extensive portions of these works; induced or at least made possible other innovations, such as greater harmonic breadth, more independent second themes, and expansion of the exposition; and, in short, imbued Haydn's symphonic style with added depth, variety, and structural clarity.

The turning point for the new style cannot be determined precisely; we do not know in what year Haydn wrote any of the seven symphonies between no. 49 (1768), definitely belonging to the old style, and no. 42 (1771), belonging to the new.[61] For the sake of convenience, we propose the year 1770, although no. 48, which includes certain ingredients of the new style, was probably composed by 1769. With this single exception, then, all symphonies Haydn composed before 1770, from his earliest efforts at Lukaveč for Count Morzin (from 1759 to 1761) to the dark-hued early "Sturm und Drang" symphonies—39 in G Minor (c. 1766/67), 49 in F Minor ("La Passione," 1768), and 26 in D Minor ("Lamentatione," c. 1768/69)—conform to one textural style. In all, this first group comprises forty-seven works: Symphonies 1-40, 41, 49, 58, 59, 72, 107 ("A"), and 108 ("B"). Between 1770 and 1772,[62] on the other hand, Haydn created a series of masterpieces, many still popular with today's concert audiences and all exhibiting many of the same techniques found in Jommelli's late Italian operas of 1770-71 and in Bach's *Temistocle* of 1772. This second group comprises, in chronological order, Symphonies 48 ("Maria Theresa"), 44 ("Trauer"), 52, 43 ("Merkur"), 42, 51, 45 ("Abschied"), 46, 47, and 65.

The ensuing study focuses exclusively on fast movements in duple meter: usually the first movement, occasionally the second (if the symphony follows *sonata da chiesa* format: slow—fast—slow—fast), but never the third (almost always a minuet). *Finali,* generally lighter, less complicated, and with a distinct character and tradition, are not considered. The repertoire under investigation therefore consists of thirty-four fast movements in duple meter, each belonging to a different symphony and falling into one of two chronological groups:

1. 1759-69: Symphonies "B," 1, 2, 4, 9-13, 15, 18, 20-22, 24-27, 30, 32, 34, 37-39, 49, 59, and 72

2. 1770-72: (in chronological order) Symphonies 48, 44, 52, 42, 46, 47, and 65

Since Haydn's symphonies are readily accessible in modern edition,[63] references to exemplary passages will specify measure numbers; also, they will cite passages only from the exposition and development sections, unless the recapitulation contains a passage of interest that has not appeared before.

In the symphonies of the first group, the Trommelbass reigns supreme. Even in the much touted "Sturm und Drang" symphony, no. 39, the bass line consists mostly of eighth notes with a few sixteenths and quarters; whole notes, half notes, dotted half notes, and dotted quarter notes are nonexistent, as are ties or syncopation of any kind. Beginning around 1770, however, the situation changed dramatically. Haydn, like Jommelli and Bach at the same time, began to dissolve the Trommelbass, employed new rhythmic patterns with rests and ties, stressed offbeats and half beats, distributed the ongoing eighth-note momentum to only one or two lines at a time, and fashioned more independent accompanying lines enriched with nonharmonic tones and melodic syncopation.

Specific bass patterns, rare or non-existent in the symphonies of the 1760s but common in those of the 1770s, include the following, most of which we have also observed in Jommelli's and Bach's operas of the later decade.

"Bass pedal for upper strings."   Like Jommelli and Bach, Haydn devised such passages only in the 1770s.[64] He allotted the pedal not only to violas, however, but sometimes also to violas and cellos, or to second violins. At the very beginning of Symphonies 42 and 48, the pedal and the sturdy, isolated notes of the bass line impart an air of grandeur and spaciousness (example 26). Significantly, if Symphony no. 48 in fact precedes all others of 1770-72—its dating is somewhat in question—then the bass pedal for upper strings which opens this work serves as a rather monumental introduction to Haydn's new symphonic style:

Example 26

(Haydn: Symphony no. 48/1)

Whole notes.   While the whole note itself hardly counts as a remarkable or particularly expressive device, its frequency conveniently monitors two elements of the new texture: the rhythmic variegation of the bass line and the distribution of the rhythmic momentum to the upper strings. Significantly, none of the bass lines Haydn composed before 1767 contains a single whole note: his rhythms are too active and nervous. Two works of the late '60s— Symphonies 26 and 59—include a few whole notes, but *all* symphonies of the second group feature them again and again.

Pattern 5 (♩ ♩ ♩ ♩).   Like Jommelli, Haydn utilized this pattern sparingly and only in the 1770s.[65]

Pattern 2 (♪ ♫♫).   In his symphonies of the 1760s, Haydn occasionally utilized patterns 2a (♪♫♫ ♪ ♫♫), 2b (♪ ♫♫ ♩), and 2c (♪ ♫♫ ♩) in the bass line. These passages have little rhythmic or melodic independence, however, and resemble most of Jommelli's early passages with this pattern. In about 50 percent of the cases, the violins also play eighth notes (or sixteenth notes) and the harmony changes at least once every beat;[66] the bass thus follows the rhythm of the melody and has no opportunity to introduce nonharmonic tones (figure 13a). In another 25 percent, the bass instruments actually double the violins in octaves, thus asserting no independence whatever;[67] or, the harmony changes more slowly, although violins still play eighth notes or sixteenth notes continuously (figure 13b).[68] Of particular interest are several fairly extensive passages where the bass follows the

shortbreathed pattern 2a with the violins sustained. While these bass lines
stand out from the melody, their pitches contain no nonharmonic tones, a
situation we have also seen in the early arias of Jommelli (see above, pp. 59-
60).[69] Such bass lines offer little of real melodic interest and sound rather
mechanical and jumpy (figure 13c). Finally, in a few isolated cases, the bass
quotes pattern 2b or 2c with the violins sustained.[70] All told, few of the early
instances of patterns 2a, 2b, and 2c in the bass differ rhythmically from the
accompanying violin parts; few contain nonharmonic tones or melodic
syncopation.

Figure 13. Haydn's Use of Pattern 2 in Early Symphonies

(Haydn: Symphony no. 30/1)

(Haydn: Symphony no. "B"/1)

(Haydn: Symphony no. 10/1)

In Haydn's symphonies of 1770-72, on the other hand, chords change more slowly and the upper string parts are more often sustained, particularly if the bass quotes patterns 2a, 2b, or 2c. Patterns 2a and 2b appear frequently in two movements apiece and almost always enhanced with nonharmonic tones and melodic syncopation (figure 14a).[71] An interesting transitional use of pattern 2b arises in Symphony no. 49, one of the last symphonies of the 1760s. Here the rhythm accompanies the second theme without syncopation or nonharmonic tones, just as one would expect in a work of this period. The passage deserves our attention instead because the pattern reappears again and again in various string parts, just as the melody itself does. A very basic, unobtrusive accompanimental figure thus becomes a motive (figure 14b). A similar technique appears in Symphony no. 44 (1770-71), where horns twice quote pattern 2b. As in Symphony no. 49, an accompanimental figure is used motivically. Even more significant, the exchange of eighth-notes with the lower strings helps integrate the horns with the rest of the orchestra (figure 14c). Such assimilation of winds and strings resembles a similar process we have already noted in Bach's *Temistocle* of 1772 (see above, p. 70).

Figure 14. Haydn's Use of Pattern 2 in Later Symphonies

(Haydn: Symphony no. 46/1)

(Haydn: Symphony no. 49/2)

c)

Allegro con brio

2 Oboi

Corno I in E/Mi

Corno II in G/Sol

Violino I

Violino II

Viola

Violoncello,
Basso
e Fagotto

(Haydn: Symphony no. 44/1)

Pattern 4 (♩♩♩, ♩♩, ○ ♩).   What is most interesting about the early passages with pattern 4 in the bass line is neither their infrequency nor their avoidance of melodic syncopation but the frequent bass imitation of the melody. Such a passage from the celebrated "Sturm und Drang" symphony, no. 49 ("La Passione"), might seem to embody Haydn's new churning Romanticism (example 27). Yet Haydn had composed similar passages years earlier, albeit in major keys.[72] More important, such imitation, although utilizing nonharmonic tones, has little in common with "classical counterpoint." Stresses are too regular, falling relentlessly and rather monotonously on all first and third beats. The phrase as a whole wanders aimlessly. The mere presence or absence of imitation thus tells us little about texture.

Example 27

(Haydn: Symphony no. 49/2)

After 1770, these patterns appear rather more frequently and always with nonharmonic tones.[73] In one case, the bass line imitates the violins—as in "La Passione"—but now with more melodic syncopation and a surer melodic direction (example 28):

Example 28

(Haydn: Symphony no. 46/1)

Interlocking bass and upper accompaniment. Since such passages feature patterns 2a or 2b in the upper string parts, it should come as no surprise that they behave much like those with patterns 2a or 2b in the bass line. In the early symphonies, accordingly, the eighth notes are always chordal[74] (example 29); in the later works, they are nonharmonic and conjunct[75] (example 30).

Example 29

(Haydn: Symphony no. 49/2)

Example 30

(Haydn: Symphony no. 46/1)

Pattern 6 (X ♩♩♩). The rhythm which Bach employed so often in *Temistocle* (1772) appears in several of Haydn's contemporary symphonies, in upper string parts as well as in the bass line.[76] In Symphony no. 42, these three quarter notes, like the seven eighth notes in figure 14b, constitute both a motive—it derives from the first bar of the symphony—and a simple accompaniment, thus exemplifying the classical style's blurring of the lines between melody and accompaniment (example 31):

Example 31

(Haydn: Symphony no. 42/1)

In Symphony no. 47, pattern 6 stamps its imprint on the entire first movement. Despite appearances to the contrary, this work closely resembles others of the early 1770s, particularly Symphonies 42, 46, and 52. In these other works, eighth notes flow back and forth between melody and bass, many short phrases or motives beginning after an eighth rest on the first or third beat. In Symphony no. 47, on the other hand, the prevailing note value is the quarter, and so quarter notes pass back and forth between melody and bass or between winds and strings, short phrases beginning after a quarter rest on the first beat (example 32):

Example 32

(Haydn: Symphony no. 47/1)

With the possible exception of the whole note, none of the patterns listed above singlehandedly dominated Haydn's symphonic style of the early 1770s. Taken together, however, these rhythmic and melodic details had enormous impact. The results can be seen most vividly in Symphony no. 42 in D Major (1771). Although written entirely in major keys and therefore generally overlooked in studies of Haydn's style of c. 1770, this work counts as one of Haydn's greatest symphonic achievements before his late "Paris" and "London" symphonies of 1785-96. The exposition is, with the exception of that of no. 48, by far the longest he had composed thus far and the longest of any he would compose until that of no. 57 (1774). (Table 3 demonstrates the gradual expansion of Haydn's first-movement expositions: each such section of the early 1770s dwarfs any of the 1760s, and the exposition of no. 48, the first of the second group, is half again as long as the longest of the earlier expositions.)

Table 3.   Length of the Exposition in the Fast Movements in Duple Meter in Haydn's Symphonies to 1772

Symphony	Number of Bars[a]	Symphony	Number of Bars[a]
1759-65[b]		**1766-69**	
B	17	39	50
1	39	59	49
2	35	38	37
4	37	49	51
9	24	26	44
10	37		
11	29	**1770-72**	
12	32	48	83
13	34	44	61
15	31	52	64
18	38	42	81
20	32	46	59
21	42	47	56
22	38	65	51
24	36		
25	31		
27	41		
30	37		
32	35		
34	39		
37	34		
38	38		

a.   In the case of movements in $\frac{2}{2}$ and of movements in ¢ where the bass line moves almost exclusively in quarter notes (rather than eighth notes, as usual), the number given here is actually the number of bars divided by two.

b.   Since the exact chronology of the pre-1766 symphonies is largely unknown, these symphonies are listed in numerical order. The symphonies of 1766-69 and 1770-72, on the other hand, are listed in the chronological order proposed by Landon (*Haydn*, pp. 285-86).

An eight-bar tonic pedal played by violas and cellos—a "bass pedal for upper strings"—opens Symphony no. 42; double basses and bassoons add their weight only at the beginning of each four-bar phrase (example 33a). After an imposing crescendo over another tonic pedal, Haydn embarks on a novel course; he expands the modulation to the unheard-of length of fifteen bars and, in the process, touches on the distant key of B Major (example 33b). Only the new textures and contours of the 1770s made possible this leisurely, but daring excursion. Each bar contains pattern 2a or 2b, always rife with nonharmonic tones. At first (mm. 26-33), melody and accompaniment alternate in quasi-imitation yet maintain separate identities; the melody alone has "sighing" half-note appoggiaturas and melodic syncopation—the highest pitch falls always on the fourth beat.

After this long digression, the V/V chord bursts in (m. 41), beginning yet another pedal point, this one lasting six bars. During the entire passage, the rhythmic equivalent of eighth notes passes back and forth between violins in thirds, on the one hand, and violas and bass instruments in octaves, on the other. Melodic interest likewise changes hands, the bass instruments playing slow eighth-note trills in the context of patterns 2b and 4c (mm. 41-43, 45). The lower auxiliary notes of these trills lend an intensity lacking in the other four pedals of the exposition (mm. 1-8, 12-18, 51-55, and 73-78), where the bass does not introduce nonharmonic tones.

The monumental tone of the exposition carries over into the development section. Its highly dramatic character derives not only from the *fausse reprise* near the beginning (mm. 89-93) but also from the mysterious passage which ensues (example 33c). Beginning in measure 94, only second violins play eighth notes, the other strings sustaining whole notes. Vague and subdued, yet anxious and menacing, this passage expresses the sort of tonal instability necessary for a development section yet allows Haydn to conserve his contrapuntal skill and use of louder dynamics for the second half of the section.

Symphony no. 42 demonstrates that the "new" rhythmic patterns and textures of the 1770s could pervade large expanses of a movement and encourage greater length, harmonic breadth, contrast, and structural clarity. The same principles underlie other first movements, chiefly those of Symphonies 46, 47, and 52, and, to a lesser extent, those of nos. 44 and 48. Further, the opening fast movements in triple meter (in Symphonies 43, 45 and 51) reveal similar techniques with patterns such as the following in the bass line:

1. ♩.   In Symphonies 43, 45, 51
2. ♪ ♫♫   In Symphonies 43, 45, 51
3. x ♩ x | x ♩ x   In Symphony no. 51
4. x x ♩ | x x ♩   In Symphony no. 51
5. x ♩ ♩   In Symphonies 45, 51

The pervasion of Haydn's new textural and rhythmic style and its similarity to that of Jommelli and Bach leads to one further conclusion: Haydn did not work in complete isolation. H.C. Robbins Landon has already shown that certain of the composer's "Sturm und Drang" traits, primarily the use of minor keys, surfaced elsewhere in Austria at roughly the same time Haydn

Example 33

(Haydn: Symphony no. 42/1)

adopted them.[77] A comparison with the operas of Jommelli and J.C. Bach reveals further shared development: much of Haydn's new style of 1770-72 appeared, even in some of its minutest details, simultaneously in the works of at least two other composers, both of whom deserve to be considered among the best of their respective generations. How this phenomenon came about is a question begging for further research. Haydn occasionally visited Vienna, particularly during winter vacation, and must have heard works of other composers. Moreover, while operas other than Haydn's were practically never performed at Eszterháza before 1776, Landon speculates that Antonio Sacchini's popular *La contadina in corte* was presented there in 1769.[78] Whatever the explanation, it is clear that Haydn's isolation and consequent originality can easily be exaggerated.

The Later 1770s and the 1780s

The agreement of detail among the changing styles of composers so geographically separated is one factor which makes the stylistic developments of c. 1770 seem so significant. Also, many of the specific rhythms, melodic contours, and accompanimental techniques which gained currency at this time also underlie the textures and rhythms of the later 1770s, the 1780s, and even beyond. As examples, we turn to some of the works—all fast and in duple meter—most praised by Edward Lowinsky and Charles Rosen in their respective analyses of classical style.

Mozart's Piano Sonata in B-flat, K. 333 (1778, example 34) is used by Lowinsky to illustrate Mozart's "inimitable verve, that quality which sets it apart from Dittersdorf or Johann Christian Bach as much as from Stamitz and Haydn".[79]

Example 34

(Mozart: Piano Sonata, K. 333. 1st mov't)

Lowinsky praises the "very subtle and almost elusive"[80] metrical stresses, yet the rhythms of the passage he quotes consist solely of two of the patterns which also underly the new texture of Jommelli, J.C. Bach, and Haydn: pattern 2b (♩♫ ♪) in the left hand and pattern 4a (♩♩ ♫♫) in the right hand. Two other traits we have seen again and again enliven the rhythmic play: melodic syncopation and nonharmonic tones. This is to suggest not that Mozart's music does not differ from that of Bach or Dittersdorf but that its distinction must lie elsewhere.

An earlier work, Mozart's Piano Concerto in E-flat, K. 271 (1776, see example 35) is proclaimed by Rosen as "perhaps the first unequivocal masterpiece in a classical style purified of all mannerist traces."[81] He points especially to the "rhythmic transition" in measure 7 where "the animation begins to increase" and where the first violins "keep the change from being obtrusive and draw the two phrases together":[82]

Example 35

(Mozart: Piano concerto in E♭, K.271)

Significantly, first violins at this point quote the equivalent of pattern 6, and second violins, the only other instruments to play through the middle of the bar, quote pattern 2b. Both parts behave exactly like the first violin part examined in Bach's *Temistocle* 18 (example 24). In both works, violins enter unobtrusively after a downbeat rest. At first they repeat notes, thus sounding accompanimental. At the beginning of the next bar, however, the violins retain the predominant note values introduced in the preceding bar but now assert a melodic preeminence as well. Both passages effect a transition to a contrasting phrase with a different pulse.

Finally, we return to Haydn's B-minor quartet of op. 33. Significantly, patterns 2a (♪ ♫♫ ♪ ♫♫), 2c (♪ ♫♫ ♩♩), and an abbreviated variant (♪ ♪♪ ♪ ♪ ♪♪ ♪) virtually saturate the opening bars (see example 13), just as all the patterns enumerated in this chapter occur again and again in so many works of the classical period. (The first movements of Mozart's Piano Concerto no. 25 in C and Beethoven's Symphony no. 5, permeated by patterns 2b or 2c, are only the most conspicuous examples.) The presence of these common rhythmic patterns in op. 33 does not of course mean that Haydn brought no originality to the fashioning of texture in these quartets. What was probably new here—if anything was—is the manner in which Haydn took standard accompanimental fragments—one can even say standard accompanimental rhythmic motives—gave them melodic identity and then carefully and consistently used them in both melody and accompaniment. The other techniques Rosen and Lowinsky point to—melodically conceived accompaniment, greater variety in the intensity and placement of accents, the transformation within one line from accompaniment to melody, the smooth transition from one predominant pulse to another, and so on—were not new in 1781 or even in the late 1770s; they did not arise first to meet the dramatic exigencies of opera buffa, nor did they remain exclusive to the music of Haydn, Mozart, and Beethoven. The repertoire examined in this chapter suggests instead that these new techniques—all involving a more subtle and complex relation of melody to accompaniment and of stress and pulse to meter—arose in the late 1760s and early 1770s as part of a general shift in style.

Wind Instruments: Variety, Ensembles, and Frequency of Use

Introduction

The second and third quarters of the eighteenth century saw momentous changes in the orchestral treatment of woodwind instruments. One development came as a result of harmonic expansion; as harmonic rhythm became slower and slower in relation to melodic rhythm, wind instruments—at first oboes and horns—assumed the function of sustaining, or otherwise drawing attention to, a chordal background. Other aspects of this veritable revolution in orchestration parallel the textural changes studied in chapter 3 in the context of string and voice parts. First, as a corollary to the increased rhythmic variegation of individual bass and accompanimental string lines, wind participation became more and more fragmentary, wind entrances serving to enhance particular chords, cadences, or entire phrases. Second, as a corollary to the rhythmically more complex and subtle vertical alignment of strings, woodwind ensembles grew in size and rhythmic intricacy. Before tracing these elements of classical orchestration in the operas of Hasse, Jommelli, and J.C. Bach, however, it is necessary to address more basic issues: what instruments were used, the frequency with which they appear, and the manner in which they combine with other winds.

The Italian opera orchestra of the 1750s differed little from that of the preceding decades,[1] the backbone remaining the same: strings, oboes, and horns. The strings consisted of first and second violins (frequently playing the same part), violas (often doubling the bass line in their own range), and cellos and double basses, this latter group, along with bassoons and cembalo, all presumably reading the same bass line. To this nucleus of four-part strings with bassoons and cembalo, a composer could add winds, usually oboes and horns. Flutes, while present in most orchestras, appeared less frequently.

The wind instrumentations specified in the thirty-five operas considered here conform to this general picture, yet vary enormously in detail, often from composer to composer, and even from opera to opera. Subject to change were not only the types of writing for each instrument (see chapters 5 and 6), but also such matters as the instruments and instrumental combinations prescribed and the number of arias per opera in which they appear (appendixes A-C list the wind instrumentation of each of the 641 arias studied here). Three forces account for this diversity: general stylistic evolution, differences among orchestras, and personal taste and habit.

Some General Conventions and their Evolution

Certain orchestrational conventions changed gradually in the operas of one composer, regardless of where his career led him. Other conventions changed gradually in the operas of two or more composers, again regardless of the peregrinations of the individuals involved. Changes of both kinds suggest an evolution from within rather than an imposition from without, a change of aesthetics rather than adaptations to suit the exigencies of particular performances. Among the three composers studied here, Hasse and Bach manifest striking similarities of this kind, thus suggesting trends which must have influenced other composers as well.

The most basic trend concerns the number of arias with winds per opera. As Michael Robinson observes, "The proportion of arias supported by strings and wind increased over the mid-century period until, c. 1765, this proportion was the major one in practically all operas."[2] To be more precise, his statement should read "strings and independent winds," since oboes and bassoons had generally served since at least the beginning of the century as ripieno instruments, doubling the strings during ritornellos. (The term "independent winds" will denote woodwinds or brass which play during the vocal sections, if only briefly.) Thus amended, Robinson's statement rings true, and certainly so in the operas of Hasse and Bach (see table 4).

Considering the geographical separation of Hasse and Bach, it is remarkable how the proportions of arias with winds increased in such parallel fashion. In the career of Hasse, three periods emerge; in the career of the much younger Bach, two:

1. 1755-60:   In Hasse's operas from *Ezio* to *Artaserse*, the proportion of arias with winds to the total number of arias per opera falls generally between 33 and 40 percent. *Nitteti*, Hasse's only opera of the period for Venice, contains an unusually low proportion: 26 percent; *Il re pastore*, an opera seria with pastoral elements, an unusually high one: 69 percent

2. 1761-c. 1765: In Hasse's operas of 1761-63 (*Zenobia, Il trionfo di Clelia,* and *Siroe*) and in most of Bach's of 1761-65 (*Artaserse, Catone in Utica, Alessandro nell'Indie,* and *Adriano in Siria*), the proportion falls generally between 50 and 61 percent. The only exception is Bach's

Table 4.   Hasse and Bach: Proportions of All Arias and of All Fast
Arias with Winds

Opera	Year	Total Arias	Arias with Winds	Total Fast Arias	Fast Arias with Winds	Percentage of Arias with Winds	Percentage of Fast Arias with Winds
Hasse							
Ezio	1755	24	9	7	1	38	14
Re pastore	1755	16	11	4	2	69	50
Olimpiade	1756	21	8	11	4	38	36
Nitteti	1758	19	5	10	2	26	20
Demofoonte	1758	20	8	8	4	40	50
Achille	1759	24	8	11	4	33	36
Artaserse	1760	21	7	12	6	33	50
Zenobia	1761	18	9	7	2	50	29
Clelia	1762	18	11	7	5	61	71
Siroe	1763	20	11	10	7	55	70
Romolo	1765	17	12	6	6	71	100
Ruggiero	1771	17	12	10	9	71	90
Bach							
Artaserse	1761	25	15	16	9	60	56
Catone	1761	17	12	7	5	71	71
Alessandro	1762	21	12	7	5	57	71
Adriano	1765	20	11	7	4	55	57
Carattaco	1767	20	16	8	7	80	88
Temistocle	1772	19	14	9	9	74	100

Catone in Utica, with 71 percent

3. 1765-72: In Hasse's last two opere serie (*Romolo ed Ersilia* and
Ruggiero) and Bach's last two before 1774 (*Carattaco* and
Temistocle), the proportions are higher still: between 71 and 80
percent

This trend particularly affected fast arias and thus reflects the gradual
process of harmonic expansion. Toward the beginning of the period 1755-72,
the vocal phrases of many fast arias had followed relentlessly one after another,
leaving little room for wind interjections. Chords had changed rapidly,
moreover, presenting scant opportunity for winds to sustain a harmonic
background. Composers therefore wrote few independent wind parts for such
arias. Later, as vocal caesuras became longer and the harmonic rhythm more
deliberate, they gradually accorded more wind parts to fast arias. In each of
Hasse's operas up to *Nitteti* of 1758, for example, the percentage of fast arias
with winds is smaller than the percentage of all arias with winds. Beginning
with *Demofoonte* of 1758, however, the situation is reversed: the percentage of

Table 5. Flute Arias: Their Numbers, Tempos, and Use of Oboes

Opera	City	Total Arias with Flutes	Tempo		Flute Arias with Oboes		Flute Arias with other Woodwinds	Remarks[a]
			Fast	Slow	Ripieno	Independent		
Hasse								
Ezio	Dresden	7	1	6	5	2	–	–
Re pastore	Dresden	8	1	7	1	6	–	–
Olimpiade	Dresden	4	–	4	1	–	1	–
Nitteti	Venice	2	1	1	–	–	–	–
Demofoonte	Naples	1	–	1	–	–	–	–
Achille	Naples	2	–	2	1	–	1	–
Artaserse	Naples	1	–	1	–	1	–	–
Zenobia	Warsaw	5	–	5	–	3	–	–
Clelia	Vienna	5	–	5	–	4	1	–
Siroe	Dresden	5	2	3	–	4	–	–
Romolo	Innsbruck	0	–	–	–	–	–	No flutes
Ruggiero	Milan	2	–	2	1	1	–	–
Total		42	5	37	9	21	4	
Bach								
Artaserse	Turin	2	–	2	–	–	1	
Catone	Naples	2	–	2	–	–	1	
Alessandro	Naples	3	–	3	–	2	1	
Orione	London	2	–	2	–	1	–	
Adriano	London	2	–	2	–	–	1	
Carattaco	London	7	–	7	–	–	3	
Temistocle	Mannheim	5	2	3	–	1	3	
Total		23	2	21	0	4	9	

Jommelli

									Remarks
Pelope	Stuttgart	1	—	1	—	—	—	—	Sinf. w. 2F, 2 Ob
Artaserse	Stuttgart	2	—	2	—	—	2	—	Sinf. w. 2F, 2 Ob
Creso	Rome	1	—	1	—	—	—	—	No flutes
Temistocle	Naples	0	—	—	—	—	—	—	Sinf. w. 2F, 2 Ob
Olimpiade	Stuttgart	0	—	—	—	—	—	—	Sinf. w. 2F, 2 Ob
Semiramide	Stuttgart	0	—	—	—	—	—	—	No flutes
Didone	Stuttgart	0	—	—	—	—	—	—	Sinf. w. 2F, 2 Ob
Demofoonte III	Stuttgart	1	—	1	—	—	—	—	Sinf. w. 2F, 2 Ob
Enea	Stuttgart	0	—	—	—	—	—	—	Sinf. w. 2F, 2 Ob
Vologeso	Stuttgart	0	—	—	—	—	—	—	Sinf. w. 2F, 2 Ob
Fetonte	Stuttgart	3	1	2	—	—	2	—	Chorus w. 2F
Armida	Naples	0	—	—	—	—	—	—	Acc. Rec. w. 2F, 2 Ob
Demofoonte IV	Naples	0	—	—	—	—	—	—	
Achille	Rome	1	—	1	—	—	—	—	
Ifigenia	Naples	0	—	—	—	—	—	—	No flutes
Ezio	Lisbon	0	—	—	—	—	—	—	Marcia w. 2F, 2 Ob
Total		9	1	8	0	0	4	0	

a. When no aria calls for flutes, the "Remarks" column notes which operas make no mention of flutes at all or lists other numbers—sinfonias, marches, or choruses—which prescribe flutes.

fast arias with winds, excepting that in *Zenobia,* exceeds the percentage of all arias with winds. In Bach's operas, the same trend is less marked, although it is important to note that his last opera of the period, *Temistocle,* is the only one to feature winds in all fast arias.[3]

While the number of independent wind parts per opera increased during the period 1755-72, the number and variety of wind instruments did not necessarily do likewise. The most important winds remained oboes and horns, occasionally in single pairs but usually combined into a four-part ensemble. Flutes appear less frequently and generally in the context of slower tempos. In the operas studied here, oboes accompany both fast and slow arias but more often fast ones; flutes, on the other hand, play almost exclusively in slow arias (see table 5). Of a total seventy-four arias with flutes, only eight are fast. In the operas of J.C. Bach, a second distinction involves the instruments with which flutes and oboes typically combine; while oboes almost automatically appear with horns, flutes combine not so much with oboes as with clarinets and bassoons (as well as horns).

A fourth wind instrument was presumably present but rarely with its own part: the bassoon. Hasse and Bach treated independent bassoons much as they did flutes (see table 6), virtually confining them to slow arias—only four of Bach's twenty-one arias with independent bassoon parts are fast. This stylistic independence of oboes and horns on the one hand, and flutes and bassoons on the other, did not last much longer, of course. Haydn's and Mozart's symphonies and operas of the 1780s already contain woodwind ensembles where flutes, oboes, bassoons, and sometimes clarinets appear in all tempos and have equal opportunity to blend with each other. Such an integrated treatment arose gradually, no doubt mostly in the 1770s, and some hints of it thus appear in the later operas of Bach and Jommelli. It is probably no coincidence, therefore, that Bach used flutes in fast arias only in *Temistocle* of 1772 or that Jommelli did likewise only in *Fetonte,* his last opera for Stuttgart (1768). By the same token, Bach used bassoons in fast arias only in *Temistocle* and in *Adriano in Siria* of 1765.

Instrumentation as a Reflection of the Size and Constitution of Orchestras in the Mid-Eighteenth Century

While virtually all orchestras of the mid-eighteenth century contained strings, oboes and horns, and flutes and bassoons, exact orchestral size and disposition varied greatly. Each ensemble possessed its own strengths and weaknesses, qualities a composer had to bear in mind as he contemplated the orchestral backdrop to his arias. Writing of a slightly earlier period, Helmut Hell reports:

> Als Kernsatz sei den Ausführungen vorangestellt, dass nicht der Komponist das Instrumentarium für sein Werk bestimmte, sondern das er sich, im instrumentalen Bereich ebenso wie im vokalen, nach den Möglichkeiten des jeweiligen Theaters zu richten hatte.[4]

Table 6. Bassoon Arias: Their Numbers, Tempos, and Use of Oboes

Opera	City	Total Arias with Bassoons	Tempo		Bassoon Arias with Oboes	Bassoon Arias with other Woodwinds
			Fast	Slow		
Hasse						
Olimpiade	Dresden	2	1	1	1	1
Demofoonte	Naples	1	1	–	1	–
Achille	Naples	1	–	1	–	1
Clelia	Vienna	1	–	1	1	1
Ruggiero	Milan	2	1	1	1	1
Total		7	3	4	4	4
Bach						
Artaserse	Turin	1	–	1	1	–
Catone	Naples	1	–	1	1	–
Alessandro	Naples	2	–	2	1	–
Orione	London	3	–	3	1	2
Adriano	London	5	1	4	1	2
Carattaco	London	4	–	4	–	4
Temistocle	Mannheim	5	3	2	3	3
Total		21	4	17	8	11
Jommelli						
Pelope	Stuttgart	1	1	–	1	–
Vologeso	Stuttgart	1	1	–	1	–
Total		2	2	0	2	0

In the period under consideration, Hasse, Jommelli, and J.C. Bach wrote for some eleven orchestras; as they went from one to another, they had to modify their styles of orchestration in certain respects. The possible discrepancies they encountered between wind sections include the following:

1. Some orchestras had no flutes
2. Some other orchestras offered flutes but only two players for both the flutes and the oboes
3. Other larger groups contained instruments that had not yet gained a regular and permanent foothold in the orchestra: clarinets and trumpets
4. Some orchestras offered trumpets but only two players for both the trumpets and the horns
5. A few larger orchestras boasted three or more players for certain instruments, particularly oboes and horns
6. The technical and expressive capabilities of the individual players varied enormously

As we shall see, however, most of these factors had limited impact. Flutes, first of all, were present in most larger orchestras of the 1750s and 1760s.[5] Consequently, of the thirty-five operas studied here, only four make no mention of the instrument: Hasse's *Romolo ed Ersilia* (Innsbruck, 1765), and Jommelli's *Temistocle* (Naples, 1757), *Didone abbandonata* (Stuttgart, 1763), and *Ifigenia in Tauride* (Naples, 1771). In only the first of these, moreover, does the lack of flutes seem to reflect the constitution of an orchestra. Since Hasse used flutes extensively in all his other operas of the period (particularly those for Germany and Austria), and since we have little other information concerning the orchestra at Innsbruck,[6] one can only speculate that Hasse ignored flutes simply because none was available. The situation with Jommelli's three operas without flutes is altogether different. Jommelli composed these works for Stuttgart and Naples, cities for which he composed numerous other operas that prescribe flutes. For example, all of his Stuttgart operas of 1755-62 and 1764-68 utilize flutes; yet his *Didone abbandonata* (Stuttgart, 1763) does not. The flute participation in the operas with flutes is minimal (see p.114), however, suggesting that Jommelli had little interest in the instrument. The absence of flute parts in *Didone abbandonata, Temistocle,* and *Ifigenia in Tauride* may thus derive not from the orchestra but from the composer, in which case only one of the thirty-five operas investigated here was affected by an outright lack of flutes.

While probably only Innsbruck lacked flutes, several other orchestras may have offered Hasse, Jommelli, and Bach only two players for both flutes and oboes. Carse claims that most large orchestras of the period included flutes, but that

> the scores and parts seem to point to the use of *either* flutes *or* oboes rather than both together.... There can be little doubt ... that in places where it was impossible to afford two pairs of players, one pair played on either of the instruments, as was required.[7]

Carse's statement applies more to the first half of the century, when the lack of sufficient players for both two flutes and two oboes was more prevalent, thus explaining why composers did not originally combine these instruments. As far as the 1750s and 1760s are concerned, however, there is little evidence that the orchestral forces which Hasse, Jommelli, and Bach encountered precluded such combinations, for twenty-one of the thirty-one operas with flutes include at least one aria—or some other number, such as a sinfonia or chorus—in which flutes and oboes sound simultaneously (see table 5). Most of the other operas were intended for Italy, although they by no means account for all the operas which Hasse, Bach, and Jommelli composed there. Oboes and flutes appear together once or twice in an opera but then are segregated entirely in another opera composed for the same house a year or two earlier or later. Hasse, for example, combined them in his last two operas for Naples, *Achille in*

Sciro (1759) and *Artaserse* (1760) but not at all in his *Demofoonte* (1758) for the same city. Similarly, Bach utilized the same instrumentation at least once in his first London opera, *Orione* (1763) but not at all in his subsequent *Adriano in Siria* (1765) and *Carattaco*[8] (1767)—both also for London. He combined flutes and oboes in *Alessandro nell'Indie* (Naples, 1762) but not in another opera he composed for the same city and same season, *Catone in Utica* (Naples, 1761).

Either the dispositions of many orchestras fluctuated wildly, or, what is more likely, the traditional stylistic independence of flutes and oboes discouraged such mixing. As evidence of this independence, Hasse, who more frequently combined flutes and oboes than Bach and Jommelli did, usually wrote very differently for each instrument, allowing flutes to accompany the voice through most of the aria but confining oboes to ritornellos, perhaps with a few brief appearances in vocal sections.[9] This contrast, as well as the small numbers of flute and oboe ensembles (particularly in Bach's operas) leads one to conclude that if the stylistic differentiation of flutes and oboes arose originally of necessity, it did not disappear immediately as orchestras added more woodwind players.

While most orchestras offered Hasse, Bach, and Jommelli flutists above and beyond the oboe players, only a few included relatively "exotic" instruments. Three of these appear in only one opera apiece: "corno inglese"in Hasse's *Il trionfo di Clelia* (Vienna, 1762),[10] "taille" in Bach's *Orione* (London, 1763),[11] and "clarinetto d'amore" in Bach's *Temistocle* (Mannheim, 1772).[12] Two others, clarinet and trumpet, both on the road towards permanent status in the orchestra, participate more frequently.

In 1755, the clarinet had only begun to take its place in the orchestra, and Rameau's *Zoroastre* of 1749 is cited often as one of the first operas to include them.[13] "In *Zoroastre*," writes Cuthbert Girdlestone, "clarinets were used for the first time at the Paris Opéra," although "Rameau wrote no special parts for them and they no doubt doubled or replaced the hautboys."[14] Rameau's *Acante et Cephise* (Paris, 1751), on the other hand, was "the first French opera in which clarinets were given individual parts."[15] Rameau and the Opéra notwithstanding, it seems that London saw the first consistent use of clarinets in the opera orchestra. Thomas Arne utilized them in *Thomas and Sally* (1760) and *Artaxerxes* (1762), and J.C. Bach did likewise soon after, in *Orione* (1763), *Zanaida* (1763), *Adriano in Siria* (1765), and *Carattaco* (1767)—all for London. Mannheim, too, was quick to appreciate the orchestral potential of the clarinet, admitting clarinettists into the orchestra in 1758 or 1759.[16] Bach, consequently, again employed the instrument, as well as "clarinetto d'amore," in *Temistocle* (Mannheim, 1772).

Among the three composers considered here, only Bach employed clarinets. He did so sparingly, moreover, confining them to two or three arias of an average of twenty per opera; the presence of clarinets did not therefore affect the bulk of his music. Much as with flutes, he associated clarinets with slow arias and never combined them with oboes (see table 7). Perhaps the dispositions of the London and Mannheim orchestras precluded such mixing, for the clarinet, having first entered the orchestra "on the pretext that it was a modified oboe,"[17] was frequently played by oboists. By the 1760s, in fact, it would be safe to assume that the clarinet had largely replaced the flute as the alternate instrument of oboists. Yet Bach may have segregated oboes and clarinets instead for purely aesthetic reasons, for it is important to note that he combined oboes with "clarinetti d'amore" in *Temistocle* and clarinets with "taille" in *Orione.*[18] If one assumes that "clarinetto d'amore" was played by clarinettists and "taille" by oboists, the one can only conclude that Bach had both clarinettists and oboists at his disposal but chose never to use them simultaneously on their principal instruments. Bach obviously thought that clarinets suited soft, slow arias and perhaps also believed that they blended best with flutes and bassoons.

Table 7.   Clarinet Arias: Their Numbers, Tempos, and Use of Oboes

Opera	City	Total Arias with Clarinets	Tempo Fast	Tempo Slow	Clarinet Arias with Oboes	Clarinet Arias with other Woodwinds
Bach						
Orione	London	2	–	2	–	1
Adriano	London	2	–	2	–	2
Carattaco	London	3	–	3	–	3
Temistocle	Mannheim	2	–	2	–	1

Unlike the clarinet, the trumpet was hardly new. Still, few orchestras of the mid-eighteenth century contained trumpeters and tympanists; when needed, they were simply borrowed from the military personnel attached to the local court.[19] In other words, trumpeters were largely available but utilized at the composer's (and ruler's) discretion. Curiously, all of Bach's London operas[20] and Jommelli's Stuttgart operas ignore trumpets completely (see table 8). In the case of Jommelli, at least, it is unlikely that this omission was imposed on the composer. Duke Carl Eugen maintained an enormous military establishment at Stuttgart and granted his Kapellmeister's every wish. Surely Jommelli could have borrowed trumpeters had he wanted them.

As with clarinets, the influence of trumpets on a composer's orchestration was rather trivial; in most operas they are confined to the sinfonia, an occasional march, and perhaps one aria. As with flutes and oboes, on the other hand, the limitations of certain orchestras might force composers to choose either horns or trumpets. As Hell reports:

Offenbar waren im Orchester nur zwei Bläser für das Blech vorhanden, so dass entweder nur Hörner oder nur Trompeten verlangt werden konnten.[21]

This problem must have confronted Hasse, Jommelli, or Bach rarely, however, for trumpets in their operas usually appear in the company of horns. The only noteworthy exceptions arise in operas for Naples, and here the evidence is inconclusive. Horns and trumpets play simultaneously in three operas composed for Naples between 1757 and 1762[22] but are segregated in three others written for the same city during the same five years.[23] Jommelli's later operas of 1770-71, on the other hand, call for "Trombe e Corni" but contain only two real parts for them.[24] Such instructions seem unambiguous, yet only Jommelli's operas for Naples limit brass parts to two; his contemporaneous *Achille in Sciro* (Rome, 1771) gives four real parts to horns and trumpets. Perhaps Naples could offer Jommelli only two brass players at this time,[25] so that Jommelli designed the parts to be performed by any pair of brass instruments: two horns, two trumpets, or one horn and one trumpet.

While some orchestras may have had fewer than the standard "classical" disposition of two players per wind instrument, others included more, such as four or five oboists or three or four horn players.[26] The three composers studied here virtually always limited parts for each wind instrument to two, nevertheless. As exceptions, Bach wrote for three "clarinetti d'amore" in *Temistocle*[27] (Mannheim, 1772), and Jommelli wrote for three horns in three Stuttgart arias.[28] In the second case, one horn performs elaborate musical acrobatics while the other two provide the usual harmonic support.

Finally, orchestras differed in the competency of their musicians, a factor which alternately sparked or dampened a composer's enthusiasm for writing unusually exposed or difficult parts. He would not assign a long "concertante" part to the bassoon if the local bassoonists were timid, sloppy, or poorly trained, just as he would not contrive string parts filled with rapid scales and arpeggios if the violinists and violists were poorly disciplined. It is not always easy to assess how and to what extent such factors affected a composer's orchestration. Unlike other influences, differences in playing ability doubtless affected not only what instruments a composer chose and how frequently he employed them but also the types of parts he wrote.

One particular type of wind writing where such cause and effect seems obvious is the "extensive independent melodic part," a term applied here to wind parts, often virtuosic, where the instrument in question not only replaces the violins as the carrier of the melody in much of the first ritornello but also competes with the voice itself: in many cases, the first and second vocal sections contain unusually long melismas where the featured wind instrument(s) accompanies the voice in thirds or sixths or else engages antiphonally with it in brilliant roulades. In the operas of Hasse, Jommelli, and Bach, such parts stand out from all other wind writing in length of exposure, melodic interest, and

Table 8. Trumpets and Their Appearance with Horns in Arias and Sinfonias

Opera	City	Arias with Two Trumpets	Arias with Trumpets and Horns	Sinfonia with Trumpets and Horns	Remarks[a]
Hasse					
Ezio	Dresden	—	—	—	Marcia w. 2H, 2T
Re pastore	Dresden	—	1	—	
Olimpiade	Dresden	—	—	—	No trumpets
Nitteti	Venice	—	—	—	No trumpets
Demofoonte	Naples	—	—	—	Marcia w. 2H, 2T
Achille	Naples	—	1	—	On-stage trumpet call
Artaserse	Naples	2	—	—	
Zenobia	Warsaw	—	1	—	No trumpets
Clelia	Vienna	—	—	x	
Siroe	Dresden	—	—	—	No trumpets
Romolo	Innsbruck	—	—	—	1st chorus w. 2H, 2T
Ruggiero	Milan	—	—	x	
Bach					
Artaserse	Turin	1	—	—	
Catone	Naples	—	1	x	
Alessandro	Naples	—	—	—	Marcia w. 2T
Orione	London	—	—	—	No trumpets[c]
Adriano	London	—	—	—	No trumpets[c]
Carataco	London	—	—	—	No trumpets[c]
Temistocle	Mannheim	—	—	x	

Jommelli

Pelope	Stuttgart	–	–	No trumpets
Artaserse	Stuttgart	–	–	No trumpets
Creso	Rome	5	x	
Temistocle	Naples	1	x	
Olimpiade	Stuttgart	–	–	No trumpets
Semiramide	Stuttgart	–	–	No trumpets
Didone	Stuttgart	–	–	No trumpets
Demofoonte III	Stuttgart	–	–	No trumpets
Enea	Stuttgart	–	–	No trumpets
Vologeso	Stuttgart	–	–	No trumpets
Fetonte	Stuttgart	–	–	No trumpets
Armida	Naples	–	x[b]	No trumpets
Demofoonte IV	Naples	–	–	No trumpets
Achille	Rome	1	–	
Ifigenia	Naples	3	x	
Ezio	Naples	2[b]	–	Sinf. w. 2T only
	Lisbon	–	–	Marcia w. 2H, 2T[b]

a. When neither arias nor the sinfonia call for trumpets or combinations of trumpets and horns, the "Remarks" column notes which operas make no mention of trumpets at all or lists other numbers—marches or choruses—which prescribe such scorings.

b. In three late operas for Naples and Lisbon, Jommelli called for "Corni e Trombe," yet composed only two parts for them (see p. 105).

c. The original sinfonias to *Orione* and *Carattaco* are lost. The sinfonia to *Adriano in Siria*, extant only in the P-La manuscript, was not available to me when I checked for trumpet scorings elsewhere than arias. (The *Orione* sinfonia was published in "Six Favourite Overtures" of 1770. The wind instrumentation, which may well depart from Bach's original, consists only of oboes and horns.)

degree of difficulty. As with trumpet and clarinet arias, however, they are few. Of the 641 arias studied here, only eighteen contain such parts and only one or two belong to any one opera (see table 9). When Bach composed *Temistocle* for Mannheim, for example, he could tailor his orchestration to an instrumental ensemble that many of his contemporaries considered the best trained and most virtuosic in Europe; many of its wind players enjoyed international reputations as performers and as composers of concertos and chamber music for their instruments. In spite of this wealth of talent, however, Bach's opera contains only two arias with extensive independent melodic wind parts, one for oboe, the other for bassoon.[29]

As further evidence that instrumental virtuosos little influenced operatic orchestrations, table 9 demonstrates that among several operas produced in the same city at more or less the same time, only one or two feature extensive independent melodic parts for the same instrument. If an excellent player was a virtual prerequisite for such parts, his presence evidently did not force the composer to design parts specifically for him. For his Dresden operas of 1755-56, for example, Hasse designed such parts for flutes in *Olimpiade* but not in *Ezio* or *Il re pastore;* he fashioned a similar part for trumpet in *Artaserse* for Naples but not in the other operas he composed for the same city, *Demofoonte* and *Achille in Sciro*. Nor, it must be added, did Jommelli or Bach do so in their roughly contemporary operas for Naples: Jommelli's *Temistocle* and Bach's *Catone in Utica* and *Allessandro nell'Indie*. Only once does the chart consistently link city and instrument: each of Jommelli's four Stuttgart operas from *Olimpiade* (1761) to *Demofoonte* III (1764) contains at least one aria with elaborate horn parts,[30] accompanied usually by equally demanding and flashy oboe parts (see example 41).

Table 9 hints at what was doubtless a greater concern for opera composers of the day: a regional disparity either in the popularity of flutes and trumpets or in the capabilities of their players. The only extensive independent melodic parts for flute appear in Dresden, Warsaw, and Vienna; the only such parts for trumpet, in Naples. This association of flutes with northern Europe and of trumpets with Italy becomes clearer when we compare the numbers of arias per opera in which flutes and trumpets participate in any capacity (see tables 5 and 8). In each of Hasse's Dresden operas of 1755-56, arias with flutes total between four and eight[31]; in each of his operas of 1758-60 for Venice and Naples, however, their numbers drop to one or two. In each of his operas of 1761-63 for Warsaw and Vienna, they total five; but in his last opera, for Milan, they number only two.[32] Similarly, Bach's operas of 1761-62 for Turin and Naples each contain two or three arias for flute. While one of his operas for London, *Adriano in Siria* (1765), likewise includes only two such arias, each of his last two operas of the period—*Carattaco* (London, 1767) and *Temistocle* (Mannheim, 1772)—boasts many flute arias: five and seven, respectively. Hasse and Bach thus fairly consistently assigned four to eight arias per opera to north European flutists but only one to three arias per opera to their Italian

Table 9. "Extensive Independent Melodic Parts" for Winds

Opera	City	Number of Arias where Found	Featured Instruments
Hasse			
Ezio	Dresden	1	Ob
Re pastore	Dresden	0	
Olimpiade	Dresden	2[a]	F; 2B
Nitteti	Venice	0	
Demofoonte	Naples	0	
Achille	Naples	1	Ob
Artaserse	Naples	1	T
Zenobia	Warsaw	1	2F
Clelia	Vienna	1	F, Ob
Siroe	Dresden	0	
Romolo	Innsbruck	0	
Ruggiero	Milan	0	
Bach			
Artaserse	Turin	0	
Catone	Naples	1	Ob, B
Alessandro	Naples	1	B
Orione	London	1	2B
Adriano	London	0	
Carattaco	London	0	
Temistocle	Mannheim	2	Ob; B
Jommelli			
Pelope	Stuttgart	0	
Artaserse	Stuttgart	0	
Creso	Rome	0	
Temistocle	Naples	0	
Olimpiade	Stuttgart	1	2 Ob. H
Semiramide	Stuttgart	2	2 Ob, H; 2 Ob, 2H[b]
Didone	Stuttgart	1	2 Ob, H
Demofoonte III	Stuttgart	1	H
Enea	Stuttgart	1	Ob
Vologeso	Stuttgart	0	
Fetonte	Stuttgart	0	
Armida	Naples	0	
Demofoonte IV	Naples	0	
Achille	Rome	0	
Ifigenia	Naples	0	
Ezio	Lisbon	0	

a. The flute in *Olimpiade* 6 and the bassoons in *Olimpiade* 10 are neither melodic nor introduced in an opening ritornello. Instead, they provide a rapid and fairly extensive sixteenth-note accompaniment. Since their parts present unusual technical demands (by Hasse's standards) and extend through much of each aria, I have classifed them as "extensive independent melodic parts."

b. The oboes and horns in *Semiramide* 16, like the flute and bassoons in Hasse's *Olimpiade* (see above), are neither very melodic nor introduced in an opening ritornello but instead execute rapid sixteenth-note passages.

counterparts. That they composed extensive independent melodic parts as well as "independent melodic ensemble" parts (see chapter 6, pp. 144-46) only for the former group of flutists suggests that higher standards of flute playing prevailed north of the Alps.

In the case of the trumpet, the evidence points instead to the superiority, or at least greater availability, of trumpeters in Italy. While most operas investigated here utilize trumpet in at most one aria, a few operas intended for Naples and Rome contain a good many more trumpet arias. Hasse's *Artaserse* (Naples 1760) and Jommelli's *Creso* (Rome, 1757), *Achille in Sciro* (Rome, 1771), and *Ifigenia in Tauride* (Naples, 1771) each contain from three to five such arias. Further, Bach and Jommelli composed no trumpet arias outside Italy. That Rome, at least, should elicit so many trumpet parts was nothing new. Helmut Hell reports of the first half of the century:

> In Rom... muss das Angebot an Trompetern reich gewesen sein. Offenbar standen hier die herrschaftlichen Trompeter im Orchester noch länger zur Verfügung. Die Besetzung mit Trompeten *und* Hörnern in der Sinfonie ist für in Rom aufgeführte Werke geradezu typisch.[33]

Trumpets also appear more frequently in the sinfonias to operas which Hasse, Jommelli, and J.C. Bach composed for Italy. As table 8 shows, eight of the thirty-five operas investigated here open with the sound of trumpets; of these eight works, six were composed for Rome, Naples, and Milan.

To sum up, the orchestras encountered by Hasse, Bach, and Jommelli differed from each other in many ways; no two were quite alike. Surprisingly, the size, constitution, and abilities of these groups influenced only a small number of arias. While a composer might have been able to write for relatively unusual instruments, such as clarinets or trumpets, design extensive independent melodic parts for particularly accomplished performers, combine oboes and clarinets, or compose parts for three horns or three oboes, he would do so rarely, in only a few arias per opera. The only really significant influence seems to have arisen in the case of flutists and trumpeters. Their standards of playing may have varied considerably, thus inspiring the composer to adjust the number and nature of their parts accordingly.[34]

By and large, convention, personal taste, and purely musical considerations governed wind instrumentation and orchestration. If they used winds at all, Hasse, Bach, and Jommelli relied mostly on oboes and horns, instruments available in any orchestra, their roles dictated by standard usage. When writing for these instruments, in fact, they could practically ignore differences between orchestras. Since oboes and horns, second-class citizens of the orchestra, generally sustained chords as a harmonic background to the strings, composers probably dashed off their parts with little thought. For the Mannheim oboists and hornists, consequently, Bach composed parts which the players of Turin and Naples (the cities for which he composed his first operas) could doubtless handle with ease.

Most important, external forces such as an orchestra (or the text) sometimes suggested or even determined merely the choice of wind instrument but not how the composer wrote for it (except in the case of the rare extensive independent melodic parts). The composer, in the end, had many options, including having the instrument double the strings sporadically or throughout an aria; present new melodic material, either throughout or only intermittently, and either alone or in the company of other winds; or provide independent harmonic support to the strings. The orchestra, moveover, could rarely determine where in an aria the composer scored for winds, whatever their relation to the strings. As the following two chapters will demonstrate, Hasse, Jommelli, and Bach positioned winds, particularly oboes and horns, according to patterns reflecting purely musical considerations, such as articulating phrases, emphasizing modulations, and reinforcing climaxes. A consideration of orchestral forces in the eighteenth century therefore only begins our study of the orchestration of these composers.

Hasse, Bach, and Jommelli: Individual Styles

With the exigencies of particular orchestras affecting instrumentation to a limited and rather superficial extent, considerable leeway remained for a composer to maintain his own style. The eighteenth-century composer of opera seria, though not the exalted and pampered figure of a Verdi or a Wagner, could still exercise his own taste and judgment, regardless of orchestra, singers, patron, and so on. Each of the three composers studied here, consequently, consistently displayed certain traits which set him apart not only from the other two but frequently from most of his other contemporaries as well.

In many ways, of course, Hasse was swayed by his environment. He composed more and more independent wind parts, most for oboes and horns accompanying fast arias. When writing for Italy, moreover, he gave fewer arias to flutes than he had when north of the Alps and fashioned no extensive independent melodic parts for that instrument. At the same time, he composed more trumpet arias as well as his only extensive melodic part for trumpet while he was in Italy. In one respect, however, Hasse held his ground: while he greatly diversified the role of oboes in his last operas (see chapter 5), he sometimes still used them—and occasionally flutes—as ripieno instruments. Even for five arias of his last opera, *Ruggiero* (Milan, 1771), he used oboes just as he had in his operas of the 1720s and 1730s; oboes double the violins in the ritornellos, neither playing their own pitches (except in isolated cases when the violins stray below the oboes' range or execute particularly rapid passages) nor appearing in vocal sections.[35] Bach and Jommelli never used oboes in such a limited capacity; their arias either contain fully written-out, independent parts for oboes or else ignore the instrument entirely.

Bach's instrumentations, as we have seen, manifest some of the same trends. He assigned winds to an ever larger proportion of arias per opera and favored trumpets in Italy and flutes in Germany and England. But here the similarities end, for Bach came to lavish attention on winds, taking advantage of their colors and resonance in a manner foreign to Hasse. For one thing, he utilized the dark hues of the clarinet. After arriving in London in 1763, he admitted these relative newcomers as standard components of his orchestra, composing at least two arias for clarinets in *Orione* (London, 1763), two in *Adriano in Siria* (London, 1765), three in *Carattaco* (London, 1767), and two in *Temistocle* (Mannheim, 1772). Second, he often amassed three pairs of woodwinds: usually flutes, clarinets, and bassoons, and always with horns (see table 10).[36]

Table 10.   Six-Part Woodwind Ensembles in the Operas of Bach

Aria	City	Wind Scoring
Alessandro 10	Naples	2F, 2 Ob, 2B, 2H
Orione 9	London	2F, 2 Ob, 2B, 2H
Orione 14		2Tailles, 2C, 2B, 2H
Adriano 11	London	2F, 2C, 2B, 2H
Carattaco 9	London	2F, 2C, 2B, 2H
Carattaco 16		2F, 2C, 2B, 2H
Temistocle 9	Mannheim	2F, 2 Ob, 2B, 2H
Temistocle 14		2F, 2C, 2B, 2H

Since *Orione,* Bach's first London opera, contains his first clarinet parts and at least two arias combining three pairs of woodwinds, one might assume that London opened Bach's eyes to a dazzling new world of orchestral color and sonority.[37] When expanding his instrumentation in *Orione,* so runs the argument, Bach was merely adapting to a larger orchestra and the expectations of a relatively sophisticated audience. Apparently quite the reverse happened, however. First, Bach had already combined three pairs of woodwinds in his second opera for Naples, *Alessandro nell'Indie* (1762). As we shall see in chapter 6, moreover, he had also begun experimenting with winds in even more significant ways before leaving Italy. Second, while Thomas Arne had already utilized clarinets in *Thomas and Sally* (London, 1760) and *Artaxerxes* (London, 1762), these operas were performed at Covent Garden, while *Orione* opened at the King's Theatre, the orchestra of which seemed "normally to have been considerably smaller than the one in Naples"[38] C.S. Terry, in fact, reports that "the advertisements in the *Public Advertiser* drew particular attention to the 'grand chorus's' and to the fact that 'several Vocal and Instrumental

Performers' were engaged outside the normal establishment."[39] One cannot simply assume, therefore, that Bach's orchestra already included clarinets, as well as the two "tailles" and separate pairs of oboists and flutists required for *Orione*. Third, Charles Burney testified to the novelty of Bach's wind parts. Of *Orione* in particular, he writes: "Every judge of Music...[was] chiefly struck with the richness of the harmony, the ingenious texture of the parts, and, above all, with the new and happy use he had made of wind-instruments."[40] Of Bach's London operas in general, he adds: "The richness of the accompaniments perhaps deserves more praise than the originality of the melodies."[41] For Burney at least, Bach's orchestration was not at all typical of London.

Bach's use of clarinets and blending of three pairs of woodwinds stand out not only in London but in a much wider context as well. Hasse and Jommelli, first of all, never wrote for clarinets, and Jommelli never combined three pairs of woodwinds (nor did Thomas Arne in *Thomas and Sally* or *Artaxerxes*). Hasse created such an ensemble but only once (and without horns), in *Il trionfo di Clelia* (Vienna, 1762).[42] Tommaso Traetta, a composer credited with developing the orchestrational potential of opera seria,[43] combined three pairs of woodwinds only once in the five opere serie he composed outside Italy during this period: *Armida* (Vienna, 1761), *Sofonisba* (Mannheim, 1762), *Ifigenia in Tauride* (Vienna, 1763), *Siroe* (Munich, 1767), and *Antigone* (St. Petersburg, 1772);[44] he used clarinets only in the last-named work. Even Gluck, so often championed for having expanded the dramatic powers of the orchestra, never combined three pairs of woodwinds in his operas of the 1760s available in modern edition: the great "reform" opera *Orfeo ed Euridice* (Vienna, 1762) and *Telemaco* (Vienna, 1765).[45] As a further indication of Bach's leading position, it seems that he was the first to introduce clarinets into operas even at Mannheim. While the orchestra there had admitted clarinettists in 1758, it does not seem that they automatically accompanied opere serie thereafter. Scores of the extant Mannheim operas of the 1760s—Traetta's *Sofonisba* (1762), di Majo's *Ifigenia in Tauride* (1764), and Piccinni's *Catone in Utica* (1770)—make no mention of the instrument. Bach's *Temistocle* (Mannheim, 1772), on the other hand, calls for clarinets as well as "clarinetti d'amore." Evidently Bach was the first—at least among Jommelli, Traetta, and Gluck—to use clarinets consistently and to join flutes, clarinets, bassoons, and horns into ensembles. As we shall see in chapter 6, moreover, he composed their parts in a style that was likewise more "modern."

Jommelli has long been acclaimed as a composer whose orchestration kept pace with or even influenced the orchestral innovations of the south German and Austrian symphonists. Helmut Hell credits him with profoundly influencing Johann Stamitz and other Mannheimers.[46] Ann Tolkoff writes of the "diversity of Jommelli's instrumental color" and of "the greater frequency of instrumental passages, the variety of the instrumentation,...[and] the size of the orchestra that distinguished Jommelli's instrumental music from that of traditional Italian opera."[47] A comparison of Jommelli's scores with those of Hasse and J.C. Bach reveals an astonishingly different picture, however, at least in the woodwind and brass components of his orchestration. In the entire period 1755-72, Jommelli generally utilized fewer wind instruments and wind combinations than Hasse or Bach did and assigned them to fewer arias. Earlier in the 1740s and early 1750s, Jommelli may have been in the vanguard of orchestrational innovation, but at least from 1755 on, his style of writing for winds ossified, changing little during the ensuing seventeen years.

Jommelli wrote nine of the sixteen operas studied here for the court of Duke Carl Eugen at Stuttgart. In all but a handful of the arias of these Stuttgart operas, Jommelli was content to use strings alone or strings with oboes and horns. Only twice did he fashion a wind accompaniment of oboes alone,[48] and he never employed horns alone. He never used clarinets or trumpets. Even more remarkable, Jommelli practically banished flutes and bassoons (independent of the continuo line) from his arias. In all nine Stuttgart operas, only seven arias, concentrated in four operas, call for flutes;[49] only two mention bassoons.[50] Concomitantly, Jommelli never combined three pairs of woodwinds, as J.C. Bach frequently did starting in 1762 with *Alessandro nell'Indie* and as even Hasse did once in *Il trionfo di Clelia* (Vienna, 1762). He rarely combined even two pairs of woodwinds in his arias.

That Jommelli composed no parts for clarinets is hardly surprising; there is no evidence that the Stuttgart orchestra of the 1750s and 1760s had admitted clarinettists into its ranks.[51] The lack of trumpet parts is not so easily accounted for (see p. 104), but the neglect of flutes virtually defies explanation. Jommelli had flutists at his disposal[52] and on a fairly regular basis allowed them to accompany most of his operatic sinfonias, choruses, and marches, where as a rule, they merely double the oboes, with occasional additions and deletions. It almost seems that Jommelli would have preferred not to use flutes at all and so tried to render them as inconspicuous as possible by burying them in large masses of instruments and voices. Even when he assigned them to arias, he slighted them, particularly towards the end of his career. Of the three arias with flutes in *Fetonte,* one (*Fetonte* 4) contains only a brief phrase for flutes and another (*Fetonte* 8) is by far the shortest aria in the opera.[53]

Of the remaining seven operas, Jommelli composed six for Rome and Naples. In certain respects, the winds in these works assume patterns slightly different from those of the Stuttgart operas. Traditions of orchestral playing and operatic accompaniment varied between South Germany and Italy, and one might suppose that Jommelli thinned out his accompaniments when confronted with Italian orchestras and audiences. Precisely the opposite was the case, however. Although he continued to deny flutes and bassoons any prominent role, he wrote quite a few trumpet arias (see p. 110), just as Hasse

Table 11.   Jommelli: Proportions of All Arias with Winds

Opera	City	Total Arias	Arias with Winds	Percentage of Arias with Winds
Pelope	Stuttgart	17	7	41
Artaserse	Stuttgart	17	9	53
Creso	Rome	20	14	70
Temistocle	Naples	20	10	50
Olimpiade	Stuttgart	16	7	44
Semiramide	Stuttgart	18	9	50
Didone	Stuttgart	18	10	56
Demofoonte III	Stuttgart	18	7	39
Enea	Stuttgart	16	7	44
Vologeso	Stuttgart	17	6	35
Fetonte	Stuttgart	14	8	57
Armida	Naples	18	10	56
Demofoonte IV	Naples	16	7	44
Achille	Rome	17	12	71
Ifigenia	Naples	18	9	50
Ezio	Lisbon	14	8	57

and Bach did in Italy.[54] More important, Jommelli generally assigned winds—mostly oboes and horns—to more arias per opera (see table 11). In Stuttgart, Jommelli generally composed wind parts for only 50 percent or less of the arias in any opera; for *Demofoonte* III (1764) and *Vologeso* (1766), in fact, he did so for only 39 and 35 percent, proportions lower than those in any of Bach's operas or in any of Hasse's after 1760. Only three of the nine Stuttgart operas—*Artaserse* (1755), *Didone abbandonata* (1763), and *Fetonte* (1768)—contain more, and the largest percentage, *Fetonte*'s 57 percent, compares with those prevailing in Hasse's and Bach's operas of 1761-65, a slightly earlier period. In Italy, on the other hand, Jommelli wrote slightly more wind parts, never as few per opera as in *Demofoonte* III and *Vologeso*. For two Roman operas—*Creso* (1757) and *Achille in Sciro* (1771)—he assigned winds to about 70 percent of the arias, the same ratio prevailing in Hasse's and Bach's last two operas of the period 1755-72.

A comparison of Jommelli's instrumentations with those of Hasse and Bach leads to two general conclusions. First, even in the relatively basic matters concerning what wind instruments were chosen, when they were used, and how they were combined, a composer could exercise his own judgment and style. Jommelli, whether in Stuttgart, Rome, or Naples, gave flutes a smaller role than they play in the overwhelming majority of operas by Bach and Hasse. Bach, whether in Naples, London, or Mannheim, blended three pairs of woodwinds with horns, producing a resonant and colorful ensemble of winds;

Hasse and Jommelli almost never did so. Hasse, whether in Naples, Milan, Dresden, or Vienna, continued to use oboes as ripieno instruments until the end of his career.

Second, one can classify the orchestras encountered by Hasse, Jommelli, and Bach into two groups: one north European (London, Mannheim, Dresden, and Vienna), and other Italian (Turin, Milan, Rome, Naples, and Venice). The former highlighted winds, particularly flutes and bassoons, and sometimes even clarinets. The latter depended more on strings and used winds—mostly oboes, horns, and trumpets—to supply a necessary but rather workaday harmonic background. The Stuttgart orchestra, accordingly, far from being typically German, maintained certain Italian characteristics: few flute parts, few independent parts for bassoons, and little blending of different woodwinds. When he began work at Stuttgart in 1753, Jommelli may have come under the sway of certain German or French attitudes, such as the desire for more accompanied recitative and chorus in opere serie, the interest in ballet, and the appreciation of opera as a serious entertainment. Concerning the technical aspects of training musicians and orchestrating music for them, however, Jommelli remained true to the land of his birth.

5

The Accompanimental Wind Ensemble: Relation to the Strings and Structural Context

Style Change in Hasse's Oboe Parts

Investigating how and why a composer selected and combined woodwinds can lead one to significant insights concerning style and style change. Still more important questions, however, involve the types of wind parts fashioned: Where in an aria do they occur? What structural purposes do they serve? How do they relate rhythmically and melodically to the string parts? When treating such issues, scholars have frequently overestimated the significance of independent melodic parts: the longer and more virtuosic, the better. Rudolph Gerber, for example, mentions woodwinds only in so far as they deliver elaborate solos.[1] Since Hasse composed such parts only sporadically throughout his long career, Gerber concludes erroneously that Hasse never expanded or otherwise altered his treatment of winds.[2] Downes and Millner concur,[3] Downes betraying a similar bias in favor of lengthy, virtuosic, and melodically independent wind parts:

> The extravagant flowering of obbligato virtuosity which now set in appears to have affected the role of the individual woodwind instruments, even when they were not being treated as obbligato solos. Within the body of the orchestra each instrument...became more of a character in its own right, valued and exploited for its individual tone quality, rather than as a mere unit of the woodwind choir.[4]

This passage exaggerates the significance of woodwind solos and overlooks one of the most crucial orchestrational developments of the late eighteenth century: the integration of flutes, oboes, bassoons, and sometimes clarinets into a self-contained ensemble. Downes also overestimates the impact of instrumental virtuosity. Supporting his view is the example of J.C. Bach, who would certainly have never devised the difficult "concertante" parts for oboe and bassoon in *Temistocle* (Mannheim, 1772)[5] had Mannheim not boasted so many outstanding wind players. Such virtuosity did not necessarily inspire other aspects of early classical orchestration, however, such as utilizing oboes and horns to sustain a harmonic background. Such chordal support, although relatively exposed, presents fewer technical difficulties than the older ripieno parts where oboes, bassoons, and sometimes flutes double the strings.

In the operas of Hasse, Jommelli, and J.C. Bach, long melodic solos are much more the exception than the rule. None of these works includes more than two arias with such solos, and most lack them entirely (see table 9). Instead, the vast majority of arias prescribe woodwinds which remain distinctly subordinate to the strings, the winds either (1) doubling the strings in ritornellos, (2) doubling the strings intermittently in the vocal sections, or (3) providing independent harmonic support. Such accompaniments, usually entrusted to oboes (along with horns), lack the glamor of virtuoso solos but yield more detailed insights into the nature and historical development of early classical orchestration.

Hasse's accompanimental parts for oboes constitute a superb repertoire in which to classify types of writing and identify style trends, for within the brief span of sixteen years—from *Ezio* of 1755 to *Ruggiero* of 1771—Hasse ran the gamut from a baroque treatment of the instrument to an essentially classical one. He was no pioneer in this regard; much of his oboe writing of 1771 resembles Jommelli's and Bach's of 1755. Rather, Hasse was apparently conforming belatedly to a widespread change in taste arising a decade or two earlier. A study of his orchestration of the 1760s and early 1770s nonetheless serves three useful functions: (1) providing analytical tools for monitoring the evolution of certain aspects of classical wind orchestration, (2) demonstrating that Hasse significantly altered his techniques of orchestration, and (3) suggesting much about orchestrational style change in the works of other composers in the 1740s and 1750s.

Hasse composed his first three operas of the period 1755-72 for Dresden, where he had held the position of Kapellmeister since 1731 and produced thirty-two of his own operas. During these twenty-four years, he had altered his style of wind orchestration little, so that *Ezio* (1755), *Il re pastore* (1755), and *Olimpiade* (1756) all preserve the typically baroque orchestration of his first operas. The first characteristic of this style concerns the structural placement of winds: instrumentation and texture remain constant throughout the A section of a da capo aria. As the only common exception, ritornellos may contrast with the vocal sections: oboes, or occasionally flutes, double the strings in ritornellos but remain silent during vocal sections. Once in a while, oboes intrude into a vocal section but only for a few bars or else for virtually its entire length.[6] The second characteristic of this baroque style concerns the relation of oboes to strings. Rarely providing independent harmonic support or melodic solos, oboes simply double violins.

After leaving Dresden for Italy in 1756, Hasse began to treat oboes differently. While he occasionally composed parts similar to those of Dresden,[7] he also fashioned others which embody two new principles. First, oboes sound sporadically, their parts consisting of phrases or phrase fragments which appear now and then and thereby can articulate important structural events. Second, while oboes frequently double the violins as before, they sometimes provide independent harmonic support as well. Hasse applied these new principles gradually, at first composing fragmented parts which simply duplicate crucial bits of the violin line. Only later, and primarily for *Ruggiero* (Milan, 1771), did he create fragmented parts which also provide independent harmonic support.

The term "independent harmonic support" defies simple definition, for an enormous grey area separates pure ripieno parts and those whose pitches and rhythms differ entirely from the strings. Contributing to this ambiguity was the frequent necessity for composers or copyists to simplify or otherwise alter certain ripieno parts. In his definition of "copiste," for example, Jean-Jacques Rousseau reports how the production of a ripieno part for oboe entailed more than simply copying the violin parts note for note:

> Les Parties de Hautbois qu'on tire sur les Parties de Violon pour un grand Orchestre, ne doivent pas être exactement copiées comme elles sont dans l'original: mais, outre l'étendue que cet Instrument a de moins que le Violon; ... outre l'agilité qui lui manque ou qui lui va mal dans certaines vitesses, le force du Hautbois doit être ménagée pour marquer mieux les Notes principales, & donner plus d'accent à la Musique.[8]

In Hasse's arias, most such simplifications arise where the violins stray below middle C (the oboe's lowest pitch) or engage in a tremolo. In the latter case, Hasse almost invariably directed oboes to sustain the same pitches with half notes or whole notes. Deviations such as these from the violin part simply reflect the technical limitations of the oboe and do not deserve the term "independent harmonic support." More problematic is figure 15a where oboes again could not easily double the violins. Instead of giving them whole notes, however, Hasse substituted a more distinctive rhythm, its syncopation countering the strings' emphasis on first and third beats and intensifying the drive to the cadence. It is impossible to determine whether this passage arose more as a necessary alteration of the violin parts or as a self-conscious attempt to create an independent woodwind accompaniment. The oboes of figure 15b, on the other hand, have a better claim to the term "independent." Although they play no new pitches, they not only introduce an independent rhythm but enter in each bar after a rest, thus sounding more distinct.

These two excerpts demonstrate the possible rhythmic differences between oboes and violins which play the same pitches. In addition, the concept of "independent harmonic support" can of course embrace a variety of

Figure 15. Independent Harmonic Support Provided by Hasse's Oboes

(Hasse: Ruggiero 17)

(Hasse: Ruggiero 7)

c)

Dal | fasto e | dal de- | coro | e dal de- | coro

(Hasse: Demofoonte 14)

d)

(cor)aggio os- | tenta per cor- aggio | forse a cambiar lin- | guag - | - (gio)

(Hasse: Romolo 10)

(Hasse: Ruggiero 4)

pitch relationships between oboes and violins. Perhaps only one of two oboes introduces notes not played by violins; or, both oboes can sound new pitches. Those of figure 15c fall in the lower register of the instrument, however, and remain somewhat obscured by the higher pitches of the violins. The oboes of figure 15d lie above the strings, although the effect of such detached chords is more rhythmic than harmonic. Finally, the oboes of figure 15e sustain relatively high notes which easily project over the strings and horns.

An understanding of such degrees of "independent harmonic support" enables one to isolate stylistic differences between composers or between periods of one composer's creative life. From *Ezio* (1755) to *Romolo ed Ersilia* (1765), for example, Hasse composed few independent supporting parts for oboes. When he did, he often fashioned the sort of brittle, unsustained support illustrated in figure 15d: oboes, usually with horns, punctuate strong beats with short detached chords.[9] By the time of *Ruggiero,* however, many more independent harmonic passages are sustained, the style of figure 15d occurring only once among the numerous instances of independent harmonic writing for oboes.[10] This development parallels the general textural and rhythmic changes of the late 1760s and early 1770s (see chapter 3). Much of Hasse's writing for oboes in the 1750s and 1760s thus regularly emphasizes strong beats, whereas his more sustained and prominent oboe parts of the 1770s produce a more lyrical and flowing accompaniment.

The many varieties and degrees of "independent harmonic support" in fact discourage a detailed and complete classification of such parts. The situation is different, however, with respect to one of the most crucial aspects of classical orchestration: the relation of fragmented parts to structure. In the case of the da capo aria, a largely formulaic structure, even in its smaller details, permits one to speak of more or less "standard" structural events. One can determine those events that a composer characteristically selected for wind articulation, trace his treatment of them over a long period of time, and compare such treatment with other composers' handling of the same events.

When writing for oboes, Hasse generally emphasized events intimately bound with the establishment of a primary tonality and with the modulation to, reinforcement of, and eventual withdrawal from, a secondary tonality. His focus on these matters therefore reflects a growing polarity between tonic and dominant keys. In the context of the mid-eighteenth-century aria, these modulatory events occur mostly in the first vocal section and the very beginning of the second vocal section. Consequently, it was here that Hasse came to treat oboes differently. Other parts of the A section—the ritornellos and the second half of the second vocal section—lack modulations; hence, Hasse there retained an earlier style. Even in *Ruggiero,* his last opera, oboes participate in ritornellos only to double the violins throughout;[11] likewise, in the second half of the second vocal section, oboes frequently accompany the strings throughout.

Within the first vocal section and beginning of the second, Hasse used oboes to articulate the following specific events:

1. A tonic cadence concluding the first phrase or "first theme"
2. An orchestral extension of the tonic resolution of the above-mentioned cadence
3. A half cadence concluding the second phrase
4. The arrival at the dominant chord of the secondary key in mid-phrase (frequently a melisma)
5. A vocal caesura between the dominant chord of the secondary key and the subsequent resolution to the new tonic
6. The beginning or all of the "tonic resolution phrase"[12]
7. The final cadence of the first vocal section
8. A sequence, usually $V^7/ii - ii - V^7 - I$ (or a similar progression emphasizing the supertonic before returning to the original tonic), near the beginning of the second vocal section

These events do not appear in every aria. The first theme in a few arias, for example, concludes with a half cadence, not a perfect one; or the first vocal section continues with a modulation uninterrupted by a half cadence. A few arias have no dominant chord before the tonic resolution in the new key, and many lack the sequence which emphasizes the supertonic. In spite of these exceptions, the events listed above occur with sufficient frequency to be considered "standard," thus providing an ideal framework in which to monitor style change in orchestration.

Bradamante's aria "Non esser troppo altero" from *Ruggiero* (Milan, 1771) exemplifies how Hasse used oboes to articulate most of the above-mentioned events (example 36). The first vocal section (mm. 6-31) consists of four phrases, the first (mm. 6-13) conforming to the typically preclassical "ABB" pattern. At the start of this phrase, the oboes are silent; the voice, doubled by violins, can clearly present the "first theme" and the first two lines of text. Oboes enter only for the conclusion of the phrase, doubling the violins on the final four beats. Their fragment, a simple cadential gesture, partakes of none of the individual qualities of the opening phrase—it could conclude almost any theme in $\frac{3}{4}$ meter[13]—yet serves two important purposes: it gives the second cadence a different tone color and rounds off the theme as a whole. The next bar extends and affirms the tonic resolution of the first theme. As in measures 12-13, the oboes (this time with horns) double the violins to separate the first theme, as well as the primary tonality in general, from the ensuing material.

The second phrase (mm. 15-20), commencing on the tonic and concluding with a half cadence, sets the stage for the eventual modulation. At the word "more," an interjection of oboes, serving no important structural function for the aria as a whole, highlights the following caesura. Three bars later, horns provide two upbeats leading to a downbeat. While rounding off the phrase, these three notes also point towards the conclusion of the half cadence with its inherent instability. The oboes, by doubling the violins immediately thereafter in m. 20, serve a similar purpose. The third phrase (mm. 21-27) completes the modulation, which actually begins with a vii^6/V chord (m. 22), the first to lie outside the original key of B-flat major. Oboes emphasize this chord by sustaining the reiterated notes of the second violins and violas. Soon thereafter follows the most important structural event of the first vocal section: the arrival at the dominant chord of the secondary key. Oboes and horns enter at this point, and, for the first time in the aria, sustain notes simultaneously. The concluding phrase (mm. 28-31) resolves to the new tonic. Its two single segments, brief and with descending melodic lines, come as something of an anticlimax. By employing winds in the second, however, Hasse increased the drive towards one of the dramatic highpoints of the aria: the repetition of part of the opening ritornello in a new key.

The beginning of the second vocal section soon lapses into the original key of B-flat (m. 37). A sequence based on the progression V^7/ii – V/V – V^7 – I confirms this return. At this point, oboes make their first appearance in the second vocal section, highlighting the expressive dominant seventh chords. By superimposing a simple rhythmic pattern over the busy violin parts, moreover, the oboes outline the structure of the sequence:

"Non esser troppo altero" thus illustrates how oboes and horns can articulate Events nos. 1, 2, 3, 5, 6, 7, and 8 listed above; an additional example shows Event no. 4. In the aria described above, the V/V chord concludes the third phrase and leads directly to a cadential phrase resolving to the new tonic. The oboes and horns in measure 26 therefore focus attention on both the V/V chord and the caesura preceding the next phrase. Some other arias utilize a

Example 36

questo è un amor che mo - re, e tut - to, tut - to a -

- mor non è. no, tut - to a -

(Hasse: Ruggiero 10)

V/V chord in another context: the chord falls in mid-phrase, frequently coinciding with the beginning of an extended melisma. Example 37, from an aria in F, shows such a phrase with melisma and oboe entrance occurring simultaneously at the V/V chord:

Example 37

(Hasse: Ruggiero 17)

These two examples, both culled from *Ruggiero* (1771), represent the culmination of a process beginning shortly after 1756 in the operas of Hasse. Table 12 traces this development chronologically, providing such details as the number of arias with articulating oboe parts per opera, the number of events with such accompaniment per aria, the identity of these events, and the type of articulation, i.e., whether oboes double the violins after a rest or provide independent harmonic support.[14] The chart reveals that Hasse at no point abruptly changed his treatment of oboes in favor of fragmented parts articulating structure. For his first post-1756 opera, *Nitteti* (Venice, 1758), he composed such parts to accompany only one aria.[15] For his next two operas, *Demofoonte* (Naples, 1758) and *Achille in Sciro* (Naples, 1759), the composer fashioned fragmented parts in the new style for only four more.[16] In no aria, moreover, did Hasse employ the principles of fragmentary doubling or of independent harmonic support to more than three standard events. In the same three operas for Italy, Hasse composed a few independent harmonic passages for oboes, but all occur in arias where oboes play throughout, mostly doubling the violins. The oboes in such independent passages therefore do not vary the orchestral color as they would if they were silent immediately before the harmonic passage. Some of these independent parts, moreover, extend through long portions of an aria and do not isolate small-scale structural events: the two lengthiest examples serve to contrast the B section as a whole from the remainder of the aria. Elsewhere, harmonic support accompanies the types of structural events listed on p. 123: in one aria, the arrival at the V/V chord; in three other arias, the sequence emphasizing the supertonic near the beginning of the second vocal section.[17]

The tentativeness with which Hasse modified his treatment of the oboe in these operas of the late 1750s makes it difficult to determine why he changed at all. Was he adapting to a specifically Italian—or more precisely, Venetian or Neapolitan—style of orchestration? Or, would he have developed along similar lines had he never left Dresden? These questions may never be answered in full, at least not without a better understanding of the operatic and symphonic repertoires of Dresden, Naples, and Venice. At least some contemporary operas composed for the Italian stage include fragmented oboe parts which draw attention to standard structural events and often provide independent harmonic support as well.[18] That J.C. Bach's *Artaserse* (Turin, 1761), his first essay in the genre of opera seria, contains such parts suggests that this style of orchestration already enjoyed wide acceptance in Italy. If so, the reserved pace at which Hasse conformed to standard practice reveals that he did not feel immediately constrained to tailor his orchestration in every detail to what his orchestra or audience expected.

After *Achille in Sciro*, Hasse gradually composed more and more fragmented parts in the new style. At the same time, more of the standard structural events came to benefit from oboe reinforcement. Beginning with *Artaserse* (1760), oboes frequently fortify the extension of the first theme's

Table 12. Standard Structural Events Articulated by Oboes in the Arias of Hasse

Aria	Aria	Tonic Cadence of 1st Theme	Extension of Tonic Cadence	Half Cadence Concluding 2d Phrase	V/V Chord,ᵃ Mid-Phrase	V/V Chord,ᵃ End of Phrase (Caesura)	Tonic Resolution Phraseᵇ	Cadence of 1st Vocal Sectionᶜ,ᵈ	"ii-I" Progression in 2nd Vocal Section	Remarks
Nitteti	1	–	x	–	–	–	–	x	*	(Oboes play throughout)ᵉ
Demofoonte	4	x	–	–	–	x	–	x	–	
	6	x	–	x	–	–	–	–	–	Oboes play throughout
	19	–	–	–	*	–	–	–	–	
Achille	2	–	x	–	–	x	–	x	*	No oboes in 1st vocal section
	14	–	x	–	–	–	x	x	–	
	22	–	–	–	–	–	–	–	*	
Artaserse	2	–	x	–	–	x	*	x	*	Ind. melodic material at Ton. Res.
	4	–	x	–	–	–	x	–	–	
	15	–	x	–	–	–	–	x	–	
	17	–	x	–	–	–	–	–	–	
Zenobia	3	x	–	–	–	–	–	x	*	Oboes nowhere else in 1st vocal section
	10	–	x	–	–	–	x	–	–	
	13	–	x	–	–	–	x	–	–	
	14	–	x	–	–	–	–	–	–	
	15	–	–	–	–	x	–	x	*	
Clelia	4	–	x	–	–	*	–	–	–	Oboes nowhere else in 1st vocal section
	13	–	x	–	–	x	x	–	–	
	16	–	–	x	–	x	x	–	–	Oboes nowhere else in 1st vocal section
	17	–	x	–	–	–	–	–	–	
	18	–	x	–	–	*	x	x	–	

Siroe	3	–	–	x	–	–	–	–	–	x	*
	12	–	–	–	–	–	–	–	–	–	*
Romolo	1	–	–	–	–	–	–	x	–	–	–
	2	–	–	x	–	x	–	x	–	x	–	Oboes nowhere else in 1st vocal section
	6	x	–	–	–	–	–	–	–	–	–	Oboes nowhere else in 1st vocal section
	10	–	–	–	–	–	–	x	–	–	–
	12	x	–	x	x	x	x	x	–	x	–
	13	–	–	–	–	–	–	x	–	x	–
	14	–	–	–	*	–	*	–	*	x	–	Ind. melodic material at Ton. Res.
	15	–	–	–	–	–	–	x	–	–	x
Ruggiero	1	x	–	–	x	–	–	–	–	–	x
	4	–	*	–	–	*	–	–	–	–	*
	5	x	–	x	–	x	–	x	–	x	–
	8	x	–	–	–	–	–	x	–	x	*
	10	x	x	–	x	–	x	x	–	x	*
	11	*	–	–	–	–	–	x	–	x	–
	12	–	*	–	*	–	*	–	*	–	–
	13	x	–	x	–	–	–	x	–	x	–
	15	x	–	x	–	–	–	x	–	x	–
	17	–	*	–	*	x	–	x	–	x	x	Ind. melodic material at Ton. Res.

Notes: The first column lists the arias where oboes articulate at least one of the standard events listed on p. 123. (As an exception, arias in which oboes double the violins only for the final cadence of the first vocal section are not included; see note c below.) Articulation consisting of oboes doubling violins after a rest is represented on the table by an "x" in the appropriate box. (As an exception, passages where oboes double violins for the final cadence of the first vocal section are listed even if oboes play immediately before the cadence as well; see below, noted.) Articulation consisting of oboes providing independent harmonic support is represented on the table by an asterisk in the appropriate box.

a. The abbreviation "V / V" is used for simplicity, although the secondary key is not invariably that of the dominant.

b. In several arias, oboes highlight the beginning or all of the tonic resolution phrase, not by doubling the violins or providing harmonic support but by introducing an independent melodic line, with strings playing a subordinate role. While a consideration of such melodic passages for winds belongs to the following chapter, the chart records these passages, since they too articulate structure: they make obvious the appearance of a new tonality.

c. In some arias (*Artaserse* 9; *Clelia* 9; *Siroe* 10, 11), oboes enter the first vocal section only at the final cadence. Since such limited doubling seems merely like a forward extension of the old-fashioned ripieno participation in the second ritornello, these arias are omitted from the chart.

d. Hasse's secondary key areas, compared with their counterparts in the arias of Jommelli and Bach, are quite short. The span from the final V / V chord to the second ritornello usually comprises but several bars. In some arias, if Hasse had wanted oboes to articulate both the beginning of the tonic resolution phrase and the final cadence, he had no choice but to double the entire passage; the tonic resolution phrase was simply too short for Hasse to insert a rest for oboes between the beginning of the phrase and the final cadence. Concerning the latter event, therefore, the chart recognizes oboe doubling which is not preceded by a rest in the oboe part.

e. The D-Mbs manuscript of *Nitteti* does not indicate unequivocally whether or not oboes should double the violins during the preceding phrase. The fact that oboes double violins throughout the remainder of the aria suggests that Hasse wanted oboes to double violins for the entire first phrase as well.

tonic cadence and occasionally highlight the beginning of the tonic resolution phrase. Starting with *Il trionfo di Clelia* (1762), moreover, oboes more frequently articulate a half cadence concluding the second phrase and separate the V/V chord from the ensuing tonic resolution phrase. Hasse's transition to independent, fragmented oboe writing reached its high water mark in his last opera, *Ruggiero* (Milan, 1771). This work boasts the most arias with fragmented parts articulating standard structural events and includes as well the greatest amount of independent part writing for oboes (whether used in the service of the specific events listed on p. 123 or elsewhere). From the standpoint of orchestration, therefore, *Ruggiero* deserves recognition as one of Hasse's most significant musical achievements. While the orchestrational style differs considerably from that which prevailed in most of his earlier opere serie, it clearly represents the culmination of new directions the composer took during the last fifteen years of his operatic career. Though conservative, Hasse was not totally rigid in matters of musical style.

Oboe and Horn Parts in the Operas of Jommelli and J.C. Bach

The metamorphosis which Hasse's orchestration underwent between 1756 and 1771 was unique only in the specific time in which it occurred. Jommelli's orchestration underwent a similar change in the 1740s and early 1750s. His *Ezio* of 1741 (Bologna) reveals a relatively old-fashioned style, where oboes in the ritornellos double violins throughout and where, in the vocal sections, the oboes double violins sporadically (and rarely for the final cadence); they seldom sustain notes on their own.[19] By 1755, the transition to a more modern style was complete: the operas of 1755-72 provide no evidence that Jommelli's oboes served as ripieno instruments. When composing *Pelope* in 1755, the Stuttgart Kapellmeister was already creating oboe parts which primarily sustain chords at standard structural locations. From then on, moreover, Jommelli did not expand, refine, or otherwise modify his treatment of oboes and horns. Significantly, the late oboe parts consisting of sustained notes pose fewer technical challenges than the earlier ones where oboes double violin lines consisting frequently of sweeping scales or rapid sixteenth-note flourishes. This distinction between Jommelli's early and later oboe parts demonstrates the shortcomings of relating style change in woodwind orchestration to any advancements in instrumental technique and virtuosity.

While the structural events Jommelli selected for wind articulation remained constant throughout the period 1755-72, they differ substantially from those Hasse came to choose. This contrast reflects certain differences in their phrase structures and harmonic rhythm. Compared with Hasse, first of all, Jommelli composed few half cadences, thus rarely interrupting the modulation to the dominant with a half cadence or inserting one after the V/V chord. (When he did so, the resulting caesura is usually insignificant, with scarcely a break in the melody and an almost immediate resolution to the tonic.) In the middle of the first vocal section, moreover, Jommelli tended to quicken the harmonic rhythm, draw out phrases, and blur their boundaries; the V/V chord is often poorly articulated, both harmonically and melodically. Often with no clearcut half cadence or V/V chord, therefore, the entire stretch from the conclusion of the first theme—or shortly thereafter—to the tonic resolution in the secondary key frequently lacks winds.

The beginning and end of the first vocal section, on the other hand, often contain balanced phrases and a harmonic rhythm slower than Hasse's. Jommelli, consequently, readily added oboes and horns to the extension of the first theme's tonic resolution, the final cadence of the first vocal section, and two other events less common in Hasse's operas:

1. A repeated progression following the first theme and emphasizing the subdominant, as $I - IV - I$, $I - IV_4^6 - I$, or $I - IV^6 - I^6 - IV$
2. Paired cadential phrases in the secondary key but preceding the final cadence of the first vocal section

The aria "Tu m'offri un regno in dono?" from *Fetonte* (Stuttgart, 1768) exemplifies the typical interaction of structure and accompanimental parts for oboes and horns in Jommelli's arias (example 38). The first six bars of the aria serve as a slow introduction, the "first theme" proper beginning in measure 7. After the initial chord of the "Grave" section, oboes and horns do not reappear until measure 13, where a C Major triad marks the end of the first theme and the beginning of the repeated harmonic progression $I - IV^6 - I^6 - IV$. At this point, horns sustain an eight-bar tonic pedal and oboes support the subdominant progression. Immediately thereafter the modulation begins, and the winds drop out for the ensuing fourteen bars where there is neither a half cadence nor a well-articulated dominant chord of the new key. (The V/V chord appears rather anticlimactically in measure 27 as the resolution of an extended I_4^6 chord in measure 26. Further, it coincides with neither the beginning nor the conclusion of the melisma as is usually the case in the arias of Hasse or Bach.) Only after a perfect cadence in the new key of G do the winds reenter: horns sustain a second tonic pedal and oboes reinforce the beginning both of measure 35 and of its varied repetition in measure 36. All winds, finally, support the strings at the final cadence of the first vocal section (m. 41).

"Tu m'offri un regno in dono?" illustrates how Jommelli's arias made a special aural impact on his listeners. While Hasse's oboes and horns often interject brief snippets between vocal phrases, Jommelli's winds generally sound simultaneously with the voice. Instead of separating phrases, they strengthen relatively slow-moving harmonic progressions involving simple tonic, dominant, and subdominant chords. Jommelli thereby fashioned large blocks of a rather massive, sustained wind sound, the tonal counterpart of the

Example 38

(Ad Orcane.)
(Zu Orcanes.)

tro - no, no, mio que-sto cuor non è. Nell' ur-na e
herr - schen! Nein, glaubst Du, mein Herz sei frei? Ob er gleich

stin-to, es - tin-to an-cor a - mo, a- -mo chi sempre a - ma - i, nè can-gia mai te-
tot ist, lebt er mir doch, lie - bend, lie- -bend denk ich des Ge - lieb-ten, so lang ich bin, wird

nor, no, non can.gia mai te . nor la mia co . stan .za, la mia co . stan . . . . .

nie, nie, so lang ich bin, soll nie die Treu.e__ schwanken, die Treu.e schwan . . . . .

za, la mi . a, la

ken, die Treu . e, die

mi a co- stan - - za, no, no,— no, no, non can-gia, ho— non cangia mai, mai,— mai—
Treu- e schwan- - -ken, nein, nein,— nein, nein, so— lang ich bin,— so lang ich bin, soll, soll,—

— te- nor, mai can- gia, no, non can- gia la mia co- stan - - - -
— soll nie, so lang ich bin, soll nie die Treu- e schwan - - - -

f assai

(Jommelli: Fetonte 5)

monumental splendor of ballet, stage design, and costume which characterized Stuttgart opera productions of the 1750s and 1760s.

Curiously, there are two contexts where Jommelli utilized winds far less frequently than Hasse did. The Stuttgart Kapellmeister, first of all, almost never permitted winds to play during melismas; only strings could accompany the virtuosic vocalizations occurring usually in the middle or near the end of each vocal section.[20] Hasse, on the other hand, readily admitted winds into such passages, particularly those proceeding over a sequence or other standard progression, such as $V - V_2^4 - I^6 - V^6$.[21] Second, Jommelli rarely extended wind parts into the B section of a da capo aria. Only a smattering of his full and half da capo arias—such arias comprise the great majority of his pre-1770 output—contain wind parts in the B section.[22] Hasse liberally bestowed winds on his B sections, however, so that a majority of his arias with winds in the A section include them in the B section as well. Both cases belie the standard assertion that Hasse kept the orchestra strictly subordinate to the voice while Jommelli encouraged his orchestra to compete with or even drown out the voice.

J.C. Bach also created fragmented oboe parts which articulate standard structural events, evidently never using oboes as ripieno instruments. Even in his first opera, *Artaserse* (Turin, 1761), he required them to supply harmonic support. Starting with *Alessandro nell' Indie* (Naples, 1762), moreover, Bach increasingly treated other woodwinds—flutes, clarinets, and bassoons—as substitutes for, or additions to, the standard accompanimental ensemble of oboes and horns (see chapter 6). His application of such accompanimental winds to structural articulation resembles elements of both Hasse's and Jommelli's styles. Like Jommelli, Bach virtually banished winds from melismas[23] and the B section of da capo arias; only one of his full or half da capo arias contains winds in the B section.[24] Like Hasse, on the other hand, he required winds to alternate with the voice more than to compete with it; winds tend to separate phrases rather than reinforce them. Of the structural events listed on p. 123 therefore, Bach's winds typically articulate (1) an extension of the first theme's tonic resolution, (2) a half cadence concluding the second phrase, (3) a vocal caesura between the new dominant chord and the subsequent resolution to the new tonic, and (4) the beginning or all of the tonic resolution phrase (which in many of Bach's arias can be considered a "second theme").

Another event, the final cadence of the first vocal section, saw a gradual shift in treatment. At first, Bach rarely added winds to this event, and in his first three operas—*Artaserse, Catone in Utica,* and *Alessandro nell'Indie*—he did so in only five arias.[25] In four of these, moreover, he limited the winds to one pair: flutes, oboes, or horns. Only one aria (*Artaserse* 9) includes two pairs— oboes and horns. After moving to London, Bach added winds to this cadence more and more consistently, the number of arias with winds here and the number of instruments so used increasing dramatically. By the time of *Carattaco* (1767), winds articulate this cadence in seven arias;[26] in four of these, such accompaniment comprises four or five parts.[27] In *Temistocle* (1772), winds support this same event in no less than ten arias;[28] in seven of these, the winds comprise between four and eight parts, such combinations including clarinets and horns (*Temistocle* 2); flutes and bassoons (*Temistocle* 4); oboes and horns (*Temistocle* 5, 8); oboes, bassoons, and horns (*Temistocle* 7); flutes, oboes, bassoons, and horns (*Temistocle* 9); and oboes and "clarinetti d'amore" (*Temistocle* 18). Each such first vocal section, as a result, concludes more colorfully, a crescendo of winds leading to the following orchestral tutti.

Although different in certain particulars, the accompanimental wind writing in the operas of Hasse, Jommelli, and J.C. Bach shares fundamental characteristics such as the alliance of oboes and horns and the articulation of standard structural events. These similarities derive from the formulaic structure of the da capo aria in the mid-eighteenth century as well as from conventions governing wind instrumentation and orchestration. With few exceptions, change came gradually, if at all. In the period 1755-72, Jommelli in fact made none. Hasse freed oboes from their dependence on violins and more and more consistently and skillfully gave them independent parts which emphasize an increasing number of important points of arrival. Bach gradually expanded the set of structural events receiving wind support and added more winds to those events. The very slow pace at which most of these innovations were adopted suggests that they did not arise to meet the immediate circumstances of an opera's performance, such as the text or the particular strengths of an orchestra. The evidence thus supports and further extends one of the conclusions of chapter 5: the differences among orchestras had limited impact not only on what instruments a composer chose but also on what kind of parts he wrote for them. A composer might weigh such considerations when he scored for flutes or trumpets; or, he might occasionally fashion an "extensive independent melodic part" for one instrumentalist. Once he chose the standard accompanimental ensemble of oboes and horns, however, he would use them in virtually the same way throughout the opera as well as in operas intended for different cities. Changes in the use of these instruments as well as of all wind instruments for purposes of structural articulation were instead bound inextricably with the emergence of classical style, contributing to the articulated and dramatic, but balanced and hierarchical, phraseology of the new style.

6

The Independent Melodic Wind Ensemble and the Expansion of the Accompanimental Ensemble

In the operas of Hasse and Jommelli and in the first operas of Bach, winds chiefly double fragments of the violin parts and sustain a harmonic background; both types of writing articulate structure. In these works, "winds" usually means an accompanimental ensemble of oboes and horns. Since three or four instruments suffice to play triads, these composers preserved a three- or four-part wind texture in most of their operas and reserved the chords for oboes and horns.[1] Other winds—flutes and bassoons—rarely augment or replace this standard accompanimental ensemble of oboes and horns; they serve more to provide color. Sometimes they double violins, although such participation differs in two important respects from oboe doubling of violins. First, flutes and bassoons play the violin part in different octaves, their timbres thus remaining distinct. Second, their parts are generally less fragmented, flutes or bassoons following the violins for entire phrases or for several phrases at a time and rarely for anything as brief as a vocal caesura. Occasionally, they play independent passages that are neither strictly accompanimental nor melodic. Such parts merit the term "independent harmonic support," although they are less sustained than most supporting oboe parts (example 39):

Example 39

(Hasse: Ezio 9)

All winds—flutes, oboes, clarinets, bassoons, horns, and trumpets—also appear as independent melodic instruments, their parts belonging to one or more of four categories:

1. Extensive parts for one instrument
2. Brief, intermittent passages for one instrument
3. Extensive parts for wind ensemble
4. Brief, intermittent passages for wind ensemble

The first two groups may be dealt with briefly. The first, actually the "extensive independent melodic parts" treated in chapter 4, affords the least opportunity for style analysis, since winds which serve as the principal orchestral carrier of the melody and challenge the voice in melodic interest and length of participation cannot articulate structure; their relation to other instruments, whether strings or other winds, generally remains straightforward and unchanging. The second group, on the other hand, is exceedingly small. The standard classical "durchgebrochene Arbeit," where solo winds exchange brief motives in rapid succession, was virtually unknown to Hasse, Jommelli, and Bach. In their operas, winds, even on the level of the phrase or phrase fragment, almost always sound in pairs. Exceptions are limited to the few extensive independent melodic parts for one instrument (see table 9), several independent bassoon parts,[2] and passages where ripieno woodwinds double the violins.[3]

The third and fourth groups constitute the "independent melodic wind ensemble," the terms "independent" and "melodic" applying not necessarily to individual lines but to an ensemble: while one or two winds introduce a melody, others double that line in thirds or octaves or provide some sort of accompaniment, usually chords or a bass line. The ensemble as a whole comes to the fore, nevertheless, the strings serving a strictly subordinate role or dropping out entirely. This "independent melodic ensemble," the counterpart to the accompanimental ensemble described in chapter 5, deserves close scrutiny. Whether appearing sporadically or dominating entire arias, such an ensemble provided the context in which Hasse, Jommelli, and particularly Bach experimented with various wind combinations and sonorities and moved towards the creation of an independent ensemble of all woodwinds (including horns).

In the operas of Hasse and Jommelli, all such ensembles are trios, two winds proceeding mostly in thirds or sixths above a bass provided by strings or a third wind instrument.[4] Such three-part writing harkens back at least to the early 1700s, when composers utilized it for contrasting solo ensembles, examples of which include the "concertino" of two violins and cello in a concerto grosso or the middle section—assigned frequently to two oboes and bassoon—of a dance movement. But tradition alone cannot explain why Hasse and Jommelli continued to find the trio so ideal for melodic ensembles.

Perhaps they conceived of winds in this context as mere substitutes for the strings, which usually sounded in three parts as well: two sections of violins with cellos and doublebasses playing the bass line. Violas, even if independent of both violins and continuo instruments, offered little of real melodic or harmonic interest. When Hasse or Jommelli gave strings a rest and allowed woodwinds to take over, they therefore maintained the trio texture.

Hasse prescribed independent melodic wind ensembles for only fourteen arias (see table 13 for the location and instrumentation of each). While he had

Table 13.　Location and Instrumentation of Hasse's Melodic Wind Ensembles

Aria			Instrumentation[a]	Remarks[b]
Ezio	13	Dresden, 1775	FF/vln	
Re pastore	1	Dresden, 1755	FF/strings	
	8		F/Ob, F/Ob[c]/vla, H	extensive
	12		F/vln	
Demofoonte	14	Naples, 1758	Ob Ob/vln	
Artaserse	4	Naples, 1760	HH/vla, bassi	Ob Ob/vla, bassi in 1st vocal section and in B section
Zenobia	3	Warsaw, 1761	Ob Ob/vla, bassi, H	
			FF/vln	extensive
	5		FF/vln, vla	
	15		FF/vln	
Clelia	14	Vienna, 1762	F Ob/vln	extensive
Siroe	10	Dresden, 1763	FF/vln, vla	
	11		Ob Ob/vla, bassi	
Romolo	13	Innsbruck, 1765	HH/strings	Ob Ob/strings. H in 1st vocal section and in B section
Ruggiero	17	Milan, 1771	Ob Ob/B HH/bassi	Ob Ob/b in 1st vocal section and in B section; Ob B H, Ob B H/bassi in 2nd vocal section[d]

a. Abbreviations preceding the slash represent instruments which play the top two lines of the trio; abbreviations following the slash, instruments which perform the bass line. (Since the instrumentation of the bass line often varies between repetitions of an ensemble passage, this chart lists only the initial instrumentation of the bass line.)

b. In several arias, the ensemble writing extends through much of the aria and therefore belongs to the third of the four categories enumerated on p. 123, "extensive" parts. The "Remarks" column identifies such arias. In the remaining arias, the ensemble appears intermittently, thus belonging to the fourth group.

c. In all independent melodic ensemble passages of *Re pastore* 8, oboes double the flutes an octave below.

d. In the second vocal section of *Ruggiero* 17, oboes, bassoons, and horns simultaneously execute the top two lines of the trio (in two different octaves).

largely reserved harmonic support for oboes and horns, he assigned melodic ensembles to all types of woodwinds—flutes, oboes, and bassoons—as well as to horns. The bass line, first of all, he entrusted once to bassoons alone (*Ruggiero* 17) and elsewhere to strings: usually violins alone, violins and violas, or just continuo instruments. For the two upper lines, he limited himself to two of the same instrument, usually flutes or oboes,[5] his choice evidently depending on external circumstances. In Germany or Austria, he seldom used oboes in this context; in Italy, he never employed flutes, thus supporting the evidence of chapter 4 to the effect that Italian flute playing was not very advanced.[6]

In three of Hasse's fourteen arias, the ensemble extends through most of the aria. In the remaining eleven, one or two brief ensemble passages appear intermittently at fairly standard locations. Introduced in the opening ritornello after the "first theme," the second type of trio usually enters on the tail of a half cadence and then extends for much of a "dominant prolongation" (example 40). The same passage then recurs near the end of the second vocal section (usually joined by the voice) and often at two other locations as well: the first vocal section after a half cadence in the secondary key,[7] and the third ritornello. In a few arias, the passage enters the second ritornello or even the B section.

Jommelli treated melodic wind ensembles similarly, inserting them at many of the same points in his arias and never deviating from three part texture.[8] At the same time, however, he prescribed such ensembles more frequently,[9] almost always assigned the top lines to oboes, and sometimes demanded considerably more technical facility, particularly in the extensive solos for two oboes and horn (see example 41, with its cascades of scales and arpeggios). With such technical brilliance, these passages must have impressed the listener in a way that Hasse's wind parts could not have.

All told, Hasse and Jommelli brought relatively little originality to bear on their independent melodic ensembles for winds. Most important, both persistently maintained the trio texture inherited from the late baroque. J.C. Bach, in his first two operas—*Artaserse* (Turin, 1761) and *Catone in Utica* (Naples, 1761)—used winds in much the same way. He employed flutes in only two arias per opera (the same number in which flutes appear in most of Hasse's operas for Italy), never combined more than one pair of woodwinds with horns, and rarely gave the winds dependent melodic material (excepting the extensive melodic parts for oboe and bassoon in *Catone* 17 and the brief trios in five arias).[10] Thereafter, however, Bach gradually but consistently varied and enlarged the independent melodic wind ensemble. He did so in two general ways. First, he added more instruments and more independent lines, thereby creating a more complex texture. Second, he gave the ensemble greater independence from the strings, by abolishing string participation outright, composing longer ensemble passages, or positioning them at structural

Example 40

(Hasse: Demofoonte 14, beginning)

Example 41

(Jommelli: Olimpiade 13)

locations of greater prominence. In time, as we have seen in chapter 5, Bach began to increase the size and scope of the accompanimental wind ensemble as well.

Why Bach first demonstrated his partiality for winds in his third opera, *Alessandro nell'Indie,* is a mystery. His previous opera, *Catone in Utica,* had received its premiere in Naples on November 4, 1761. Presumably because of the opera's great success, Bach was commissioned almost immediately to compose another opera for the same house. This next work, *Alessandro nell'Indie,* was first performed only two and a half months later, on January 20, 1762. Although these two operas were composed for the same opera house during the same season, the disparity between the wind writing of *Alessandro* and that of *Catone* is enormous indeed.

Alessandro nell'Indie requires no more winds than does *Catone in Utica;* the Naples orchestra had doubtless not changed in the two and a half months since the premiere of the earlier work. Rather than demanding more instruments, Bach composed more independent melodic passages for winds and grouped winds into larger, more complex ensembles. Bach, in fact, gave some sort of independent melodic material to winds in all but two of the twelve arias with wind accompaniment. For *Alessandro* 13, he fashioned an extensive solo for bassoon. For six of the remaining arias, he composed brief ensemble passages differing from Hasse's only in their greater frequency[11]—the texture remains three-part with two oboes playing mostly in parallel thirds. Again like Hasse, such passages first appear after a half cadence in the first ritornello and then recur near the conclusions of the first and second vocal sections. Most important, Bach constructed most ensembles of *Alessandro,* as well as those of his subsequent operas, over simple, slow-moving progressions: $I - V - I - V$ or the closely related $I_4^6 - V - I_4^6 - V$.[12]

In the remaining three arias with independent melodic material, Bach expanded the instrumentation of both melodic and accompanimental ensemble passages. He allotted a brief melodic passage in *Allesandro* 8 to four instruments: two flutes and two horns, again in the context of the progression $I - V - I - V$. In *Alessandro* 17, he combined pairs of flutes, oboes, and horns, and constructed not only the usual trios (with oboes and flutes playing in octaves) but also several five-part ensembles (minus a separate part for second horn) to sustain chords (example 42). In each vocal section of *Alessandro* 10, finally, Bach fashioned the most radical departure from the standard trio: a seven-part melodic ensemble for pairs of flutes, oboes, bassoons, and horns (again playing the same part). To do so, he simply required certain winds to supply a harmonic background to other winds, just as they normally did to strings. Flutes and horns thus sustain a three-octave dominant pedal, while oboes and bassoons engage in two simultaneous duets over the progression $V^7 - I_4^6 - V^7 - I_4^6 - V^7 - I_4^6 - V^7 - I$ (example 43).

Example 42

(viole col basso)   (Bach: Alessandro 17)

The association of most melodic ensemble passages in *Alessandro* with such simple and repetitive harmonic progressions merits further elaboration. At several crucial junctures in an aria—a half cadence in the first ritornello, a half cadence on V/V in the first vocal section, and a "second theme" in the first ritornello and both vocal sections—Bach often alternated simple tonic and dominant chords, each extending for one bar or half a bar and conferring harmonic and rhythmic stability. He composed such passages so frequently that it seems he must have conceived of them first in harmonic terms, only later "filling in" the melody and other voice leadings from tonic to dominant and back to tonic, and so on. This primarily harmonic conception and the relative slowness with which these chords change doubtless facilitated Bach's new handling of winds. When placing independent melodic ensembles in such a context, Bach was less interested in creating a good melody than in providing emphatic and resonant chords on strong beats. He consequently saw no reason to limit himself to three instrumental lines and utilized all available wind instruments. Sonority took precedence over purity of voice leading.

Example 43

(viole col basso)

(Bach: Alessandro 10)

In little more than a year after *Alessandro*, Bach composed *Orione* for London. While a complete score has not survived, the extant arias reveal advances which by no means outweigh those of *Alessandro nell'Indie* over *Catone in Utica*. Bach's ensemble writing thus reinforces the evidence of chapter 4 to the effect that the move to London in itself did not substantially alter Bach's treatment of winds. Three of the five extant arias in *Orione* call for winds other than the standard quartet of oboes and horns. In one (*Orione* 1), Bach entrusted brief melodic fragments alternately to two clarinets and two horns and occasionally molded all four into an accompanimental ensemble much like that of oboes and horns. For another (*Orione* 9), he composed a passage similar to one in *Alessandro* 10 (example 43); flutes sustain a dominant pedal while oboes and bassoons engage in two duets of steady quarter notes over the progression I – V – I – V. Only the third (*Orione* 14) reveals new

Example 44

(Bach: *Orione* 14)

techniques. In the first ritornello of this aria, the independent melodic wind ensemble plays extensively (example 44), mostly unsupported by strings. In the fourth bar of this ritornello, the bass line initially passes back and forth between lower strings and bassoon; the former, rather than playing throughout, mark each down beat, after which the latter arpeggiates slow-moving I, I$_4^6$, and V chords. These undulating triadic fragments serve simultaneously as bass line and harmonic support. They enter repeatedly on the second half beat of each bar and thus anticipate the development of "classical counterpoint" in the later 1760s and early 1770s (see chapter 3).

In the wind ensemble writing of his third London opera, *Adriano in Siria* (1765), Bach offered little new; but in that of his fourth, *Carattaco* (1767), he completely excelled all of his earlier efforts, utilizing more of the rhythmic and textural innovations associated with the rise of classical counterpoint. All independent melodic wind writing of his earlier *Alessandro nell'Indie* (1762) had sounded "busy," the upper parts maintaining a steady, sometimes plodding succession of eighth notes or quarter notes (see example 43). The string accompaniment, in addition, frequently consisted of repeated eighth- or sixteenth-note chords. Melody and accompaniment thus emphasized each beat

Example 45

(Bach: Carattaco 2)

of each measure, producing a rather monotonous rhythmic effect. The first ritornello of *Carattaco* 2 (example 45), however, begins with a very different sort of melodic ensemble passage. In measure 7, a solo clarinet intones a lyrical theme repeated immediately by solo horn. Both phrases contain a variety of note values, and the tie over the third beat insures that only the first beat of each measure receives stress. Violins do not repeat chords but engage in rapid arpeggiations, a technique Hasse and Jommelli never used. These accompanimental sixteenths flow so quickly that they do not emphasize individual beats but simply sustain a harmonic background. Melody and accompaniment, here more rhythmically independent of each other, unite to produce a phrase whose linear elements are not marred by too frequent and too regular rhythmic stresses.

Carattaco 9 opens with a similarly lyrical passage (example 46). Again the third beat is avoided, this time by means of the rhythm ♩ ♩ ♩ . More important, strings and winds exchange roles for much of the ritornello. Flutes, clarinets, horns, and bassoon (supported by cellos and double basses) present the first theme. The remaining strings enter only to reinforce the theme's tonic resolution, just as oboes and horns often do in the arias of Hasse and Jommelli. In the following phrase (mm. 5-8), the woodwinds again take the lead. Strings finally assume control of both melody and bass in m. 9, winds reverting to their customary role of providing harmonic support. Ironically, however, this phrase functions as a "dominant prolongation," the one standard location in the first ritornello where a composer would allow winds to come to the fore. Role reversal is thereby maintained.

Example 46

(Bach: Carattaco 9)

Other details of these two ritornellos reveal the care and skill with which Bach constructed his independent melodic ensembles. First, in the thirty-five operas studied here, the duet between clarinet and horn in *Carattaco* 2 (mm. 11-13) is the only instance where two instruments of a duet lie more than an octave apart. While the lower part in other duets usually runs in thirds or sixths with the upper part, Bach here assigned it to another instrument in a different octave. Second, the opening of *Carattaco* 9 shows Bach giving four pairs of winds different functions. Clarinets introduce the melody; bassoons provide an arpeggiated bass line in a different rhythm; horns sustain the harmonic background; flutes play chords as well, but only at the cadence, thus providing fragmentary harmonic support to other winds.

Five years later, Bach composed *Temistocle* (Mannheim, 1772), his last opera of the period. Here he did not lavish as much attention on independent melodic ensembles for winds but instead further expanded the accompanimental ensemble. Two aspects of this development deserve special notice. First, he now more than ever allowed flutes, clarinets, and bassoons to sustain chords. In *Temistocle* 1, consequently, he replaced the typical harmonic support of oboes and horns with one of flutes; in *Temistocle* 2, he combined horns with clarinets, and in *Temistocle* 9, he combined four pairs of winds—flutes, oboes, bassoons, and horns—all for the same purpose. Second, Bach consistently applied a new principle which he had used before only sporadically: octave doublings within the accompanimental ensemble. Like Hasse and Jommelli, Bach had occasionally required several winds to play an independent melody in their respective registers. Purely accompanimental parts, however, such as sustained harmonic support or short interjections between vocal phrases, he had almost always limited to four instruments: two oboes and two horns. *Temistocle* marks a turning point, however. Bach allowed other woodwinds, playing notes of the same pitch class but in their own registers, to enter the traditional domain of oboes and horns and thereby fashioned a harmonic support with more sonority and variety of color. In most arias with at least two pairs of woodwinds, in fact, Bach required one pair to double the other in octaves, such combinations including flutes and oboes (*Temistocle* 9), oboes and bassoons (*Temistocle* 9), flutes and clarinets (*Temistocle* 14), oboes and "clarinetti d'amore" (*Temistocle* 18), and flutes and horns (*Temistocle* 19). In one aria, Bach even massed three pairs of woodwinds—flutes, oboes, and bassoons—all of which at times play the same notes in three different octaves (example 47).

Whether the road Bach took from the wind writing of *Catone in Utica* to that of *Temistocle* was uncharted or well-traveled cannot easily be determined. Bach was no doubt influenced by symphonists active in London or Mannheim, but the present state of research into the preclassical symphony does not permit us to evaluate precisely such cause and effect. At least some of the innovations of *Temistocle* must reflect a general shift in style, for Jommelli and Hasse each composed one late opera in which they incorporated a few of the same techniques. In *Fetonte* (Stuttgart, 1768), Jommelli not only admitted flutes to a fast aria for the first time[13] but also required them to sustain chords along with oboes and horns. In *Ruggiero* (Milan, 1771), Hasse retained some old-fashioned characteristics—all arias with flutes are slow and confine oboes to ritornellos—but in one aria adopted two new techniques.[14] First, flutes and bassoons play accompanimental material in octaves; second, bassoons provide sustained harmonic support with horns.

These two isolated examples show that the new directions Bach had taken since the mid-1760s found echoes in some operas of older composers. *Fetonte*

Example 47

(Bach: Temistocle 9)

and *Ruggiero* notwithstanding, however, Bach far surpassed Hasse and Jommelli in the extent to which he abandoned conventions of the past and molded all woodwinds (with horns) into an ensemble capable of providing a powerful harmonic support to the strings or replacing them entirely. In this regard, he may in fact have exceeded most other composers as well. Gluck, for example, practically never utilized octave doublings for harmonic support. Even as late as his *Iphigénie en Tauride* (Paris, 1779), as in his other operas of the 1760s and 1770s, three pairs of woodwinds, in various permutations, usually play only three pitches.[15] Furthermore, oboes frequently double the violins, bassoons rarely depart from the continuo line, and independent ensemble passages maintain a three-part texture.

Comprehensive analysis of Gluck's wind orchestration, as well as that of others, such as Piccinni or Traetta, lies beyond the scope of this book. As such studies are undertaken, Bach's position in the history of opera instrumentation and orchestration will doubtless be modified. It seems likely, just the same, that of all composers of Italian opera in the third quarter of the eighteenth century, Bach will emerge as the one who made the most extensive, varied, and skillful use of woodwinds.

Conclusion

Of the various aspects of style change in the mid-eighteenth century, the fundamental and most decisive was doubtless harmonic expansion. We have seen its beginning ca. 1720—the harmonic rhythm of the arias of the 1710s hardly differs from that of Bach and Handel—and have followed its course through the 1730s, '40s, '50s, '60s, and '70s. How much longer the process continued was not determined, although it must be said that the harmonic rhythm of Haydn and Mozart in the 1780s does not seem significantly slower than that of J.C. Bach and Jommelli in the 1770s. Harmonic expansion thus had probably begun to abate by 1770, at which time a movement towards greater textural and accentual variegation was well under way. This later development, while not the inevitable result of harmonic expansion, would nonetheless have been impossible much before 1770. In other words, classical counterpoint, so often described as a return to baroque practices, would have been inconceivable in the context of baroque harmonic and phrase rhythm. The new texture instead required that the pace of harmonic change be substantially slower than the prevailing note values of the melody and various accompanimental lines. Harmonic expansion also set the stage for the more independent and structural roles given to woodwinds during the course of the century. As harmonic and melodic rhythms grew farther and farther apart, woodwinds tended more and more to sustain a harmonic background. Also, as phrases and even individual chords became more distinct, winds lent their various colors to highlight further these events.

The existence of these general areas of style change and the gradualness with which they occurred point to what must be considered the central thesis of this book: the third quarter of the eighteenth century was a time not of stylistic chaos but of widespread and consistent stylistic evolution leading in the general direction of the mature classicism of Haydn and Mozart. Not all composers participated in equal measure. Hasse adjusted his style rather late, as we have seen, and hardly took part in the development of classical counterpoint. Such an exception hardly invalidates the general thesis, however. At no time in the history of music have all composers shared equally in what are later considered to be the major style shifts of that period.

Viewed from the perspective of these fundamental issues involved in the transformation from late baroque style to mature classicism, the four particular composers studied here emerge in a new light. Hasse, the oldest of the three opera composers, employed the fastest harmonic rhythms and certain obsolete techniques of orchestration. Yet he still changed, although slowly. He decreased the rate of harmonic change, expanding some of his thematic and cadential constructions, and he partially freed winds from their ripieno functions, giving oboes lines which provide harmonic support. He also began to combine flutes, bassoons, and horns into an independent ensemble counterbalancing the strings.

The investigation of Jommelli reveals the most surprises, the scores demonstrating that Jommelli had scant interest in orchestral color. He limited himself to strings, oboes, and horns and virtually ignored flutes, bassoons, and trumpets, instruments that both Hasse and J.C. Bach used more frequently. Further, he treated wind instruments rather inflexibly, rarely allowing them to accompany melismas or the B section of da capo arias, functions Hasse frequently granted winds. Jommelli seems instead to have lavished far more care on strings, but in this respect the Stuttgart operas prove less masterful and less "classical" than the later operas for Naples and Rome. There Jommelli fashioned a texture in which the preclassical Trommelbass gives way to a more variegated bass line, in which the relentless stressing of downbeats gives way to a more graded and subtle accentuation, in which textural monotony gives way to continual textural contrast, and in which a continuously heavy combination of string parts gives way to a blend marked by greater transparency and independence of voices.

Viewed in terms of these textural and accentual matters, even the stylistic growth of Joseph Haydn emerges more clearly, for the same new textural details pervading Jommelli's last operas also revolutionized Haydn's symphonic style at the same time (1770). These changes affected practically every aspect of his symphonies and thus accounts for Haydn's early stylistic development far better than the standard emphasis on "Sturm und Drang," minor keys, and rhythmic drive. Significantly, these textural changes include most of the stylistic innovations often attributed instead to the early 1780s in general and to Haydn's op. 33 string quartets in particular.

J.C. Bach, the youngest of the three opera composers, developed the most varied, colorful, and "modern" wind accompaniments by combining flutes, oboes, clarinets, bassoons, and horns in virtually every possible permutation; by allowing all winds (not only oboes and horns) to provide harmonic support; and by occasionally relegating strings to a position subordinate to winds. These techniques have virtually no parallel in the available operas of other leading Italian opera composers of the day—Jommelli, Tommaso Traetta, Nicola

Piccinni, and even Gluck. On the basis of his orchestration alone, Bach deserves greater attention in histories of eighteenth-century opera.

Results such as these suggest that we have far more to learn by investigating further the style trends of the eighteenth century through the medium of Italian opera. Such research requires great care. First, the terminology must be precise, for the stylistic elements are too varied and subtle for us to settle for brief descriptions. We have seen, for example, that the concept of "independent harmonic support" (provided by winds) embraces a multitude of pitch and rhythmic relationships between oboes and violins. Any study of the evolution of such parts must therefore account for all of this complexity. Second, works should be compared extensively, both with works of the same composer as well as with those of other composers. As we have seen, Jommelli's *Fetonte,* with its large numbers of ensembles, choruses, and flute arias, does not speak for all of Jommelli's Stuttgart operas; and Haydn's symphonies in minor keys—particularly the early ones, such as nos. 26, 39, and 49—do not tell us everything we need to know about Haydn's symphonies of 1766-75. By the same token, Jommelli's Stuttgart wind orchestrations may first appear "German," "modern," or "complex." Such an impression vanishes, however, when these wind parts are compared with those of Hasse and J.C. Bach. Extensive comparison is thus necessary to gain perspective on even one opera. Third, the concept of "reform" should be used with care, since reform elements appeared in the 1750s, 1760s, and 1770s in a great variety of contexts and combinations. Hasse's *Ruggiero* (Milan, 1771), for example, contains more accompanied recitative than do several of Jommelli's Stuttgart operas; and Bach's *Carattaco* (London, 1767) contains more choral writing and variety of aria forms than do most of Jommelli's Stuttgart operas. Also, the composer who most expanded the woodwind component of orchestration was not a "reformer," such as Jommelli, Traetta, or Gluck, but J.C. Bach. We should probably not classify composers or even single operas as "reform" but should recognize individual reform traits wherever they arise. Fourth, the search for evidence of the evolution of classical style must extend beyond German and Austrian repertoires, since much of the process transpired elsewhere. Jommelli's handling of classical counterpoint reached its zenith in Naples and Rome; J.C. Bach's original approach to winds began in Naples and matured in England; Hasse's most "classical" woodwind orchestration appeared only in Milan. To focus only on music of Germany and Austria thus produces a rather incomplete picture of classical style.

Further research can expand in two directions. First, we should investigate other elements of style, such as the evolution of the "second theme," the pitch content of melodies, texture in slow movements and slow arias, modulatory progressions used to reach the dominant key, first theme structures other than "ABB," and so on. We should also study the operas of other composers. I would argue strongly for the early opere serie of Mozart and the opere serie of Tommaso Traetta, Francesco di Maio, and Antonio Sacchini, as well as the opere buffe of Haydn, Florian Leopold Gassmann, and Baldassare Galuppi. Hidden in the scores to these and many other works is doubtless a wealth of information illuminating the evolution from the preclassical style to the mature classicism of Haydn and Mozart.

Appendix A

Thematic Catalog of the Opera Seria Arias by J.C. Bach, 1755-72

Appendix A lists the arias of the seven J.C. Bach operas investigated in this book. The operas are listed alphabetically; the arias, in the order in which they appear in each opera. Each aria entry provides the first verse line of text and an incipit of the vocal line with the original clef preceding the modern clef. To the right of the text incipit, an Arabic numeral indicates the number of syllables per line. To the right of the vocal incipit, data pertaining to the aria's tempo, wind instrumentation, and thematic structure are recorded.

First, "fast arias" (see above, p. 13) are designated by the word "Fast." In "two-tempo arias" (see below, p. 282), a fast second section is designated as follows: "Fast (second section.)"

Second, wind parts are listed according to the following abbreviations:

F—flute
Ob—oboe
C—clarinet
B—bassoon
H—French horn
T—trumpet

"Extensive independent melodic parts" for winds (see above, pp. 105-10) are indicated by the underlining of the appropriate instrumental abbreviation, as in "2 Ob" or "H."

Third, first themes with phrase structure ABB or AA are indicated by the designation "ABB" or "AA."

Adriano in Siria

1. **Dal labbro, che t'accende**   7

   Andante

   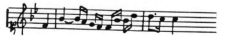   First theme: ABB

2. Disperato in mar turbato   8

Allegro

Fast
Winds: 2 Ob, 2H
First theme: ABB

3. Sprezza il furor del vento   7

Allegro di molto

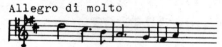

Fast
Winds: 2H

4. Dopo un tuo sguardo, ingrata!   7

Andante

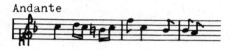

First theme: ABB

5. Vuoi punir l'ingrato amante?   8

Allegretto

First theme: ABB

6. Chi mai d'iniqua stella   7

Andante

Winds: 2F, 2H
First theme: ABB

7. Numi, se giusti siete   7

Allegro moderato

Fast
Winds: 2B
First theme: ABB

8. Non è la mia costanza   7

    Allegro   Fast

9. Leon piagato a morte   7

    Maestoso   Winds: 2 Ob, 2H

10. Quanto grato nell'amore   8

    Allegretto

   First theme: AA

11. Deh! lascia, o ciel pietoso   7

    Andantino   Winds: 2F, 2C, 2B, 2H

12. Volga il ciel, felici amanti   8

    Allegretto

   First theme: ABB

13. Cara la dolce fiamma   7

    Largo   Winds: 2 Ob, B, 2H
                                             First theme: ABB

14. Tutti nemici e rei   7

    Allegro assai   Fast
                                          Winds: 2 Ob, 2H

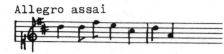

15. Digli ch'è un infedele   7

    Allegretto

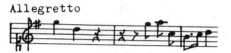

16. Più bella al tempo usato   7

    Allegro   Fast

                                          First theme: ABB

17. Se l'amistà tu sdegni   7

    Moderato
                                          Winds: 2H
                                          First theme: ABB

18. Oh Dio! mancar mi sento   7

    Andante espressivo
                                          Winds: 2B
                                          First theme: ABB

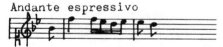

19. Non ritrova un' alma forte   8

    Allegro moderato   Fast

20. Son sventurato; ma pure, o stelle 10

Andante

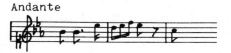

Winds: 2C, 2B, 2H
First theme: AA

Alessandro nell'Indie

1. È prezzo leggiero   6

Andante maestoso

First theme: ABB

2. Vil trofeo d'un'alma imbelle   8

Allegro

Fast
Winds: 2 Ob, 2H
First theme: ABB

3. O su gli estivi ardori   7

Allegro

Fast

First theme: ABB

4. Se mai più sarò geloso   8

Andante

5. Se mai turbo il tuo riposo   8

Allegro

Fast
Winds: 2 Ob, 2H
First theme: ABB

6. Se possono tanto   6

Andantino espressivo

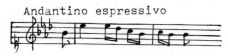

First theme: ABB

7. Compagni nell' amore   7

Allegretto

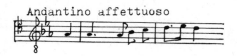

First theme: ABB

8. Se amor a questo petto   7

Andantino affettuoso

Winds: 2F, 2H
First theme: ABB

9. Non sarei sì sventurata   8

Allegro

Fast

First theme: ABB

10. Oh Dio! la man mi trema   7

Largo

Winds: 2F,[1] 2 Ob, 2B, 2H
First theme: ABB

11. Digli, ch'io son fedele   7

Andante

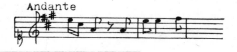

First theme: ABB

---

[1]Although I-Nc and I-Mc prescribe "Trombe" for these
parts, P-La calls for "Traversi," and the style and range of
the parts clearly indicate that Bach wanted flutes.

12. Destrier, che all'armi usato   7

Allegro

Fast
Winds: 2 Ob, 2H
First theme: ABB

13. Se è ver che t'accendi   6

Andante

Winds: B, 2H

14. Se il ciel mi divide   6

Allegretto

Winds: 2 Ob
First theme: AA

15. Di rendermi la calma   7

Allegro

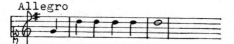

Fast
Winds: 2 Ob, 2H
First theme: ABB

16. Se troppo crede al ciglio   7

Allegretto

Winds: 2 Ob, 2H
First theme: ABB

17. Non so d'onde viene   6

Andante

Winds: 2F, 2 Ob, 2H

18. Trafiggerò quel core   7

Allegro assai   Fast
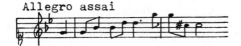   Winds: 2H
                                                   First theme: ABB

19. Mio ben ricordati   5

Andante
   First theme: ABB

20. Son confusa pastorella   8

Allegretto
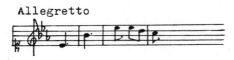

21. Ombra del caro sposo   7

Larghetto   Winds: 2 Ob, 2H
   First theme: ABB
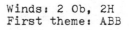

Artaserse

1. Conservati fedele   7

Andante   Winds: 2 Ob, 2H

2. Fra cento affani e cento   7

Allegro di molto   Fast
   Winds: 2H
                                                   First theme: ABB

3. Sulle sponde del torbido Lete   10

(no tempo indication)

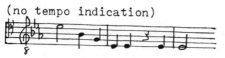

Winds: 2 Ob, 2H

4. Per pietà bell' idol mio   8

Allegro

Fast

5. Bramar di perdere   5

Allegretto

6. Non ti son padre   5

Allegro assai

Fast
Winds: 2 Ob, 2H
First theme: ABB

7. Torna innocente e poi   7

Allegro

Fast

First theme: ABB

8. Dimmi ch'un empio sei   7

Allegro assai

Fast
Winds: 2H

9. Vo solcando un mar crudele   8

Allegro   Fast
   Winds: 2 Ob, 2H

10. Rendimi il caro amico   7

Allegro moderato   Fast
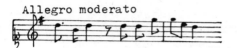   First theme: ABB

11. Mi scacci sdegnato   6

Allegro con expressione   Fast
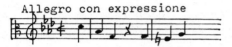   First theme: ABB

12. Non temer ch'io mai ti dica   8

Allegro   Fast
   First theme: ABB

13. Se d'un amor tiranno   7

Andante

14. Per quel paterno amplesso   7

Largo
   Winds: 2 Ob, 2H
                                             First theme: ABB

15. Va tra le selve ircane   7

Allegro di molto   Fast
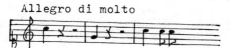   Winds: 2 Ob, 2H
                                             First theme: ABB

16. Fra tanti miei tormenti   7

Allegro   Fast
   Winds: 2H
                                             First theme: ABB

17. Non conosco in tal momento   8

Andante
   First theme: ABB

18. Così stupisce e cade   7

Allegro   Fast
   Winds: 2 Ob, 2T

19. Perché tarda è mai la morte   8

Larghetto
   Winds: 2F, 2H

20. Vivrò se vuoi così   7

Andantino
   Winds: 2 Ob, B, 2H

21. Nuvoletta opposta al sole   8

   Allegro

Fast
Winds: 2 H
First theme: ABB

22. Ardito ti renda   6

   Allegro

Fast
Winds: 2H

23. Figlio, se più non vivi   7

   Allegro

Fast

24. Mi credi spietata   6

   Allegro

Fast

25. Non è ver che sia contento   8

   Andante

Winds: 2F

Carattaco

1. Perfidi non osate   7

   Allegro assai

Fast
Winds: 2 Ob, 2H
First theme: ABB

2. Allor che in campo armato   7

   Andante maestoso

                                            Winds: 2C, B, 2H

3. Se a quei detti a quello sdegno   8

   Allegretto

                                            First theme: ABB

4. I primi affetti miei   7

   Andante

                                            Winds: 2F
                                            First theme: AA

5. Vanne superbo audace   7

   Allegro di molto   Fast
   Winds: 2 Ob, 2H
                                            First theme: ABB

6. Cara sposa amato figlia   8

   Andante con moto

                                            Winds: 2H
                                            First theme: ABB

7. Accender mi sento   6

   Allegretto

8. Quando infiamma un cor gentile   8

Andantino
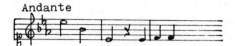

Winds: 2F, 2B
First theme: AA

9. Fra l'orrore di tanto spavento   10

Andante
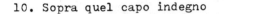

Winds: 2F, 2C, 2B, 2H

10. Sopra quel capo indegno   7

Allegro assai
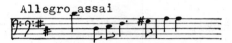

Fast
Winds: 2 Ob, 2H
First theme: ABB

11. Già m'abbandona la mia costanza   10

Allegro moderato

Fast

12. Sposa raffrena il pianto   7

(no tempo designation)
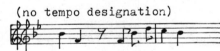

Winds: 2F, 2H
First theme: ABB

13. È costume ognor di Roma   8

Andante

14. Ho fra catene il piede

Allegro

7

Fast
Winds: 2 Ob, 2H
First theme: ABB

15. Ah mi sento già strideo d'intorno 10

Allegro

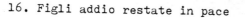

Fast
Winds: 2 Ob, 2H

16. Figli addio restate in pace

Larghetto

8

Winds: 2F, 2C, 2B, 2H
First theme: ABB

17. Se la pietà co' vinti

Allegro

7

Fast
Winds: 2H
First theme: ABB

18. Non è ver che assisa in Trono

Andante

8

Winds: 2F, 2H
First theme: ABB

19. Sfida il ciel non cura e sprezza

Allegro

8

Fast
Winds: 2 Ob, 2H
First theme: ABB

20. Se amico mi chiami   6

Tempo di Menuetto

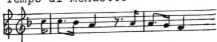

Winds: 2F, 2H

Catone in Utica

1. Con sì bel nome in fronte   7

Andante maestoso

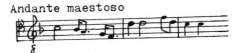

Winds: 2 Ob, 2H
First theme: ABB

2. Non ti minaccio sdegno   7

Allegro

Fast
Winds: 2 Ob, 2H
First theme: ABB

3. Fiumicel che s'ode appena   8

Andantino

Winds: 2F
First theme: ABB

4. O nel sen di qualche stella   8

Allegro

Fast
Winds: 2 Ob, 2H
First theme: ABB

5. Chi un dolce amor condanna   7

Largo

Winds: 2 Ob, 2H
First theme: ABB

6. È in ogni core   5

Andante

7. È follia se nascondete   8

Allegro

Fast
Winds: 2 Ob, 2H
First theme: ABB

8. Va ritorno al tuo tiranno   8

Allegro con brio

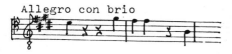

Fast

9. Nacqui agl'affanni in seno   7

Allegretto

First theme: ABB

10. Se in campo armato   5

Allegro con spirito

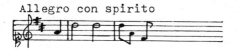

Fast
Winds: 2 Ob, 2H, 2T
First theme: ABB

11. Dovea svenarti allora   7

Allegro assai

Fast

First theme: ABB

12. So che godendo vai   7

Andante

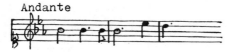

13. Così talor rimira   7

Allegro

Winds: 2 Ob, 2H
First theme: ABB

14. La fronda che circonda   7

Allegro

Fast
Winds: 2 H
First theme: ABB

15. Confusa smarrita   6

Andante

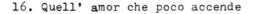

Winds: 2F
First theme: AA

16. Quell' amor che poco accende   8

Allegretto

Winds: 2 Ob, 2H
First theme: ABB

17. Per darvi alcun pegno   6

Larghetto

Winds: O, B
First theme: ABB

<u>Orione</u>

1. Frena crudel lo sdegno   7

   Andante di molto

   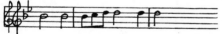

   Winds: 2C, 2H
   First theme: ABB

2. Per questa volta almeno   7

   (music lost)

3. Della misera germana   8

   (music lost)

4. Nel' trionfare il fato   7

   (music lost)

5. Solcar pensa un mar sicuro   8

   Allegro   Fast

   First theme: ABB

6. Andrò dal colle al prato   7

   Andante

   Winds: 2F
   First theme: ABB

7. Bella diva calma omai   8

(music lost)

8. Se de' miei strali

(music lost)

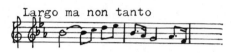

9. Se mi è caro l'idol mio   8

Largo ma non tanto

Winds: 2F, 2 Ob, 2B, 2H

10. Il figlio tuo   5

(no tempo designation)

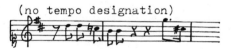

11. Più madre non sono   6

Allegro assai

Fast
Winds: 2 Ob, 2H

12. A mi basta o cara Tirsi   8

Allegretto

13. Nocchier che si abbandona   7

    (music lost)

14. Di quest' alma desolata   8

    Largo
   Winds: 2 Tailles, 2C,
                                                2B, 2H

15. Bene adorato addio   7

    Andantino
   First theme: ABB

16. Se volete eterni dei   8

    Allegretto
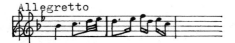   Winds: 2B

17. Del fato il giusto sdegno   7

    (music lost)

18. Cara Nice, io ti parlai   8

    (music lost)

19. Alfin fra tanti affanni   7

   (music lost)

<u>Temistocle</u>

1. Ch'io speri? ah Padre amato   7

   Allegro non tanto   Fast
      Winds: 2F

2. Fosca nube il sol ricopra   8

   Andante con moto
      Winds: 2C, 2H
                                              First theme: ABB

3. Basta dir ch'io sono amante   8

   Andante
      First theme: ABB

4. Chi mai d'iniqua stella   7

   Andante espressivo
                                              Winds: 2F, 2B
                                              First theme: ABB

5. Ch'io parta! il comando   6

   Largo   Allegro assai   Fast (second section)
                                              Winds: 2 Ob, 2H
                                              First theme: ABB

6. Contrasta assai più degno   7

Winds: 2H
First theme: ABB

7. Non m'alletta quel riso fallace   10

Fast
Winds: 2 Ob, B, 2H
First theme: AA

8. Si scorderà l'amante   7

Fast
Winds: 2 Ob, 2H

9. Del terreno nel concavo seno   10

Fast (second section)
Winds: 2F, 2 Ob, 2B, 2H

10. È specie di tormento   7

First theme: ABB

11. Or a' danni d'un ingrato   8

Fast
Winds: Ob, 2H
First theme: ABB

12. No quel labbro non parmi verace   10

Allegretto

First theme: ABB

13. Serberò fra ceppi ancora   8

(no tempo designation)

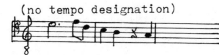

First theme: ABB

14. Sordo al suon de miei queruli accenti   10

Allegro moderato/Allegro assai

Fast
Winds: 2 Ob, 2H[1]

15. A quei sensi di gloria d'onore   10

Andante

Winds: 2H
First theme: ABB

16. Ah frenate il pianto imbelle   8

Allegro moderato

Fast
Winds: 2 Ob, 2B, 2H
First theme: ABB

17. Di quella fronte un raggio   7

Andante

First theme: ABB

---

[1]In the B section, however, the winds are as follows:
2F, 2C, 2B, 2H.

18. Ah si resti onor mi sgrida   8

Allegro con spirito

Fast
Winds: 2 Ob, 3 Clarinetti
     d'amore
First theme: ABB

19. Ma di Serse in petto amore   8

Largo

Winds: 2F, 2H

Appendix B

Thematic Catalog of the Opera Seria Arias by Hasse, 1755-72

Appendix B lists the arias of the twelve Hasse operas investigated in this book. The operas are listed alphabetically; the arias, in the order in which they appear in each opera. Each aria entry provides the same type of information given in appendix A for the Arias of J.C. Bach (see above, p. 165). In addition, ripieno parts for oboe—only Hasse composed such parts—are listed only for arias that also feature flutes and are represented with parentheses, as follows: "(2 Ob)."

Achille in Sciro

1. No ingrato amor non senti   7

   Vivace

First theme: ABB

2. Involarmi il mio tesoro   8

   Allegro assai

Fast
Winds: 2 Ob, 2H

3. Fra l'ombre un lampo solo   7

   Andante spiritoso

First theme: ABB

4. Alme incaute che torbide ancora   10

   Allegro di molto

Fast

5. Sì ben mio sarà qual vuoi   8

   Un poco lento ed amoroso

Winds: 2F, (2 Ob), 2H

6. Si varia in ciel talora   7

   Allegro

First theme: ABB

Fast

First theme: ABB

7. Intendo il tuo rossor   7

Allegretto

First theme: ABB

8. Del sen gl'ardori   5

Allegro e con spirito

Fast
Winds: 2H

9. Risponderti vorrei   7

Lento

First theme: ABB

10. Chi mai vide altrove ancora   8

Allegro ma non troppo

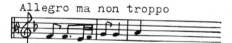

Fast
Winds: 2H

11. Quando il soccorso apprenda   7

Allegro

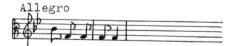

Fast

12. Fa che si spieghi almeno   7

Spiritoso non presto

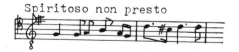

13. Potria fra tante pene   7

Allegretto

First theme: ABB

14. Così leon feroce   7

Allegro

Fast
Winds: 2 Ob, 2H
First theme: ABB

15. Ah se veder potessi   7

Un poco lento

First theme: ABB

16. Dille che si consoli   7

Allegro

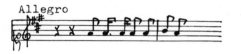

Fast

17. Disse il ver? parlò per gioco?   8

Allegro di molto

Fast

18. Pastorella abbandonata   8

Andantino

Winds: <u>Ob</u>

19. No ingrati non saremo   7

    Allegro   Fast

                                          First theme: ABB

20. Quel cor che sembra ingrato   7

    (no tempo designation)

                                          First theme: AA

21. Sento ch'al cor la speme   7

    Allegretto

22. Dal terreno nel concavo seno   10

    Andante e con spirito   Winds: 2 Ob, 2H

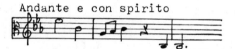

                                        First theme: AA

23. Tornate serene   6

    Non troppo lento   Winds: 2F, 2B

24. Chi può dir che rea son io   8

    Allegro non troppo però   Fast

                                        First theme: AA

Artaserse

1. Conservati fedele   7

   Un poco moderato ma poco
      First theme: ABB

2. Fra cento affanni e cento   7

   Presto e con molto spirito   Fast
      Winds: 2 Ob, 2H
                                                        First theme: ABB

3. Per pietà bell' idol mio   8

   Andantino
   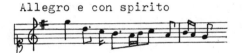   First theme: ABB

4. Sogna il guerrier le schiere   7

   Allegro e con spirito   Fast
      Winds: 2 Ob, 2H
                                                        First theme: AA

5. Deh respirar lasciatemi   7

   Andante
      First theme: ABB

6. Non ti son padre   5

   Allegro   Fast

7. Torna innocente e poi   7

  Allegro assai   Fast

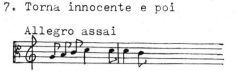

                                        First theme: ABB

8. Se al labbro mio non credi   7

  Un poco lento ma non troppo patetico

                                        First theme: ABB

9. Se vendetta io chiedo oh Dio   8

  Allegro   Fast
                                        Winds: 2 Ob, T, T

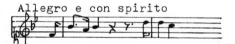

10. Mi scacci sdegnato   6

  Allegro e con spirito   Fast

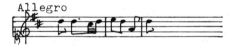

                                        First theme: ABB

11. Non temer ch'io mai ti dica   8

  Allegro   Fast

12. Se d'un amor tiranno   7

  Moderato

13. Se del fiume altera l'onda   8

   Allegro di molto   Fast

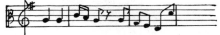

                                        First theme: ABB

14. Per quel paterno amplesso   7

   Lento

                                        Winds: 2F, 2 Ob, 2H

15. Va tra le selve ircane   7

   Presto di molto   Fast
                                        Winds: 2 Ob, 2H, 2T
   First theme: ABB

16. Non conosco in tal momento   8

   Allegretto

17. Così stupisce e cade   7

   Allegro   Fast
                                        Winds: 2 Ob, 2H

18. L'onda dal mar divisa   7

   Allegro e con spirito   Fast

   First theme: AA

19. Figlio se più non vivi   7

    Allegro di molto   Fast
    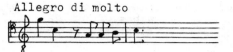   Winds: 2 Ob, 2T

20. Mi credi spietata   6

    Allegretto
       First theme: ABB

21. Non è ver che sia contento   8

    Allegretto

Demofoonte

1. O più tremar non voglio   7

   (no tempo designation)
      Winds: 2 Ob, 2H

2. In te spero, o sposo amato   8

   Andantino amoroso
      First theme: AA

3. Per lei fra l'armi dorme il guerriero   10

   Allegro non troppo   Fast

   First theme: AA

4. Sperai vicino il lido   7

   Un poco lento   Allegro di molto   Fast (second section)
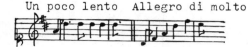
                                            Winds: 2 Ob, 2H
                                            First theme: ABB

5. Non curo l'affetto   6

   Allegro   Fast

6. Il suo leggiadro viso   7

   A tempo giusto ma non lento
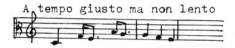   Winds: 2 Ob, 2H
                                            First theme: ABB

7. Padre perdona oh pene   7

   Moderato   Allegro   Fast (second section)
   Winds: 2 Ob, B, 2H

8. Per lei mi nacque amore   7

   Andante amoroso

9. Tu sai chi son; tu sai   7

   (no tempo designation)
   First theme: ABB

10. Prudente mi chiedi?   6

    Allegro   Fast

                                   First theme: ABB

11. Se tronca un ramo un fiore   7

    Andante

12. Se tutti i mali miei   7

    Andante amoroso   Winds: 2F

13. No non chiedo amate stelle   8

    Piuttòsto andante

                                   First theme: AA

14. Felice età dell' oro   7

    (no tempo indication)   Winds: 2 Ob, 2H
                                   First theme: AA

15. Perfidi già che in vita   7

    Allegro   Fast
                                   Winds: 2 Ob, 2H

16. Non odi consiglio?   6

    Allegro   Fast

17. Nel tuo dono io veggo assai   8

    Allegretto

18. Misero pargoletto   7

    Lento

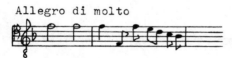

                                    First theme: ABB

19. Odo il suono de' queruli accenti 10

    Allegro di molto   Fast
                                         Winds: 2 Ob, 2H
                                         First theme: AA

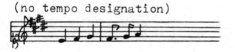

20. Che mai risponderti   5

    (no tempo designation)

Ezio

 1. Se tu la reggi al volo   7

    Allegro   Fast

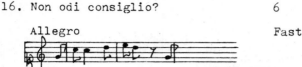

2. Pensa a serbarmi o cara   7

Non troppo lento

First theme: ABB

3. Caro padre a me non déi   8

Allegretto

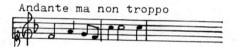

First theme: AA

4. Il nocchier che si figura   8

Fast

Allegro assai

First theme: ABB

5. Se un bell' ardire   5

Andante ma non troppo

6. Quanto mai felici siete   8

Comodetto

Winds: 2F, (2 Ob), 2H
First theme: AA

7. So chi t'accese   5

Andante e per lo più staccato

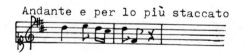

8. Se fedele mi brama il regnante   10

    Allegro assai   Fast

9. Finchè un zeffiro soave   8

    Andantino

Winds: 2F, 2 Ob, 2H
First theme: AA

10. Vi fida lo sposo   6

    Allegretto

11. Va dal furor portata   7

    Allegro   Fast

First theme: ABB

12. Recagli quell' acciaro   7

    Poco andante e maestoso

Winds: 2F, (2 Ob), 2H
First theme: ABB

13. Quel finger affetto   6

    Andante

Winds: 2F, (2 Ob)
First theme: AA

14. Nasce al bosca in rozza cuna   8

Allegro

Fast
Winds: 2F, 2 Ob, 2H
First theme: ABB

15. Finchè per te mi palpita   7

Andante

First theme: ABB

16. Caro mio bene addio   7

Adagio

Winds: 2F, (2 Ob), 2H
First theme: ABB

17. Svenami pur tiranno   7

Allegro

Fast

First theme: ABB

18. Che mi giova impero e soglio   8

Andante maestoso

Winds: 2F, (2 Ob), 2H
First theme: ABB

19. Peni tu per un' ingrata   8

Allegretto

First theme: ABB

20. Già del mio zelo antico   7

Allegretto

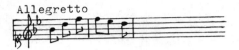

21. Dona si grande invero   7

Grave   Allegretto

   Winds: 2 Ob, 2H

22. Per tutto il timore   6

Allegro di molto   Fast

   First theme: ABB

23. Tergi l'ingiuste lagrime   7

Andante

   First theme: ABB

24. Ah s'io respiro e parto   7

Lento

   Winds: <u>Ob</u>

Nitteti

1. Sono in mar non veggo sponde   8

Allegro di molto   Fast
                                               Winds: 2 Ob, 2H
                                               First theme: ABB

2. Se il labbro nol dice   6

Andantino

First theme: AA

3. Tu sai che amante io sono   7

Allegro

Fast

First theme: AA

4. Se d'amor se di contento   8

Adagio

First theme: ABB

5. Non ho il core all' arti avvezzo 8

Allegro

Fast

First theme: AA

6. Già vendicato sei   7

Andante ma non troppo

Winds: 2 Ob, 2H

7. Tutte fin or dal cielo   7

Andante con spirito

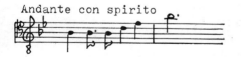

First theme: ABB

8. Povero cor tu palpiti   7

    Allegro   Fast
                                            Winds: 2F

9. Puoi vantar le tue ritorte   8

    (no tempo designation)   Fast

                                            First theme: AA

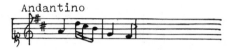

10. Per costume o mio bel nume   8

    Andantino   Winds: 2F
                                            First theme: AA

11. Sol può dir come si trova   8

    Andante ma non troppo   Winds: 2 Ob, 2H
                                            First theme: ABB

    (aria borrowed from Re pastore 15)

12. Chi sa qual core   5

    Non troppo lento

13. Se fra gelosi sdegni   7

    (no tempo designation)

                                            First theme: AA

14. Se può tradire il perfido   ˉ7

Presto   Fast

                                        First theme: ABB

15. Più della sorte o stelle   7

Andantino

                                        First theme: ABB

16. Sol car pensa un mar sicuro   8

Allegro   Fast

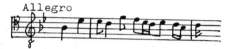

                                        First theme: AA

17. Deh rispetta il padre amato   8

Allegro molto   Fast

                                        First theme: AA

18. Non dimandar ti prego   7

Allegro   Fast

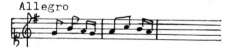

                                        First theme: ABB

19. Per tutto il timore   6

Allegro di molto   Fast

                                        First theme: ABB

(aria borrowed from Ezio .22)

Olimpiade

1. Superbo di me stesso   7

   Allegro e con spirito   Fast
                                                 Winds: 2 Ob, 2H
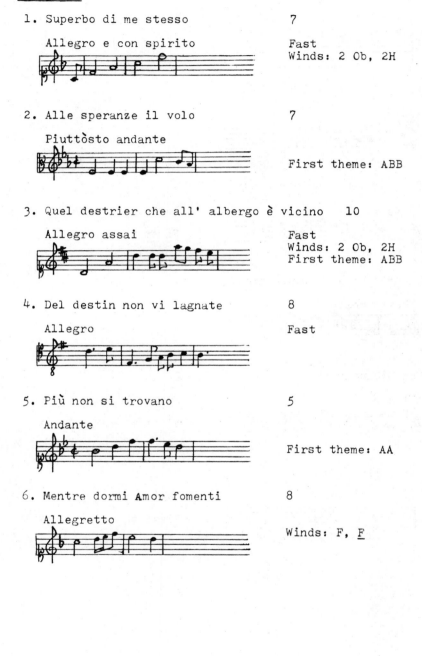

2. Alle speranze il volo   7

   Piuttòsto andante

                                                 First theme: ABB

3. Quel destrier che all' albergo è vicino   10

   Allegro assai   Fast
                                                 Winds: 2 Ob, 2H
                                                 First theme: ABB

4. Del destin non vi lagnate   8

   Allegro   Fast

5. Più non si trovano   5

   Andante

                                                 First theme: AA

6. Mentre dormi Amor fomenti   8

   Allegretto

                                                 Winds: F, F

7. Parto ma so che degno   7

   Allegro non troppo

8. Grandi è ver son le tue pene   8

   Non troppo andante

First theme: AA

9. Che non mi disse un dì?   7

   Allegro   Fast

10. Siam navi all' onde algenti   7

   Allegro di molto

Fast
Winds: 2 Ob, 2B̲

11. So ch'e fanciullo **Amore**   **7**

   Allegretto

First theme: ABB

12. Se cerca se dice   6

   Andantino

First theme: ABB

13. Tu me da me dividi   7

    Allegro assai   Fast

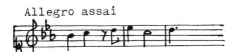

First theme: ABB

14. No la speranza   5

    Allegro   Fast

15. Gemo in un punto e fremo   7

    Allegro assai   Fast
                                     Winds: 2 Ob, 2H

First theme: ABB

16. Caro son tua così   7

    Allegretto

   Winds: 2F, 2B

17. Placa lo sdegno ormai   7

    Lento   Allegro di molto   Fast (second section)

First theme: ABB

18. Fiamma ignota nell' alma mi scende   10

    Allegro   Fast

   First theme: AA

19. Son qual per mare ignoto — 7

Allegro di molto

Fast

First theme: ABB

20. Non so d'onde viene — 6

Andantino

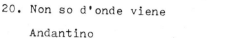

Winds: 2F, (2 Ob)

21. Consola il genitore — 7

Lento

Winds: 2F

Il re pastore

1. Intendo amico rio — 7

Un poco lento

Winds: 2F
First theme: ABB

2. Alla selva al prato al fonte — 8

Allegro e con spirito

Fast
Winds: 2F, 2 Ob, 2H

3. So che pastor son io — 7

Allegretto

Winds: 2F, (2 Ob)

4. Si spande al sole in faccia   7

Andante e con spirito

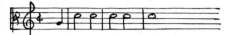

Winds: 2 Ob, 2H
First theme: ABB

5. Per me rispondete   6

Un poco lento

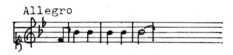

6. Di tante sue procelle   7

Allegro

Fast
Winds: 2 Ob
First theme: ABB

7. Al mio fedel dirai   7

Allegretto

Winds: 2F, 2 Ob

8. Barbaro oh Dio mi vedi   7

Lento

Winds: 2F, 2 Ob, 2H
First theme: ABB

9. Ogn'altro affetto ormai   7

Allegro

Fast

First theme: ABB

10. Ah per voi la pianta umìle   8

Moderato

Winds: 2F, 2 Ob, 2H

11. Se vincendo vi rendo felici   10

Allegretto

Winds: 2H
First theme: AA

12. L'amerò sarò costante   8

Allegretto

Winds: 2F, 2 Ob
First theme: AA

13. Io rimaner divisa   7

Presto

Fast

First theme: ABB

14. Se tu di me fai dono   7

Allegretto

15. Sol può dir come si trova   8

Piuttòsto andante

First theme: ABB

16. Voi che fausti ognor donate   8

Maestoso ma non troppo lento

Winds: 2F, 2 Ob, 2H, 2T

Romolo ed Ersilia

1. Questa è la bella face   7

Lento ma non troppo

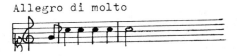

Winds: 2 Ob, 2H
First theme: ABB

2. Sorprendermi vorresti   7

Allegro di molto

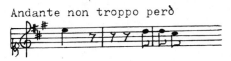

Fast
Winds: 2 Ob
First theme: ABB

3. Sì m'inganni e pure oh Dio   8

Andante non troppo però

4. Molli affetti dall' alma fuggite   10

Allegro di molto e con spirito

Fast
Winds: 2 Ob, 2H
First theme: ABB

5. Con vanto menzognero   7

Andante

Winds: 2 Ob

6. Nel pensar che padre io sono   8

   Larghetto ma poco   Winds: 2 Ob, 2H

7. Con le stelle invan s'adira   8

   Allegro ma non troppo presto

   First theme: ABB

8. Ah perchè quando appresi   7

   Andantino

9. Se talun non qual sia   7

   Andantino ma che sia vivo non languente

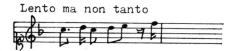

10. Sprezzami pur per ora   7

   Allegro   Fast
                                     Winds: 2 Ob, 2H
                                     First theme: ABB

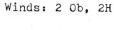

11. Basta così vincesti   7

   Lento ma non tanto

                                     First theme : ABB

12. Con gli amorosi mirti   7

    Allegro di molto   Fast
   Winds: 2 Ob, 2H
                                    First theme: ABB

13. Respira al solo aspetto   7

    Allegro   Fast
   Winds: 2 Ob, 2H
                                    First theme: ABB

14. Perdono al primo eccesso   7

    Andante
   Winds: 2 Ob
                                    First theme: ABB

15. Fra quelle tenere   5

    Andantino
   Winds: 2 Ob, 2H
                                    First theme: AA

16. Un istante al cor talora   8

    Allegro   Fast
   Winds: 2 Ob
                                    First theme: ABB

17. Il tenor de' fati intendi   8

    Un poco maestoso
   Winds: 2 Ob, 2H

<u>Ruggiero</u>

1. Farò ben io fra poco   7

   Molto allegro e staccato

                                   Fast
                                   Winds: 2 Ob, 2H
                                   First theme: ABB

2. Io non so nel mio martiro   8

   Allegretto

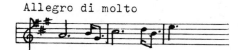

3. Otterrò felice amante   8

   Allegro di molto   Fast

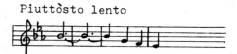

                                   First theme: AA

4. Ah se morir di pena   7

   Piuttòsto lento

                                   Winds: 2 Ob, 2H

5. Di marziali allori   7

   Molto allegro   Fast

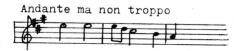

                                   Winds: 2 Ob, 2H
                                   First theme: ABB

6. So che un sogno è la speranza   8

   Andante ma non troppo

7. È dal corso altero fiume   8

Molto allegro

Fast
Winds: 2 Ob, 2H
First theme: ABB

8. Non esser a te stesso   7

Allegro

Fast
Winds: 2 Ob, 2H
First theme: ABB

9. Quel ira istessa che in te favella 10

Andantino

First theme: ABB

10. Non esser troppo altero   7

Molto allegro

Fast
Winds: 2 Ob, 2H
First theme: ABB

11. Lo sdegno ancor che fiero   7

Allegro di molto   Un poco lento

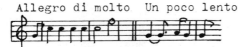

Winds: 2F, 2 Ob
First theme: ABB

12. Di quello ch'io provo   6

Allegro assai

Fast
Winds: 2 Ob, 2H

13. Di pietà d'aita indegno   8

Allegro   Fast
   Winds: 2 Ob, 2H

14. T'ubbidirò ben mio   7

Larghetto
   Winds: 2F, (2 Ob), 2B, 2H
                                         First theme: ABB

15. Ho perduto il mio tesoro   8

Allegro   Fast
   Winds: 2 Ob, 2H
                                         First theme: ABB

16. Ah come tu non sai   7

Andantino grazioso

17. Si correr voglio anch'io   7

Allegro e con spirito   Fast
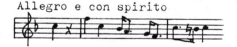   Winds: 2 Ob, 2B, 2H

Siroe

1. Se il mio paterno amore   7

Allegro e con spirito   Fast
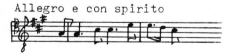
                                         First theme: ABB

2. D'ogni amator la fede   7

Andante

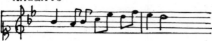

First theme: ABB

3. O placido il mare   6

Allegro e con molto spirito

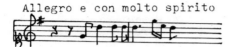

Fast
Winds: 2 Ob, 2H
First theme: ABB

4. Contente non siete   6

Andantino

5. La sorte mia tiranna   7

Largo

First theme: ABB

6. Fra l'orror della tempesta   8

Allegro e con brio

Fast
Winds: 2F, 2 Ob , 2H

7. Mi lagnerò tacendo   7

Andantino

First theme: AA

8. Mi credi infedele   6

Allegretto

   Winds: 2F

9. Sgombra dall' anima   5

Allegro   Fast

   First theme: AA

10. Tu decidi del mio fato   8

Andantino

   Winds: 2F, 2 Ob

11. Se pugnar non sai col fato   8

Allegro e con molto spirito   Fast
                                        Winds: 2 Ob, 2H
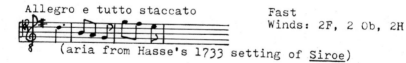   First theme: ABB

12. Tu di pietà mi spogli   7

Allegro e tutto staccato   Fast
                                        Winds: 2F, 2 Ob, 2H

(aria from Hasse's 1733 setting of <u>Siroe</u>)

13. Fra dubbi affetti miei   7

Allegro ma non troppo

                                        First theme: ABB

14. Non vi piacque ingiusti Dei   8

   Andante

       (from 1733 <u>Siroe</u>)

Winds: 2H

15. Se il caro figlio   5

   Allegro di molto
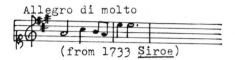
       (from 1733 <u>Siroe</u>)

Fast

16. Che furia! che mostro   6

   Allegro di molto

       (from 1733 <u>Siroe</u>)

Fast
Winds: 2H

17. Gelido in ogni vena   7

   Lento

       (from 1733 <u>Siroe</u>)

Winds: 2F, 2 Ob, 2H

18. L'alma a goder prepara   7

   Allegretto

First theme: ABB

19. Se l'amor tuo mi rendi   7

   Allegro e nel giusto polacco

Fast
Winds: 2H

20. Torrente cresciuto

6

Allegro assai

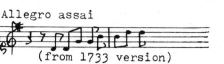

(from 1733 version)

Fast
Winds: 2H

Il trionfo di Clelia

1. Sì tacerò se vuoi

7

Andante

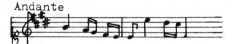

First theme: ABB

2. Ah celar la bella face

8

Allegro

Fast

3. Resta o cara e per timore

8

Andantino

4. Tempeste il mar minaccia

7

Allegro

Fast
Winds: 2 Ob, 2H
First theme: ABB

5. Sai che piagar si vede

7

Allegro

Fast
Winds: 2 Ob, 2H
First theme: ABB

6. Saper ti basti o cara   7

Lento

Winds: 2F, 2H

7. Mille dubbi mi destano   in petto   10

Andante

First theme: ABB

8. Dei di Roma ah perdonate   8

Largo

Winds: 2F, 2 Ob, 2B

9. Sol dal Tebro in su la sponda   8

Andante ma non presto

10. Dico che ingiusto sei   7

Allegro ma non troppo

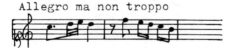

11. Vorrei che almen per gioco   7

Winds: 2F, 2 Ob, 2H

Allegretto vivo

12. Io nemica? a torto il dici   8

Allegro con spirito   Fast

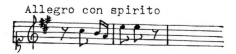

First theme: ABB

13. Non speri onusto il pino   7

Allegro di molto   Fast
                                        Winds: 2 Ob, 2H

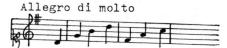

14. Tanto esposta alle sventure   8

Andantino moderato

   Winds: <u>F</u>, <u>Ob</u>

15. Ah ritorna età dell' oro   8

Allegretto

   Winds: 2F, 2 Ob, 2H

16. Spesso se ben l'affretta   7

Allegro con spirito   Fast
                                        Winds: 2 Ob, 2H
   First theme: ABB

17. In questa selva oscura   7

Andante moderato

   Winds: 2 Ob, 2H

18. De' folgori di Giove   7

Presto

Fast
Winds: 2 Ob, 2H, 2T
First theme: ABB

Zenobia

1. Oh almen qualor si perde   7

Allegretto vivo e con spirito

First theme: ABB

2. Cada l'indegno e miri   7

Allegro di molto   Fast

3. Resta in pace e gli astri amici   8

Andante grazioso ma non patetico, non languente
Winds: 2F, 2 Ob, 2H

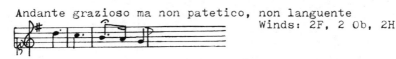

4. Di ricche gemme e rare   7

Allegro di molto e con spirito   Fast

5. Lasciami o ciel pietoso   7

Allegretto vivo

Winds: 2F

6. Ch'io parta? m'accheto   6

   Allegro   Fast

7. Vi conosco amate stelle   8

   Un poco lento e maestoso ma che non languisca . . .
                                    Winds: 2F, 2 Ob, 2H

8. So che sognata ancora   7

   Allegretto vivace e con spirito

                                    First theme: ABB

9. Ha negl' occhi un tale incauto   8

   Allegretto vivo e che arrivi quasi all' allegro intiero

10. Oh che felici pianti   7

    Allegretto con spirito, molto staccato . . .
                                    Winds: 2 Ob, 2H

11. Non respiro che rabbia e veleno   10

    Presto e con molto spirito   Fast
                                    Winds: 2 Ob, 2H
                                    First theme: ABB

12. Salvo tu vuoi lo sposo?   7

Allegro ma non troppo   Fast

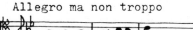

13. Voi leggete in ogni core   8

Andantino vivo

Winds: 2 Ob, 2H

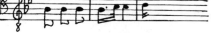

14. Ah perchè s'io ti detesto   8

Allegro di molto e con spirito   Fast
Winds: 2 Ob, 2H

15. Pace una volta e calma   7

Allegretto grazioso

Winds: 2F, 2 Ob, 2H
First theme: ABB

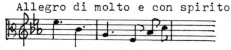

16. Si soffre una tiranna   7

Allegretto vivo

17. Pastorella io giurerei   8

Allegro e con spirito   Fast

First theme: ABB

18. Fra tutte le pene   6

Andantino grazioso

Winds: 2F

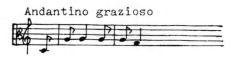

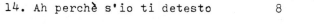

Appendix C

Thematic Catalog of the Opera Seria Arias by Jommelli, 1755-72

Appendix C lists the arias of the sixteen Jommelli operas investigated in this book. The operas are listed alphabetically; the arias, in the order in which they appear in each opera. Each aria entry provides the same type of information given in appendix A for the arias of J.C. Bach (see above, p. 165). (It is important to note that three of the aria texts Jommelli set do not employ a consistent verse type for the entire strophe: *Didone* 1, 9, 16.)

Achille in Sciro

1. No ingrato amor non senti

   Allegro moderato

   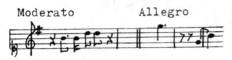

   7

   Fast

   First theme: AA

2. Involarmi il mio tesoro

   Moderato   Allegro

   8

   Fast (second section)
   Winds: 2 Ob, 2H

3. Fra l'ombre un lampo solo

   Allegro moderato

   7

   Fast
   Winds: 2 Ob, 2H
   First theme: ABB

4. Sì ben mio sarò qual vuoi

   Andante affettuoso

   8

   Winds: 2F, 2H
   First theme: ABB

5. Sì varia in ciel tall' ora

   Allegro

   7

   Fast

   First theme: AA

6. Intendo il tuo rossor

   Andantino

   7

   Winds: 2 Ob, 2H
   First theme: AA

7. Del sen gl'ardori

Allegro

5

Fast
Winds: 2 Ob, 2H
First theme: AA

8. Passaggier che su la sponda

Allegro con spirito

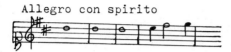

8

Fast
Winds: 2 Ob, 2H

9. Quando il soccorso apprenda

Andante vivace

7

Winds: 2 Ob, 2H
First theme: ABB

10. Fa che si spieghi almeno

Allegro spiritoso

7

Fast

First theme: ABB

11. Così leon feroce

Allegro

7

Fast
Winds: 2 Ob, 2T

12. Dille che si consoli

Andantino

7

Winds: 2 Ob, 2H, 2T

13. Lungi da tuoi bei rai   7

    Allegro vivace   Fast

                                           First theme: ABB

14. Ira furor dispetto   7

    Allegro molto   Fast
                                            Winds: 2 Ob, 2H, 2T

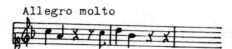

                                           First theme: AA

15. Ch'io speri ma come   6

    Allegretto

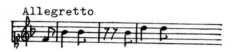

16. Di pietà spogliato il core   8

    Allegro maestoso   Fast
                                            Winds: 2 Ob, 2H

                                           First theme: ABB

17. Del terreno nel concavo seno   10

    Allegro moderato   Fast
                                            Winds: 2 Ob, 2H, 2T

<u>Armida</u>

1. Non è viltà s'io cedo   **7**

    (no tempo designation)

    (Fast)
    Winds: 2 Ob, 2H
    First theme: ABB

2. Da quel primiero istante   **7**

    Andante moderato

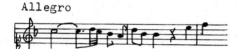

    First theme: ABB

3. Resta ingrata io parto addio   **8**

    Allegro

    Fast
    Winds: 2 Ob, 2H
    First theme: ABB

4. Non ti sdegnar mio bene   **7**

    Andantino

    Winds: 2 Ob, 2H
    First theme: AA

5. Se la pietà l'amore   **7**

    Allegro spiritoso   Fast

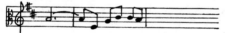

6. Odo che un zefiro   **5**

    Andante

7. Cercar fra perigli   6

   Allegretto   Fast
      Winds: 2 Ob, 2H
                                     First theme: AA

8. Caro mio ben mia vita   7

   Andantino affettuoso

9. Troppo di me pretendi   7

   Allegro vivace   Fast
      Winds: 2 Ob, 2H
                                     First theme: ABB

10. Ah ti sento mio povero core   10

    Adagio
       First theme: ABB

11. L'arte e l'ingegno   5

    Andante
       First theme: AA

12. Fra l'orror di notte oscura   8

    Allegro moderato   Fast
       Winds: 2 Ob, 2H

13. Guarda chi lascio ascolta

Andante

7

Winds: 2 Ob, 2H

14. Odio furor dispetto

Allegro assai

7

Fast
Winds: 2 Ob, 2H

15. Vieni ove onor ti chiama

Allegro moderato/Andantino

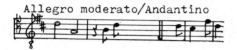

7

Fast (first section)
Winds: 2 Ob, 2H

16. L'onor tradito

Un poco andante

5

17. Giusto cielo s'è ver che m'accendi **10**

Andantino

Winds: 2 Ob, 2H
First theme: ABB

18. Ah non ferir t'arresta

Un poco adagio

7

<u>Artaserse</u>

1. Conservati fedele   7

    Andantino

   First theme: ABB

2. Fra cento affanni e cento   7

    Allegro   Fast
                                           Winds: 2 Ob, 2H
   First theme: ABB

3. Sulle sponde del torbido Lete   10

    Andante spiritoso
                                           Winds: 2 Ob, 2H
   First theme: ABB

4. Per pietà bell' idol mio   8

    Andante moderato

   First theme: AA

5. Sogna il guerrier le schiere   7

    Andante
                                           Winds: 2F, 2 Ob, 2H

6. Bramar di perdere   5

    Allegro   Fast

   First theme: AA

7. Rendi il mio caro amico   7

Andante moderato

First theme: ABB

8. Mi scacci sdegnato   6

Adagio   Andantino

Winds: 2 Ob, 2H

9. Se d'un amor tiranno   7

Andante moderato

First theme: ABB

10. Per quel paterno amplesso   7

Andantino affettuoso

Winds: 2 Ob
First theme: ABB

11. Va tra le selve ircane   7

Allegro di molto

Fast
Winds: 2 Ob, 2H
First theme: ABB

12. Così stupisce e cade   7

Allegro

Fast
Winds: 2 Ob, 2H

13. L'onda dal mar divisa   7

Andante

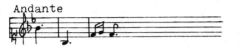

First theme: ABB

14. Quando il mar biancheggia e freme 8

Allegro

Fast
Winds: 2 Ob, 2H

15. Figlio se più non vivi   7

Larghetto   Allegro

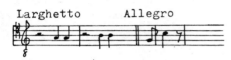

Fast (second section)

16. Mi credi spietata   6

Andante moderato

First theme: AA

17. Non è ver che sia contento   8

(no tempo designation)

Winds: 2F, 2 Ob, 2H

Creso

1. Tu sei padre io sono amante   8

Allegro

Fast
Winds: 2 Ob, 2H, 2T

2. Se in amor volete pace   8

Andantino

First theme: ABB

3. Se un ingrata un empia figlia   8

Andante

Winds: 2 Ob, 2H
First theme: AA

4. Di! che pietà non speri   7

Allegro

Fast
Winds: 2 Ob, 2H, 2T
First theme: ABB

5. Partirò non posso ancora   8

Andantino moderato

First theme: ABB

6. Placido lenti voli   7

Andante

First theme: AA

7. Questo è il mio stato   5

Andante moderato

8. Al tuo valor m'accendo   7

Allegro   Fast
   Winds: 2 Ob, 2H

9. Non so trovar l'errore   7

Andante affettuoso
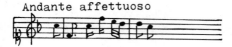   Winds: 2F, 2H
                                              First theme: ABB

10. Ah mio cor che mai prevedi   8

Andante
   Winds: 2 Ob, 2H

11. Confusa oh Dio prevedo   7

Andante
   Winds: 2 Ob, 2H

12. Il reo disegno intendo   7

Allegro con spirito   Fast
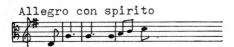   Winds: 2 Ob, 2H
                                              First theme: ABB

13. Per me solo oh Dio credea   8

Andante affettuoso
   First theme: ABB

14. Empia conosco assai   7

    Allegro molto spirito   Fast
    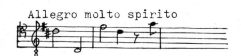   Winds: 2 Ob, 2H, 2T
                                            First theme: ABB

15. Là nel torbido fiume diletto   10

    Allegro spiritoso   Fast
       Winds: 2 Ob, 2H

16. Infidi amanti   5

    Allegro   Fast
       Winds: 2 Ob, 2H, 2T
                                            First theme: ABB

17. Amato genitore   7

    Andante
       First theme: ABB

18. Ma quel voce qual torrido gelo   10

    Andante
       Winds: 2 Ob, 2H

19. Imiterò sovente   7

    Andante vivace
       Winds: 2 Ob, 2H, 2T
                                            First theme: ABB

20. Ah padre io venni aspetta   7

Un poco andante

Winds: 2 Ob, 2H
First theme: ABB

Demofoonte III

1. Per lei fra l'armi dorme il guerriero   10

Allegro

Fast
Winds: 2 Ob, 2H

2. O più tremar non voglio   7

Allegro

Fast
Winds: 2 Ob, 2H

3. In te spero o sposo amato   8

Andantino affettuoso

First theme: AA

4. Sperai vicino il lido   7

Allegro

Fast

5. Non curo l'affetto   6

Allegro vivace

Fast
Winds: 2 Ob, 2H
First theme: AA

6. Il suo leggiadro viso

7

First theme: ABB

7. Tu sai chi son tu sai

7. Tu sai chi son tu sai

7

8. Prudente mi chiedi?

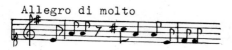

6

Fast
Winds: 2 Ob, 2H

9. Se tronca un ramo un fiore

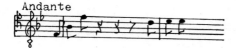

7

10. È soccorso d'incognita mano

10

11. Se tutti i mali miei

7

Winds: 2F
First theme: AA

12. No non chiedo amate stelle   8

Andante moderato

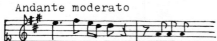

First theme: ABB

13. Perfidi già che in vita   7

Allegro di molto

Fast
Winds: 2 Ob, 2H
First theme: ABB

14. Non odi consiglio?   6

Allegro

Fast

15. Misero pargoletto   7

Larghetto

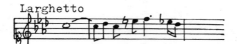

First theme: ABB

16. Odo il suono de' queruli accenti   10

Allegro

Fast
Winds: 2 Ob, 2H, <u>H</u>

17. Che mai risponderti   5

Larghetto   Allegro assai

Fast (second section)

First theme: AA

18. Non dura una sventura   7

Allegro   Fast

Demofoonte IV

1. Oh più tremar non voglio   7

Allegro moderato   Fast
                                   Winds: 2 Ob, 2H
   First theme: ABB

2. In te spero o sposo amato   8

Andantino

   First theme: AA

3. Per lei fra l'armi dorme il guerriero   10

Allegro moderato   Fast
                                   Winds: 2 Ob, 2H

4. Sperai vicino il lido   7

Allegro   Fast

5. Non curo l'affetto   6

Allegro   Fast

   First theme: AA

6. Il suo leggiadro viso   7

   Andante affettuoso

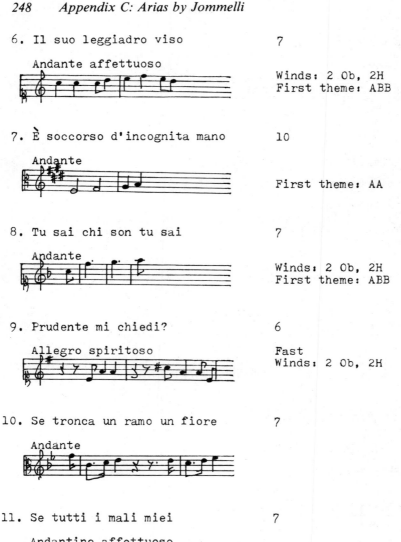

Winds: 2 Ob, 2H
First theme: ABB

7. È soccorso d'incognita mano   10

   Andante

First theme: AA

8. Tu sai chi son tu sai   7

   Andante

Winds: 2 Ob, 2H
First theme: ABB

9. Prudente mi chiedi?   6

   Allegro spiritoso

Fast
Winds: 2 Ob, 2H

10. Se tronca un ramo un fiore   7

    Andante

11. Se tutti i mali miei   7

    Andantino affettuoso

12. No non chiedo amate stelle   8

    Andante moderato

First theme: AA

13. Perfidi! già che in vita   7

    Allegro spiritoso

Fast
Winds: 2 Ob, 2H

14. Non odi consiglio?   6

    Moderato

15. Misero pargoletto   7

    Affettuoso

First theme: ABB

16. Che mai risponderti   5

    Un poco andante/Allegro spiritoso Fast (second section)
                               Winds: 2 Ob, 2H

Didone abbandonata

1. Dovrei... ma no...   5,7 (see above, p. 231)

    (no tempo designation)

2. Dirò che fida sei   7

   Andantino

3. Son regina e sono amante   8

   Allegro   Fast
                                           Winds: 2 Ob, 2H

4. Tu mi scorgi al gran disegno   8

   Andante

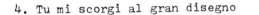

                                           First theme: AA

5. Se dalle stelle tu non sei guida   10

   Andante spiritoso

                                           Winds: 2 Ob, 2H

6. Quando saprai chi sono   7

   (no tempo designation)   (Fast)

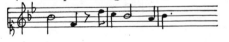

7. Son quel fiume che gonfio d'umori   10

   Allegro   Fast
                                           Winds: 2 Ob, 2H

8. D'atre nubi è il sol ravvolto   8

Allegro   Fast
                                          Winds: 2 Ob, 2H

9. Ah non lasciarmi no   7,5 (see above, p. 231)

Andantino affettuoso

10. Fosca nube il sol ricopra   8

Andante   Winds: 2 Ob, 2H

11. Ah non sai bella Selene   8

Adagio

   First theme: ABB

12. Ogni amator suppone   7

Allegretto   Winds: 2 Ob, 2H
                                          First theme: AA

13. La caduta d'un regnante   8

Allegro   Fast

14. A trionfar mi chiama   7

Allegro   Fast
   Winds: 2 Ob, H, 2H

15. Io d'amore oh Dio mi moro   8

Andantino
   First theme: ABB

16. Va crescendo   4,5 (see above, p. 231)

Larghetto
   Winds: 2 Ob, 2H

17. Cadrà fra poco in cenere   7

Allegro   Fast
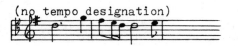   Winds: 2 Ob, 2H

18. Su procelle omai cessate   8

(no tempo designation)   (Fast)
   Winds: 2 Ob, 2H

Enea nel Lazio

1. Da cento furie e cento   7

Allegro   Fast
                                        Winds: 2 Ob, 2H
                                        First theme: ABB

2. Ch'io t'ami! chi sa   6

(no tempo designation)

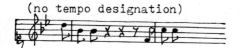

First theme: ABB

3. La cerva ferita   6

Andante

First theme: AA

4. S'io son d'amor nemica   7

Andante

First theme: ABB

5. Quando amor giunge all' eccesso   8

(no tempo designation)

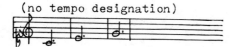

First theme: ABB

6. Se non senti in petto amore   8

Larghetto

7. Fa ritorno a Lete intorno   8

Allegro

Fast
Winds: 2 Ob, 2H

8. Sdegno e amore m'infiamma m'accende 10

Allegro di molto

Fast
Winds: 2 Ob, 2H
First theme: ABB

9. Quel ruscel che bagna appena   8

Allegro

Fast
Winds: 2 Ob, 2H

10. L'usignuolo imprigionato   8

Allegro spiritoso

Fast

First theme: ABB

11. M'insulti? m'inganni?   6

Con spirito

Fast
Winds: 2 Ob, 2H

12. Rendimi tu la pace   7

Andantino affettuoso

Winds: Ob, Ob, 2H

13. Un sospiro un guardo un riso   8

(no tempo designation)

(Fast)

First theme: ABB

14. Figlia addio dammi un amplesso   8

   Adagio

   First theme: ABB

15. Se l'innocenza in voi   7

   Andante

   First theme: ABB

16. Di giusto sdegno armato   7

   Allegro con spirito

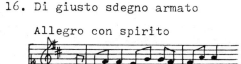

   Fast
   Winds: 2 Ob, 2H

Ezio

1. Se tu la reggi al volo   7

   Allegro non presto

   Fast
   Winds: 2 Ob, 2H

2. Pensa a serbarmi o cara   7

   Andantino affetto

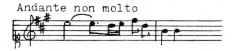

3. Caro padre a me non déi   8

   Andante non molto

4. Il nocchier che si figura   8

   Allegro moderato   Fast
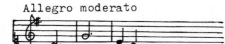   Winds: 2 Ob, 2H

5. Quanto mai felici siete   8

   Andante
   Winds: 2 Ob, 2H

6. So chi t'accese   5

   Maestoso e staccato
   Winds: 2 Ob, 2H

7. Va dal furor portata   7

   Allegro   **Fast**
   Winds: 2 Ob, 2H

8. Recagli quell' acciaro   7

   Maestoso
   Winds: 2 Ob, 2H

9. Tenterò per l'idol mio   8

   Andantino

10. Nasce al bosco in rozza cuna   8

Andante vivace

11. Finchè per te mi palpita   7

Andante moderata

12. Tutto il mio sangue   5

Moderato   Winds: 2 Ob, 2H

13. Per tutto il timore   6

Allegro   Fast

14. Ah non son io che parlo   7

Allegro   Fast
                                            Winds: 2 Ob, 2H

Fetonte

1. Tacito e lento il fuoco   7

Allegro   Fast
                                            Winds: 2 Ob, 2H

2. Voi che sortir d'affanno   7

Andante moderato

First theme: AA

3. Le mie smanie celarti io dovrei   10

Allegro

Fast

First theme: ABB

4. Spargerò d'amare lagrime   8

Andante vivace

Winds: 2F, 2 Ob, 2H
First theme: AA

5. Tu m'offri un regno in dono?   8

Grave   Allegro moderato

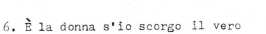

Fast (second section)
Winds: 2 Ob, 2H
First theme: ABB

6. È la donna s'io scorgo il vero   9[a]

Andante moderato

7. Penso scelgo mi pento poi torno   10

Allegro spiritoso

Fast
Winds: 2F, 2 Ob, 2H

---

[a]Alone among the 641 arias studied, Fetonte 6 has a text with nine syllables per line (novenario).

8. Spiegarmi vorrei   6

Larghetto   Andantino

Winds: 2F, 2H

9. Sempre fido il primo affetto   8

Andantino

10. Leggi sdegno non soffro consigli   10

Allegro spiritoso

Fast
Winds: 2 Ob, 2H
First theme: AA

11. Ombre che tacite   5

Adagio

Winds: 2 Ob, 2H
First theme: AA

12. Tu che ognor l'ardir proteggi   8

Andante vivace

First theme: AA

13. Son quel fiume che gonfio d'umori 10

Allegro

(aria borrowed from Didone 7)

Fast
Winds: 2 Ob, 2H

14. È un' ombra labile   5

Andante moderato

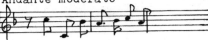

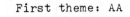   First theme: AA

Ifigenia in Tauride

1. De' tuoi mali esulterei   8

Allegretto

Fast
Winds: 2 Ob, 2H
First theme: ABB

2. Fra cento belve e cento   7

Allegretto

First theme: ABB

3. È specie di follia   7

Andante

Winds: 2 Ob, 2H
First theme: ABB

4. Per pietà deh nascondimi almeno   10

Andantino

First theme: ABB

5. Tardi rimorsi atroci   7

Allegro

Fast
Winds: 2 Ob, 2H (in the
        B section only)

6. Sagace rammenta   6

Andante vivace

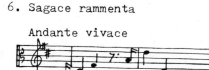

Winds: 2 Ob, 2H, 2T

7. Non m'irritate o perfidi   7

Allegro

Fast
Winds: 2 Ob, 2T
First theme: ABB

8. Ombra cara che intorno t'aggiri   10

Allegro di molto

Fast
Winds: 2 Ob, 2H

9. È lo sdegno degl' amanti   8

Andante moderato

First theme: AA

10. Qual nave in mezzo all' onde   7

Non molto allegro

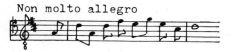

First theme: ABB

11. Ah non voler ch'io sveli   7

Andantino

12. Non paventa di Borea sdegnato   10

Allegro moderato   Fast

Winds: 2 Ob, 2H

13. Prendi l'estremo addio   7

Adagio

14. Per un ingrata   5

(no tempo designation)

15. Sol di mia voce il tuono   7

Andante

Winds: 2 Ob, 2H, 2T

16. Non temer sicuro sei   8

Andante moderato

First theme: ABB

17. Tornò la mia speranza   7

Andantino

First theme: AA

18. Quà la fiamma là il fumo che inciampo **10**

Allegro

Fast
Winds: 2 Ob, 2H
First theme: AA

Olimpiade

1. Superbo di me stesso   7

Allegro

Fast
Winds: 2 Ob, 2H
First theme: ABB

2. Quel destrier che all' albergo è vicino   10

Allegro

Fast
Winds: 2 Ob, 2H

3. Del destin non vi lagnate   8

Andante moderato

First theme: ABB

4. Tu di saper procura   7

Andantino

First theme: AA

5. Più non si trovano   5

Andante moderato

Winds: 2 Ob, 2H
First theme: AA

6. Grandi è ver son le tue pene   8

Andantino

First theme: AA

7. Che non mi disse un dì?   7

Allegretto

First theme: AA

8. So ch'è fanciullo Amore   7

Andante spiritoso

First theme: AA

9. Se cerca se dice   6

Andante

Winds: 2 Ob, 2H

10. Tu me da me dividi   7

Allegro di molto

Fast

First theme: ABB

11. Gemo in un punto e fremo   7

Allegro

Fast
Winds: 2 Ob, 2H

12. Caro son tua così   7

Fast

First theme: AA

13. Lo seguitai felice   7

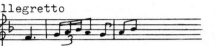

Winds: 2 Ob, H
First theme: ĀA

14. Fiamma ignota nell' alma mi scende   10

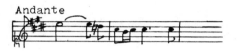

15. Son quel per mare ignoto   7

Fast

First theme: ABB

16. Non so donde viene   6

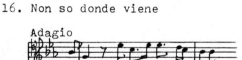

Winds: 2 Ob, 2H

Pelope

1. Scende dal monte e balza   7

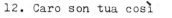

Fast
Winds: 2 Ob, 2H
First theme: AA

2. Così diletta e piace   **7**

Andantino

First theme: ABB

3. Digli che fosti e sei   **7**

Andantino

4. Morirò ma a te ben mio   **8**

Non molto adagio

Winds: 2 Ob, 2H

5. Fra speme e timore   **6**

Allegro spiritoso

Fast

First theme: ABB

6. Non si può senza periglio   **8**

Allegro moderato

Fast
Winds: 2 Ob, 2H
First theme: AA

7. Sperar quel ciglio amabile   **7**

Andantino

First theme: AA

8. Ah quel guardo quel sospiro   8

Andante

First theme: AA

9. Salda rupe invan percuote   8

Con spirito

Winds: 2 Ob, 2H
First theme: AA

10. Delusa schernita   6

Andante

First theme: AA

11. Perder l'amato bene   7

Andante moderato

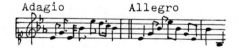

Winds: 2F, 2H
First theme: ABB

12. Un alma invitta e forte   7

Adagio   Allegro

Fast (second section)

13. Va trionfa in sì bel giorno   8

Allegro

Fast
Winds: 2 Ob, 2H & 2 Ob,
    B, 2H[1]
First theme: ABB

---

[1]The bassoon and extra oboes and horns constitute a
separate stage band.

14. Siam qual nave all' onde in seno   8

Allegro

Fast
Winds: 2 Ob, 2H

15. La figlia m'offende   **6**

Allegro con spirito

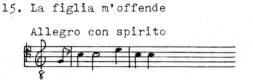

Fast

First theme: ABB

16. Sono amante e son guerriero   **8**

Andante moderato

First theme: AA

17. Se in ciel vedeste   **5**

Moderato

First theme: AA

<u>Semiramide riconosciuta</u>

1. Non so se più t'accendi   7

Allegro

Fast
Winds: 2 Ob, 2H
First theme: AA

2. Vorrei spiegar l'affanno   7

Adagio moderato

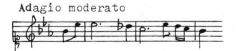

First theme: ABB

3. Che quel cor quel ciglio altero   8

   Allegro vivace   Fast

                                          First theme: ABB

4. Maggior follia non v'è   7

   Moderato

                                            Winds: 2 Ob, 2H
                                            First theme: ABB

5. Bel piacer saria d'un core   8

   Andantino

                                            First theme: ABB

6. Come all' amiche arene   7

   Allegro   Fast

                                            Winds: 2 Ob, 2H
                                            First theme: ABB

7. Se intende sì poco   6

   Andantino affettuoso

                                            First theme: ABB

8. Passaggier che su la sponda   8

   Allegro vivace   Fast
                                       Winds: 2 Ob, 2H

9. Tu mi disprezzi ingrato   7

Allegro   Fast
                                    Winds: 2 Ob, 2H
   First theme: ABB

10. Voi' che le mie vicende   7

Allegro spiritoso   Fast
                                    Winds: 2 Ob, 2H

11. Saper bramate   5

Larghetto/(no tempo indication)

12. Il pastor se torna aprile   8

Andantino   Winds: 2 Ob, H, 2H
                                    First theme: ABB

13. Vieni ché in pochi istante   7

Allegretto
   First theme: AA

14. Or che sciolta è già la prora   8

Allegro   Fast

                                    First theme: AA

15. Fuggi dagl' occhi miei   7

Allegro spiritoso

Fast
Winds: 2 Ob, 2H
First theme: ABB

16. Odi quel fasto   5

Maestoso/(no tempo indication)

Winds: 2 <u>Ob</u>, 2<u>H</u>

17. D'un genio che m'accende   7

Andantino affettuoso

First theme: ABB

18. Sentirsi dire   5

Andante

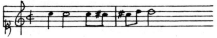

First theme: AA

<u>Temistocle</u>

1. Al furor d'avversa sorte   8

Allegro non presto

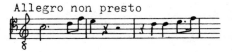

Fast
Winds: 2 Ob, 2T
First theme: ABB

2. Basta dir ch'io sono amante   8

Allegro vivace

Fast

First theme: AA

3. Chi mai d'iniqua stella   7

Andante moderato

First theme: AA

4. Io partirò ma tanto   7

Andante

5. Contrasto assai più degno   7

Allegro

Fast
Winds: 2 Ob, 2H

6. Non m'abbaglia quel lampo fugace   10

Allegro di molto

Fast
Winds: 2 Ob, 2H
First theme: AA

7. È specie di tormento   7

Allegro con molto spirito

Fast

First theme: ABB

8. Fremea del mare in seno   7

Allegro con molto brio

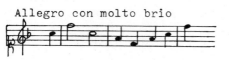

Fast
Winds: 2 Ob, 2H

9. Tal per altrui diletto   7

   (no tempo designation   (Fast)

                                             Winds: 2 Ob, 2H
                                             First theme: ABB

10. Quando parto e non rispondo   8

    Moderato

   Winds: 2 Ob, 2H

11. Ammiro quel volto   6

    Andantino

12. Vicino al tuo sembiante   7

    (no tempo designation)

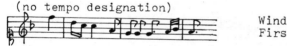   Winds: 2 Ob, 2H
                                             First theme: AA

13. A dispetto d'un tenero affetto   10

    Allegretto

   First theme: ABB

14. Serberò fra' ceppi ancora   8

    Allegro   Fast

   Winds: 2 Ob, 2H

15. Oh Dèi che dolce incanto   7

Adagio assai

First theme: ABB

16. Se più fulmini vicino   8

Allegro

Fast
Winds: 2 Ob, 2H

17. Ah frenate il pianto imbelle   8

Larghetto

First theme: AA

18. Ah si resti onor mi sgrida   8

Allegro vivace

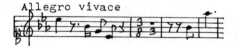

Fast
Winds: 2 Ob, 2H

19. Non tremar vassallo indegno   8

Allegro vivace

Fast

First theme: AA

20. Aspri rimorsi atroci   7

(no tempo designation)

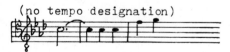

Vologeso

1. In van minacci e credi   7

   Allegro   Fast
   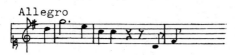   Winds: 2 Ob, 2H

2. Luci belle più serene   8

   Andantino
      First theme: ABB

3. Se vive il mio bene   6

   Allegro vivace   Fast
      First theme: AA

4. Tutti di speme al core   7

   Andante moderato   Winds: 2 Ob, 2H
      First theme: ABB

5. Crede sol che a nuovi ardori   8

   Allegro spiritoso   Fast
   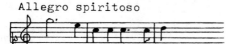   First theme: AA

6. So ben comprenderti   5

   Allegro moderato   Fast
   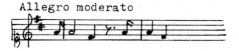   First theme: ABB

7. Sei tra' ceppi e insulti ancor   **8**

Allegro con molto spirito

Fast
Winds: 2 Ob, 2H

8. Cara deh serbami   **5**

Andantino

First theme: ABB

9. Tu chiedi il mio core   **6**

Andantino

Winds: 2 Ob, 2H
First theme: ABB

10. Che faro? privarmi io deggio   **8**

Andante

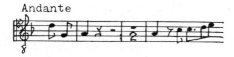

First theme: AA

11. Rammentagli chi sei   **7**

Andante

First theme: AA

12. Partirò se vuoi cosi   **8**

Allegro

Fast

First theme: ABB

13. Uscir vorrei d'affanno   **7**

Larghetto   Allegro

Fast (second section)
Winds: 2 Ob, 2H

14. Amor che sa che sia   **7**

Andantino

First theme: ABB

15. Ah sento che in petto   **6**

Allegro

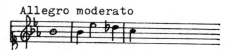

Fast

First theme: AA

16. Ombra che pallida   **5**

Allegro moderato

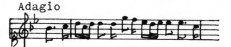

Fast
Winds: 2 Ob, B, 2H
First theme: AA

17. Su quel caro volto esangue   **8**

Adagio

Notes

Chapter 1

1. For a vivid description of the decline of opera seria in Dresden, Stuttgart, and Berlin, see Alan Yorke-Long, *Music at Court: Four Eighteenth-Century Studies* (London: Weidenfeld & Nicolson, 1954).

2. Daniel Heartz, "The Genesis of Mozart's *Idomeneo*," *Musical Quarterly* 55 (1969):1-19.

3. Distinguished exceptions are Reinhard Strohm, *Italienische Opernarien des frühen Settecento (1720-1730)*, 2 vols., Analecta musicologia, vol. 16 (Cologne: Arno Volk, 1976), and Helmut Hell, *Die neapolitanische Opernsinfonie in der ersten Hälfte des 18. Jahrhunderts. N. Porpora—L. Vinci—G.B. Pergolesi—L. Leo—N. Jommelli*, Münchner Veröffentlichungen zur Musikgeschichte, vol. 19 (Tutzing: Hans Schneider, 1971).

4. Charles Rosen, *The Classical Style: Haydn, Mozart, Beethoven*, rev. ed. (London: Faber, 1976).

5. Ibid., p. 22.

6. Ibid., p. 47.

7. Ibid., p. 44.

8. Ibid., p. 164.

9. Frederick Millner, *The Operas of Johann Adolf Hasse* (Ann Arbor: UMI Research Press, 1979), pp. 380-91.

10. Marita McClymonds, "Jommelli," *The New Grove Dictionary of Music and Musicians* (London: Macmillan, 1980), 9:686-95.

11. Edward O. Downes, "The Operas of Johann Christian Bach as a Reflection of the Dominant Trends in *opera seria*, 1750-1780" (Ph.D. dissertation, Harvard University, 1958).

12. Hasse may have composed two additional opere serie during this time: (1) a fourth version of *Leucippo*, the production of which was scheduled for Dresden in 1756 but cancelled upon the outbreak of the Seven Years' War, and (2) a fifth version of *Leucippo*, the production of which was scheduled for Dresden in 1763 but cancelled upon the sudden death of the Elector. (The score which may correspond to the first work primarily contains arias that Hasse composed in 1747 for his first version of *Leucippo*. No score for the second work exists. See Millner, *Hasse*, pp. 110-11, 112-16.)

13. The first opera, *La clemenza di Tito* (Naples, 1758) borrows much from Hasse's *Il re pastore* (Dresden, 1755) and *Olimpiade* (Dresden, 1756). Doubtless other arias of *La clemenza di Tito* derive from even earlier Hasse operas not studied here.

The second opera, a second version of *Olimpiade* (Turin, 1765), consists mostly of arias that Hasse borrowed from his first setting of the same libretto (for Dresden in 1756). Only seven arias are new: these will not be considered here.

14. *Il re pastore* was actually first performed by Dresden forces on this date at the royal hunting lodge at Hubertusberg. Since it was soon performed in Dresden itself, *Il re pastore* will be referred to simply as a Dresden opera.

15. It is not certain whether *Siroe* was first performed in Warsaw or in Dresden after the court returned from exile (Millner, *Hasse*, pp. 30-31).

16. Nine operas are lost: *Enea nel Lazio,* first version (Stuttgart, 1755), *Tito Manlio* (Stuttgart, 1758), *Ezio,* third version (Stuttgart, 1758), *Nitteti* (Stuttgart, 1759), *Alessandro nell'Indie* (Stuttgart, 1760), *Cajo Fabrizio* (Mannheim, 1760), *Il re pastore* (Stuttgart, 1764), *La clemenza di Tito* (Stuttgart, 1765), and *Temistocle,* second version (Stuttgart, 1765).

17. After 1764, Jommelli's operas for Duke Carl Eugen were actually first performed in the new opera house in suburban Ludwigsburg. For the sake of simplicity, *Enea nel Lazio, Vologeso,* and *Fetonte* will always be referred to here as Stuttgart operas.

18. Hasse, Jommelli, and Bach each frequently set the same libretto more than once. Considering the surviving settings of 1755-72, however, this practice occurred only once: Jommelli composed his third and fourth versions of *Demofoonte.* These works will be referred to subsequently as "*Demofoonte* III" and "*Demofoonte* IV."

19. The librettos of these five subsequent performances are listed in Claudio Sartori, "Primo tentativo di catalogo unico dei libretti italiani a stampa fino all'anno 1800" (Milan, 1968 et seq.).

20. Of the eight operas Bach composed during this time, two survive in fragmentary form. In one, *Zanaida* (London, 1763), only eight of an original twenty-one arias survive; this work will not be considered here. In the other, *Orione* (London, 1763), ten of an original nineteen arias survive. Since a majority of the arias survive and thus give us a glimpse of Bach's first London opera, *Orione* will be considered.

21. Mozart's attendance at these performances is recorded in letters written by him or by his father, Leopold Mozart (*Mozart: Briefe und Aufzeichnungen,* eds. Wilhelm A. Bauer and Otto Erich Deutsch [Kassel: Bärenreiter, 1962], 1:179, 335, 358, 448, 449).

22. For a discussion of and further bibliography on this matter, see Downes, "Johann Christian Bach," 2:277-78.

23. Donald Jay Grout, *A Short History of Opera,* 2d ed. (New York: Columbia University Press, 1965), p. 190.

24. Ibid.

25. Of the scores examined for this study, five contain substitute arias: the I-Mc autograph of Hasse's *Olimpiade* (Dresden, 1756) with some of the new arias for the 1765 Turin revival, the D-Mbs score of Hasse's *Nitteti* (Venice, 1758) with one substitute aria, the A-Wn score of Hasse's *Romolo ed Ersilia* (Innsbruck, 1765) with one substitute aria, and the D-Sl autograph and B-Bc copy of Jommelli's *Demofoonte* III (Stuttgart, 1764), both with six new arias for the Stuttgart revival of the following year. The last-named two scores exemplify two methods of incorporating old and new arias into one score. The D-Sl autograph presents each of the new arias immediately before each of the corresponding original ones. The B-Bc score, on the other hand, records the 1765 version of the opera and relegates the old arias (for which substitutes were composed) to an appendix.

26. This in fact happened in Dresden in 1763 upon the death of Elector Friedrich August II and the ascension of his grandson Friedrich August III, who better appreciated the severity of Saxony's financial straits and preferred opera buffa anyway. Similarly, the production of new serious operas in Stuttgart came to a virtual halt in the late 1760's when Duke Carl Eugen, facing rebellion by his Estates and mounting pressure from King Frederick the Great of Prussia, inaugurated a period of political and financial retrenchment (Yorke-Long, *Music at Court*, pp. 62, 88.)

27. The information on reperformances is taken from Millner, *Hasse*, pp. 319-37; and Sartori, "Libretti italiani," passim.

28. *Demofoonte* III was reperformed in Stuttgart in 1778; *Didone abbandonata*, in 1777, 1780, and 1782; and *Fetonte*, in 1770, 1771, 1772, and 1773.

29. The reperformances of Jommelli's operas for the court of King José I (1750-77) in Lisbon constitute a fascinating chapter in the history of eighteenth-century opera seria (see Marita McClymonds, "Niccolò Jommelli: The Last Years," [Ph.D. dissertation, University of California at Berkeley, 1978]). For these performances, Jommelli's original work was extensively revised by the court maestro di capella, Joáo Cordeiro da Silva. Scores preserving these Lisbon versions are located in Lisbon, Biblioteca da Ajuda.

30. *Armida abbandonata* was reperformed in Naples in 1771 and 1781.

31. Most of these scores are located in Milan, Biblioteca di Conservatorio "Giuseppe Verdi." The scores were identified as Hasse's autographs only as recently as 1965 by Sven Hansell (see Sven Hansell, "The Solo Cantatas, Motets, and Antiphons of Johann Adolf Hasse," [Ph.D. dissertation, University of Illinois, 1966], pp. 473-74). The two operas of this period for which the autographs do not survive are *Nitteti* and *Romolo ed Ersilia*.

32. Hasse's *Artaserse, Demofoonte, Nitteti, Olimpiade, Il re pastore*, and *Il trionfo di Clelia* were reperformed in Warsaw in the years 1759-62 (Millner, *Hasse*, pp. 319-37).

33. Sven and Kathleen Hansell, Review of *Johann Adolf Hasse: Ruggiero, ovvero L'eroica gratitudine*, Concentus musicus, Vol. 1 (Cologne: Arno Volk, 1973) in *Journal of the American Musicological Society* 29 (1976):318-19.

34. Millner, *Hasse*, pp. 39-40.

35. Elsewhere in this book, the second complete setting of the first stanza of text will be referred to as the "second vocal section." The setting of the second stanza of text will be referred to as the "B section."

36. In arias of the "half da capo" variety, the first stanza reappears only once after the second stanza. There were many ways to achieve this abbreviation, although the basic idea can be diagrammed as follows:

A rit.	A₁ stanza	A₁ rit.	A₂ stanza	A₂ rit.	B stanza	B rit.	A₃ stanza
I---I	I-------V	V----V	V(I)----I	I----I	vi---iii	iii-I(V)	I(V)---I

In arias of the "simple ternary" or "modified da capo" variety, the first stanza appears only twice, the setting of the second stanza separating the two settings of the first. This scheme can be diagrammed as follows:

A rit.	A₁ stanza	A₁ rit.	B stanza	B rit.	A₂ stanza	A₂ rit.
I---I	I-------V	V----V	V----I(iii)	I(iii)-I	I-------I	I----I.

37. As exceptions, most of the few "Allegro non troppo" arias as well as a few "Allegro" arias contain many sixteenth-note triplets, sixteenth notes in the bass, etc., and therefore will not be considered as fast arias: Hasse's *Olimpiade* 7, *Clelia* 10, *Siroe* 13, *Romolo* 7; and Bach's *Catone* 13. On the other hand, the rest of the "Allegro non troppo" arias as well as a few "Allegretto" arias contain almost no sixteenth-note triplets, sixteenth notes in the bass, etc., and therefore will be considered as fast arias: Hasse's *Demofoonte* 3; *Achille* 10, 24; *Zenobia* 12; and Jommelli's *Armida* 7, *Ifigenia* 1.

38. A few arias contain two tempos within the A section. These "two-tempo arias" (not to be confused with arias where the tempo and meter change at the beginning of the B section) have much in common. Most lack an introductory ritornello and proceed from a slow to a fast tempo. The first section is invariably shorter; it sets one or usually two verses, often to an "ABB phrase." The second section, beginning immediately thereafter, includes the modulation and secondary key area, the medial ritornello, and most of the second vocal section as well. Two-tempo arias with a fast second tempo are counted as fast arias.

39. Duke Carl Eugen of Württemberg, for example, dictated the subjects of the operas Jommelli composed for him at Stuttgart (Yorke-Long, *Music at Court*, p. 54).

40. See, for example, John Walter Hill, "Vivaldi's *Griselda*," *Journal of the American Musicological Society* 31 (Spring 1978):53-82.

41. See below, chapters 4-6.

42. They may not even change when a composer self-consciously attempts to write in another style, as Edward Lowinsky has shown in the case of Mozart's fugues. Edward Lowinsky, "On Mozart's Rhythm," *The Creative World of Mozart*, ed. Paul Henry Lang (New York, Norton, 1963), pp. 31-32.

43. McClymonds, "Jommelli: The Last Years," 2:625. McClymonds translates this passage as follows: "Those eternal four lines per part in every aria, and always at the most, seven or eight feet [?syllables] each, and worse then, that further repetition in so small a number of lines of the same words, almost as if the poet had to buy them at the market and pay a high price for them."

44. Five-line strophes appeared mostly in Metastasio's earliest dramas, particularly *Catone in Utica* (1728) and *Semiramide* (1729), each containing five such texts. They soon dwindled in number, however, and virtually disappeared after *Ciro riconosciuto* (1736). Strophes of more than seven or of only two lines are even more exceptional and likewise confined mostly to Metastasio's dramas of the 1720s.

45. See, for example, *Clelia* 2; *Romolo* 9; and *Ruggiero* 2, 4, 6.

46. Two exceptions: Hasse's *Artaserse* 4 and Bach's *Temistocle* 7.

47. *Artaserse* (Turin, 1760) contains the smallest proportion: eleven of twenty-five. *Alessandro nell'Indie* (Naples, 1762) and *Catone in Utica* (Naples, 1761), contain the highest: sixteen of twenty-one and thirteen of seventeen (see appendix A).

48. *Demofoonte* (Naples, 1758) contains the smallest proportion: five of twenty; *Romolo ed Ersilia* (Innsbruck, 1765), the highest: ten of seventeen (see appendix B).

49. This strophe translates literally as follows:

> I would not be so unfortunate,
> If, being born among the ranks
> Of the Amazon warriors,
> I had learned to wage war.

50. The standard accentual patterns for these verse types in Metastasio are:

    Quinario: ⌣/⌣/⌣   (iambic) /⌣⌣/⌣   (dactylic)
    Settenario: ⌣/⌣/⌣/⌣ (iambic) /⌣⌣/⌣/⌣ (dactylic-trochaic)

51. This convention survived well into the nineteenth century. Verdi's "La donna è mobile" *(Rigoletto)* and "Di quella pira" *(Il trovatore)* are only two of the best known examples.

52. The standard accentual pattern for *ottonario* in Metastasio is trochaic: /⌣/⌣/⌣/⌣ .

53. *Ottonario* thus does not inevitably contain, as Reinhard Strohm asserts, "vier fast gleichwertige Wortakzente" (four almost equivalent word accents). Strohm, *Italienische Opernarien,* 1:127-28.

Chapter 2

1. See, for example Donald Jay Grout, *A Short History of Opera,* 2d ed. (New York: Columbia University Press, 1965), pp. 182-84; Daniel Heartz, "Critical Years in European Musical History, 1740-1760," International Musicological Society, *Report of the Tenth Congress. Ljubljana, 1967* (Kassel: Bärenreiter, 1970), pp. 160-68; Helmut Hucke, "Die neapolitanische Tradition in der Oper," International Musicological Society, *Report of the Eighth Congress, New York City, 1961* (Kassel: Bärenreiter, 1961), pp. 253-77; and Reinhard Strohm, *Italienische Opernarien des frühen Settecento (1720-1730),* 2 vols. Analecta musicologica, vol. 16 (Cologne: Arno Volk, 1976).

2. Charles Rosen, *The Classical Style: Haydn, Mozart, Beethoven,* rev. ed. (London: Faber, 1976), pp. 116-19.

3. Grout, *Opera,* p. 222.

4. Charles Burney, *A General History of Music from the Earliest Ages to the Present Period,* 4 vols. (London: 1776-89), 4:547.

5. Ibid., 4:557.

6. For *Idomeneo,* Mozart composed ABB first themes for the following arias: "Padre, germani, addio!," "Non ho colpa e mi condanni," "Tutte nel cor vi sento," "Se il tuo duol, se il mio desio," and "Se colà ne'fati è scritto."

7. Manfred Bukofzer, *Music in the Baroque Era* (New York: W.W. Norton, 1947), pp. 221-22.

8. The operas included in the second and third categories are merely those of which scores are presently available to me. These scores derive from three sources: the facsimile editions comprising *Italian Opera: 1640-1770,* eds. Howard Mayer Brown and Eric Weimer (New York: Garland, 1978 et seq.), modern editions (see Bibliography), and microfilms belonging to the extensive personal collection of Professor Howard Mayer Brown, University of Chicago. Despite the apparent haphazard nature of this selection, many of the operas studied represent a good sample of each composer's work. In the case of each of many composers, the works studied constitute the only surviving operas, the last operas to survive complete, or operas particularly significant in the composer's career. (Such features will be pointed out in subsequent footnotes.)

9. First themes which do not conform to the ABB formula will not be considered.

10. The musical examples in this chapter will also eliminate the variable of tonality. All examples of ABB themes will thus appear transposed to the key of C; all examples of first vocal section cadences will appear transposed to the key of G.

11. *Griselda* was Bononcini's last opera seria to survive complete (Strohm, *Opernarien,* 2:151-52).

12. *Il Bajazet* was Gasparini's last full scale "dramma per musica" to survive complete (Strohm, *Opernarien,* 2:166-68).

13. *Alessandro Severo* was Lotti's last opera for Italy before his two-year sojourn in Dresden and subsequent retirement from the theatre (Anna Mondolfi, "Lotti," *Die Musik in Geschichte und Gegenwart,* 8:1227-28).

14. These works constitute three of Scarlatti's last four serious operas (Roberto Pagano and Lino Bianchi, *Alessandro Scarlatti* [Turin: Radiotelevisione Italiana, 1972], pp. 355-57).

15. *Artaserse* was the last opera Vinci composed before his untimely death in 1730 (Strohm, *Opernarien,* 2:233-34).

16. A few such themes occur in Giacomelli's *Lucio Papirio Dittatore,* Lotti's *Alessandro Severo,* Scarlatti's *Attilio regolo,* Vinci's three operas, and Vivaldi's *Tito Manlio.*

17. The arias in question are "Fiume altier va pur con l'onde" from Giacomelli's *Lucio Papirio Dittatore,* "Perche t'amo mia bella vita" from Vivaldi's *Tito Manlio,* and "Torno ai ceppi" from Sarri's *Arsace.*

18. *Andromaca* (1730) is Feo's last surviving opera seria before his *Arsace* of 1740. Hanns-Bertold Dietz, "Feo," *The New Grove Dictionary of Music and Musicians* (London: Macmillan, 1980) 6:466.

19. It was with *Cleofide* that Hasse launched his brilliant career as maestro di capella at Dresden.

20. *Demetrio, Demofoonte,* and *Andromaca* constitute Leo's last opere serie (Helmut Hell, *Die neapolitanische Opernsinfonie in der ersten Hälfte des 18. Jahrhunderts. N. Porpora—L. Vinci—G.B. Pergolesi—L. Leo—N. Jommelli,* Münchner Veröffentlichungen zur Musikgeschichte, vol. 19 [Tutzing: Hans Schneider, 1971], pp. 561-70). Although composed in the early 1740s, these three works will be considered along with those of the 1730s since Leo died in 1744 and his last operas, as we shall see, maintain style traits of the 1730s.

21. *Olimpiade* was Pergolesi's last and probably most popular opera seria (Helmut Hell, "Pergolesi," *Die Musik in Geschichte und Gegenwart,* 10:1055).

22. *Vologeso* is Rinaldo's only surviving opera seria before 1751. Claudio Gallico, "Rinaldo di Capua," *The New Grove Dictionary of Music and Musicians* (London: Macmillan, 1980) 16:43.

23. Themes in $\frac{2}{4}$ meter will be counted as if in $\frac{4}{4}$ meter. The number of bars listed here in such arias would thus be the actual number of bars divided by two.

24. Rarely, each B segment lasts one and a half bars. Themes with such dimensions will nevertheless be counted among those with one-bar B segments.

25. The numbers enclosed in parentheses indicate the range of possible lengths of the A segment. In this case, the A segment may be as short as half a bar or as long as two bars. For the purpose of listing the dimensions of ABB themes, the points of division between the A segment and the first B segment and between the two B segments will correspond not to rests in the vocal line but to the final tonic accent of each corresponding segment of text. In figure 2a, where the text reads "Vanne infedel, che tardi? / Che pensi? che brami?", the point of demarcation between the A segment and the first B segment falls on the first syllable of "tardi" and thus occurs on the downbeat of the second measure.

26. These themes begin three of the ten fast duple-meter arias that open with **ABB** themes: "Talor, che irato è il vento," "Prendi quel ferro, o barbaro," and "Paventa, o traditore."

27. These themes begin three of the ten fast duple-meter arias that open with **ABB** themes: "Tu me da me dividi," "Torbido in volto e nero," and "Son qual per mare ignoto."

28. This theme begins the aria "Scocca dardi l'altero tuo ciglio."

29. For the purposes of this chapter, "cadential phrase" is defined as the span from the penultimate cadence (in the secondary key) of the first vocal section to the final cadence of that section. The former cadence may be perfect, imperfect, or deceptive.

30. Significantly, such cadences occur mostly in the same early operas that also contain **ABB** themes: Giacomelli's *Lucio Papirio Dittatore*, Lotti's *Alessandro Severo*, Vivaldi's *Tito Manlio*, and Vinci's three operas.

31. "Saldo scoglio fra l'urti dell'onde."

32. "Torbido in volto e nero."

33. "Quel destrier, che all'albergo è vicino."

34. "Benche turbar si veda" and "Scende da giogo Alpino."

35. "O più tremar non voglio" and "Perfidi! già che in vita."

36. These operas are Hasse's *Ezio* (Dresden, 1755), *Il re pastore* (Dresden, 1755), *Olimpiade* (Dresden 1756), *Nitteti* (Venice, 1758), *Demofoonte* (Naples, 1758), *Achille in Sciro* (Naples, 1759), and *Artaserse* (Naples, 1760); and Jommelli's *Pelope* (Stuttgart, 1755), *Artaserse* (Stuttgart, 1756), *Creso* (Rome, 1757), and *Temistocle* (Naples, 1757).

37. *Semiramide riconosciuta* was the first opera that Gluck composed for Vienna and one of the first of all his opere serie to survive complete. *Il re pastore,* on the other hand, is the last opera seria Gluck composed before 1762, the year of his famous "reform" opera *Orfeo ed Euridice* (Anna Amalie Abert, "Gluck," *Die Musik in Geschichte und Gegenwart,* 5:347).

38. *Ezio* and *Semiramide* were Jommelli's third and fifth opere serie, Jommelli having launched his career as a composer of opera seria in 1740 (Marita McClymonds, "Jommelli," *The New Grove Dictionary of Music and Musicians* [London: Macmillan, 1980], 9:686-95.

39. *Merope* and *Sesostri* are two of the only three fully extant operas by Terradellas, whose operatic career extended for only twelve years from 1739 to 1751 (Henry Bloch, "Terradellas," *Die Musik in Geschichte und Gegenwart,* 13:244).

40. Helga Scholz-Michelitsch, "Wagenseil," *Die Musik in Geschichte und Gegenwart,* 14:68-69.

41. The shorter themes occur in the following arias: "Done si vide mai," "Sarò de'cenni tuoi," "Un raggio de speme," "Un empio m'accusa," "Ombre, o perché tornate?," and "Cada qual empio."

42. The themes with dimensions (½-2) + 1 + 1 occur in *Ezio* 11, 17, 22; *Re pastore* 6; and *Olimpiade* 3, 19. The themes with dimensions (1-4) + 2 + 2 occur in *Ezio* 4 and *Re pastore* 9. (Another **ABB** theme, that to *Olimpiade* 15, belongs in a category by itself, see p. 34).

43. These short themes occur in *Achille* 14 and *Artaserse* 13, 20. Six arias in these four operas composed for Italy contain longer **ABB** themes with dimensions (1-2) + 2 + 2: *Nitteti* 1, 14; *Demofoonte* 10; and *Artaserse* 2, 10, 15.

44. The themes with a three bar B segment occur in the arias "Talor se freme irato," "Serbami al grande impero," "Talor se perde i figli," "Fidarsi della sorte," and "Tremate, si tremate." The theme with a six-bar A segment occurs in the aria "Di quel superbo core."

45. The dimensions of the themes in question are $1 + 4 + 4$ and $3 + 3 + 3$, respectively.

46. The aria in *Ezio* is "In braccio a mille affanni" with dimensions $2 + 4 + 4$; the aria in *Semiramide riconosciuta* is "Talor se il vento freme" with dimensions $7 + 4 + 4$.

47. Only Wagenseil's *Ariodante* and Gluck's *Il re pastore* do not utilize the ascending bass formula.

48. Such cadences are found in "Done si vide mai."

49. Such cadences are found in the arias "Non so se più t'accendi" and "Tu mi disprezzi ingrato."

50. *Olimpiade* 1; and *Nitteti* 1, 9.

51. *Ezio* 11, 14; *Olimpiade* 19; *Nitteti* 16; *Demofoonte* 3, 16; *Achille* 1, 8, 17; and *Artaserse* 9, 15.

52. Such a three-bar ascending cadence occurs in "O più tremar non volgio" from *Demofoonte*, second version. The other cadences with whole note I $^6_4$ and V chords occur in "Per lei fra l'armi dorme il guerriero" from the same opera and in *Artaserse* 12 and *Temistocle* 1 and 8.

53. *La clemenza di Scipione* was the last opera seria Bach composed and the only such work that he composed after 1772, except for *Lucio Silla* (Mannheim, 1774).

54. *Armida* is Haydn's only surviving opera seria of the 1770s and 1780s.

55. Like Vinci, Pergolesi, and Terradellas, di Maio died young; his career in opera seria extended only from 1758 to 1770.

56. These four works constitute Mozart's entire output of opere serie before his *La clemenza di Tito* of 1791.

57. These five works constitute all but one of the extant operas Traetta composed for theaters outside Italy. The remaining work is *Lucio vero* (St. Petersburg, 1774). Daniel Heartz, "Traetta," *The New Grove Dictionary of Music and Musicians* (London: Macmillan, 1980) 19:113-14.

58. Actually only thirty-eight operas will be discussed here since none of the fast duple-meter arias of Jommelli's *Didone abbandonata* (Stuttgart, 1763) commences with an ABB theme.

59. Such themes occur in *Zenobia* 11; *Clelia* 4, 5, 18; *Siroe* 1, 3, 11; *Romolo* 2, 12, 13; and *Ruggiero* 1, 5, 7, 11, 15.

60. Such themes appear in *Romolo* 10 and 16. (Perhaps Hasse borrowed these themes from earlier operas?)

61. An eight-bar B segment occurs only once among the operas represented here, in "Con si bel nome in fronte" from Piccinni's *Catone in Utica* (Mannheim, 1770).

62. *Olimpiade* 15 and *Semiramide* 6.

63. *Enea* 10, 13; *Vologeso* 12; *Achille* 10; and *Ifigenia* 1.

64. See, respectively, *Armida* 1, *Achille* 3, and *Ifigenia* 7.

65. *Armida* 3 and 9.

66. Jommelli fashioned such B segments first in *Enea* 13 and then in *Vologeso* 12, *Achille* 10, and *Ifigenia* 1.

67. He did so first in *Semiramide* 6 and then in *Enea* 10; *Vologeso* 12; *Armida* 1, 9; and *Ifigenia* 1.

68. The aria in which such a cadence concludes the first vocal section is *Demofoonte* III 14. In two other arias, *Vologeso* 13 and *Fetonte* 3, the same cadence occurs near the end (but not at the very end) of the first vocal section.

69. *Artaserse* 18 and *Temistocle* 7. Both arias utilize the three-bar variant of the ascending bass formula.

70. Cadential I⁶₄ chords longer than one bar are rare, however. As far as the thirty-nine operas of 1761-84 are concerned, such chords occur in only two additional arias: "Infelice in van m'affanno" from Bach's *La clemenza di Scipiono* and Jommelli's *Achille* 5.

71. *Ruggiero* 17.

72. Charles Burney, *The Present State of Music in Germany, the Netherlands, and United Provinces,* 2d ed., corr. (London, 1775), 1:238-39. For more on Hasse's conservative orchestration, see below, chapter 5, passim.

73. Haydn, of course, never set foot in Italy, but he had produced many Italian operas at Eszterháza since 1776 and thus acquainted himself with current Italian styles.

74. Bernasconi and Jommelli left Italy in 1753 for Munich and Stuttgart, respectively. Their music of the 1760s kept pace with that of composers who remained in Italy, however, thus suggesting that southern Germany, at least by the third quarter of the century, was far more influenced by Italian styles than was northern Germany.

Chapter 3

1. H.C. Robbins Landon, *The Symphonies of Joseph Haydn* (New York: Macmillan, 1956), p. 307.

2. Ibid., p. 317.

3. For the origin and history of Haydn's early string quartets, see James Webster, "The Chronology of Haydn's String Quartets," *Musical Quarterly* 61 (1975):17-46.

4. *Joseph Haydn: Gesammelte Briefe und Aufzeichnungen,* ed. Dénes Bartha (Kassel: Bärenreiter, 1965), p. 107. H.C. Robbins Landon, in *The Collected Correspondence and London Notebooks of Joseph Haydn* (London: Barrie & Rockliff, 1959), p. 33, translates the passage as follows: "They are written in a new and special way, for I have not composed any for 10 years."

5. Adolf Sandberger, "Zur Geschichte des Haydn'schen Streichquartetts," *Altbayerische Monatschrift* 2 (1900):41-64.

6. See, for example, Jens Peter Larsen, *Die Haydn-Überlieferung* (Copenhagen: Einar Munksgaard, 1939), pp. 83-84.

7. See Friedrich Blume, "Josef Haydns künstlerische Persönlichkeit in seinen Streichquartetten," *Jahrbuch der Musikbibliothek Peters* 38 (1931):24-48.
   On the subject of texture in Haydn's string quartets, see also Reginald Barett-Ayres, *Joseph Haydn and the String Quartet* (London: Barrie & Jenkins, 1974); Ludwig Finscher, *Studien zur Geschichte des Streichquartetts,* vol. 1: *Die Entstehung des klassischen Streichquartetts. Von den Vorformen zur Grundlegung durch Joseph Haydn* (Kassel: Bärenreiter, 1974); Karl Geiringer, *Haydn: A Creative Life in Music,* rev. ed. (Berkeley: University of California Press, 1968); Adolf Hinderberger, *Die Motivik in Haydns Streichquartetten* (Turbenthal: Robert Furrers Erben, 1935); H.C. Robbins Landon,

Haydn: Chronicle and Works, vol. 2: *Haydn at Eszterháza 1766-1790* (Bloomington: University of Indiana Press, 1978), pp. 576-82; Orin Moe, "Texture in the String Quartets of Haydn to 1787" (Ph.D. dissertation, University of California at Santa Barbara, 1970); and James Webster, "The Bass Part in Joseph Haydn's Early String Quartets and in Austrian Chamber Music, 1750-1780" (Ph.D. dissertation, Princeton University, 1973).

8.   Charles Rosen, *The Classical Style: Haydn, Mozart, Beethoven,* rev. ed. (London: Faber, 1976), pp. 116-17.

9.   Ibid., p. 117.

10. Ibid., p. 117.

11. For a summary of eighteenth-century criticism of Jommelli's operas, see Marita McClymonds, "Niccolò Jommelli: The Last Years" (Ph.D. dissertation, University of California at Berkeley, 1978), 1:149-54, 160-63, 167, 183-84; and Audrey Lynn Tolkoff, "The Stuttgart Operas of Niccolò Jommelli" (Ph.D. dissertation, Yale University, 1974), pp. 53-87.

12. Donald Jay Grout, *A Short History of Opera,* 2d ed. (New York: Columbia University Press, 1965), p. 222.

13. Anna Amalie Abert, "Opera in Italy and the Holy Roman Empire," *The New Oxford History of Music,* vol. 7, *The Age of Enlightenment 1745-1790* (London: Oxford University Press, 1973), p. 34.

14. Tolkoff, "Stuttgart Operas," p. 220.

15. Hermann Abert, *Niccolo Jommelli als Opernkomponist* (Halle: Max Niemeyer, 1908).

16. Charles Burney, *A General History of Music from the Earliest Ages to the Present Period,* 4 vols. (London: 1776-89), 4:565.

17. Another opera of the period 1755-72 survives: Jommelli's *Ezio* (Lisbon, 1772). Since Jommelli composed the work specifically for Lisbon and included in it only three fast arias in duple meter, I omit consideration of *Ezio* from this chapter.

18. "Melodic syncopation"—the effect produced when the highest pitch in a series of quarters or eighths falls on an offbeat or even-numbered half beat.

19. In *Armida* 1, 3, 5, 9; *Demofoonte* IV 1, 3, 4, 5, 14, 16; *Achille* 1, 3, 5, 8, 10, 13, 16, 17; *Ifigenia* 1, 5, 12. (This chapter recognizes this pattern and all others discussed below only if they occur in sections with voice, i.e., the first vocal section, the second vocal section, and the B section. Ritornelli, which generally do not offer material not presented elsewhere, are not represented.)

20. In *Pelope* 1, 12; *Artaserse* 8; *Temistocle* 1, 5, 9, 16, 19; *Olimpiade* 12; *Semiramide* 3; *Didone* 13.

21. Numerous variants of pattern 4 employ sixteenth notes. Examples include the following:

In all cases, nonetheless, the tied note still begins on the beat and the eighth or sixteenth notes resume on the second or sixth half beat.

22. For the purposes of the following data, "melodic syncopation" exists in either of two cases: (1) in a group of three eighth notes (some perhaps divided into sixteenths), the first, occurring on the second or sixth half beat, carries the highest pitch; (2) in a group of three eighth notes (some again perhaps divided into sixteenths), the second, occurring on the second or fourth beat, carries the highest pitch, which is higher also than that of the following strong beat. This second note, if it were pitched lower than the following strong beat, would have the character not of a syncopation but of a stepping-stone to the stronger beat and higher pitch:

Example 48

One further qualification: a note pitched an octave higher than the surrounding notes is not a "melodic syncopation" at all but a variant of the standard preclassical Trommelbass:

Example 49

23. *Armida* 1, 3; *Demofoonte* IV 4; *Achille* 3, 5, 11; *Ifigenia* 1, 10.

24. *Artaserse* 11; *Temistocle* 5.

25. *Armida* 1, 5, 9; *Demofoonte* IV 1, 3, 5; *Achille* 1, 3, 8, 14; *Ifigenia* 5, 12.

26. *Temistocle* 1, 5, 9, 16, 19; *Olimpiade* 11; *Semiramide* 8.

27. In the vocal lines, both types of syncopation arise concurrently in *Armida* 3; *Achille* 3, 5; and *Ifigenia* 1 and 10; in the bass line, only in *Ifigenia* 12.

28. "Bass" in this context refers to chordal structure: the pedal functions as the bass of the chord. "Upper strings" refers to violins, violas, or cellos. As with pattern 5, this orchestrational technique assumes importance because Haydn began to use it at the same time (see p. 80). Jommelli composed such passages only in *Achille* 10 and 14.

29. These patterns must occur at least twice in succession to be counted as examples of "interlocking bass and upper accompaniment." (The bass line is occasionally sustained as in example 50.)

Example 50

30. These patterns appear in only three arias: *Temistocle* 14, *Olimpiade* 12, and *Didone* 6.

31. In *Armida* 1, 5; *Achille* 1, 3; *Ifigenia* 1, 5.

32.   In *Armida* 1; *Demofoonte* IV 16; *Achille* 10, 13; *Ifigenia* 10. A few other arias contain these patterns, although in neither of the two structural contexts mentioned above: *Achille* 16 and *Ifigenia* 17.

33.   See also *Ifigenia* 8 with similar patterns. *Armida* 10 features another powerful ostinato figure with a similar bass but without rests for the violins:

Example 51

34.   In *Pelope* 1, 12; *Temistocle* 1, 5, 16; *Didone* 13.

35.   In *Temistocle* 9, 16, 10; *Didone* 6.

36.   In *Temistocle* 1, 9, 19; *Olimpiade* 12.

37.   In *Artaserse* 8, *Temistocle* 5, *Semiramide* 3.

38.   In *Temistocle* 1, 5, 9, 16, 19; *Olimpiade* 11.

39.   See, in particular, *Armida* 1, 3; *Demofoonte* IV 1, 5; *Achille* 1, 3, 5, 8; *Ifigenia* 1, 5.

40.   Pattern 2 appears in mm. 6 (bass), 8 (second violins, bass), 11 (second violins, bass), 14 (first violins, bass), and 26 (first and second violins, then violas and bass). Pattern 3 appears in mm. 15 (second violins), 16 (first violins), and 24-25 (second violins). Pattern 4 appears in mm. 4-5 (voice) and a close variant appears in mm. 16-17 (first violins).

41.   Melodic emphasis of the second beat occurs in mm. 2 (voice), 5 (voice), 6 (bass line), 7 (all strings), 10 (all strings), 13 (all strings), 15 (bass), 17 (bass), 18 (bass), 22 (bass), 25 (voice, first violins), and 27 (all violins). Melodic emphasis of the second or sixth half beat occurs in mm. 7 (bass), 10 (bass), 14 (bass), 15 (second violins), 17 (first violins), and 26 (violas and bass).

42.   Prominent nonharmonic tones are found in mm. 6 (bass), 8 (bass), 11 (bass), 17 (bass), and 18-23 (viola).

43.   When the composer applied for a leave of absence from Stuttgart in 1769, Duke Carl Eugen "denied Jommelli both the originals and copies of his work as a means of insuring his return and as a retaliation for supposed disloyalty"(McClymonds, "Jommelli: The Last Years," 1:110).

44.   Another extant opera, *Adriano in Siria* (London, 1765), was not available to me when I conducted this comparative survey.

45.   Unlike Jommelli with his typically frantic rhythms, Bach often wrote a Trommelbass of quarter notes only (see *Artaserse* 8, 11; *Catone* 10; *Alessandro* 15).

46.   Pattern 2 occurs in four early arias (*Artaserse* 16, 21, 22, 24). Interlocking bass and upper accompaniment patterns also appear in four early arias (*Artaserse* 8, 16, 18; *Catone* 10).

47.   In *Temistocle* 1, 5, 7, 11, 18.

48.   In *Temistocle* 7, 14. In *Temistocle* 18, moreover, Bach took the function of the bass pedal from the strings and gave it to a wind instrument, the "clarinetto d'amore." (Bach had also written a "bass pedal for upper strings" once at the outset of his operatic career, in *Artaserse* 11.)

49. In the second themes of *Temistocle* 5, 7, and 18. Bach had used this pattern before, in *Artaserse* 8 and *Catone* 10, but only in the B section. There it had the effect of cutting the tempo of the entire section in half; Bach, it would seem, was unable to integrate the quarter notes of this pattern with the predominantly eighth-note rhythms of the A section.

50. Théodore de Wyzewa, "A propos du centenaire de la mort de Joseph Haydn," *Revue des deux mondes* 51 (1909):935-46.

51. H.C. Robbins Landon, *Haydn: Chronicle and Works*, vol. 2: *Haydn at Eszterháza 1766-1790* (Bloomington: Indiana University Press, 1978), pp. 266-71. See also Barry Brook, "Sturm und Drang and the Romantic Period in Music," *Studies in Romanticism* 9 (1970):269-84; H.C. Robbins Landon, "La crise romantique dans la musique autrichienne vers 1770: Quelques précurseurs inconnus de la symphonie en sol mineur (KV 183) de Mozart," *Les influences étrangères dans l'oeuvre de W.A. Mozart*, ed., André Verchaly (Paris: n.p., 1956), pp. 27-47; J.A. Westrup, "The Paradox of Eighteenth Century Music," *Studies in Musicology: Essays in the History, Style, and Bibliography of Music in Memory of Glen Haydon*, ed. James W. Pruett (Chapel Hill: University of North Carolina Press, 1969), pp. 118-32.

52. H.C. Robbins Landon and Jens Peter Larsen, "Haydn," *Die Musik in Geschichte und Gegenwart*, 5:1901-1902. The passage translates as follows: "But in a series of symphonies, which should belong to the time around 1768/69 (26, 39, 49, 59), there arises such a striking intensification of expression that one may speak almost of a new style. What in these symphonies strikes one as especially characteristic is, next to the strong rhythmic impulse which comes to the fore in the fast movements, the choice of the minor mode."

53. Landon, *Haydn*, pp. 273-76.

54. H.C. Robbins Landon, *The Symphonies of Joseph Haydn* ((New York: Macmillan, 1956), pp. 317-35.)

55. Landon, *Haydn*, p. 273.

56. Landon, *Symphonies*, p. 258.

57. Ibid., p. 319.

58. Ibid., p. 320.

59. Ibid., p. 317.

60. Brook, "Sturm und Drang," p. 270.

61. According to Landon, Haydn composed these seven symphonies in the following order: 58 (c. 1768), 26 (c. 1768-69), 41, 48, 44 (c. 1770-71), 52, and 43. (This and all further data on the chronology of Haydn's symphonies are based on Landon, *Symphonies*, pp. 174-75, 230, 271, 307; and Landon, *Haydn*, pp. 285-86.)

62. The list could well include Haydn's symphonies of 1773 and 1774. The cut-off date of 1772 simply ensures that this study of Haydn remain within the specific chronological limits of this book.

63. *Joseph Haydn: Critical Edition of the Complete Symphonies*, ed. H.C. Robbins Landon (Vienna: Universal Edition, 1964-68).

64. In Symphonies 42 (mm. 1-8), 47 (mm. 82-89), and 48 (mm. 1-8, 18-21).

65. In Symphonies 52 (mm. 36, 56, 95) and 65 (mm. 41-43).

66. In Symphonies "B" (mm. 8, 11), 2 (mm. 25, 27), 4 (mm. 1, 2, 5, 38, 39), 12 (m. 53), 15 (mm. 37, 38), 21 (mm. 43, 50), 25 (mm. 76-78, 121, 143-46), 30 (mm. 10, 11), and 72 (m. 38).

67. In Symphonies 4 (m. 36), 9 (mm. 83, 85, 87), 18 (m. 24), 20 (m. 15), and 49 (m. 12).

68. In Symphonies "B" (m. 24), 1 (mm. 18, 19), 12 (mm. 22, 84, 86, 88), 13 (mm. 40, 71), and 34 (mm. 50-52).

69. In Symphonies 10 (mm. 12-15, 26, 28, 30-31, 45-47), 11 (mm. 14-17, 26-34), 12 (mm. 17-20, 50-51, 55-56), and 25 (mm. 63-68).

70. In Symphonies "B" (mm. 1, 18), 1 (m. 13), 4 (mm. 8, 11, 23, 25), 11 (mm. 81, 83, 85), 39 (m. 16), and 49 (mm. 1, 14).

71. Pattern 2a occurs in Symphonies 42 (mm. 169-71) and 46 (mm. 95-96); pattern 2b occurs in Symphonies 42 (mm. 27, 29, 31, 33, 41, 167, 168) and 52 (mm. 22, 67, 71).

72. In Symphonies 2 (mm. 45-51) and 27 (mm. 32-33).

73. In Symphonies 42 (mm. 42-45), 44 (m. 42), and 46 (mm. 43-44, 48-49).

74. In Symphonies 21 (mm. 60-65), 27 (mm. 28-29), and 49 (mm. 65-69).

75. In Symphonies 42 (mm. 34-40) and 46 (mm. 33-34, 45-47, 54-55, 89-94, 99-104).

76. Earlier works had employed the pattern on occasion, but it is always obscured by continuous "busy" writing elsewhere in the string orchestra.

77. Landon, "La crise romantique."

78. Landon, *Haydn*, p. 158.

79. Edward Lowinsky, "Mozart's Rhythm," *The Creative World of Mozart*, ed. Paul Henry Lang (New York: Norton, 1963), pp. 31-55.

80. Ibid., p. 36.

81. Rosen, *Classical Style*, p. 59.

82. Ibid., p. 60.

Chapter 4

1. For an examination of the instrumental forces employed by Leo, Porpora, Pergolesi, and Jommelli in the earlier period, see Helmut Hell, *Die neapolitanische Opernsinfonie in der ersten Hälfte des 18. Jahrhunderts. N. Porpora—L. Vinci—G.B. Pergolesi—L. Leo—N. Jommelli*, Münchner Veröffentlichungen zur Musikgeschichte, vol. 19 (Tutzing: Hans Schneider, 1971), pp. 39-60. For other general introductions to orchestration in the early and mid-eighteenth century, see Edward O. Downes, "The Operas of Johann Christian Bach as a Reflection of the Dominant Trends in *opera seria*, 1750-1780" (Ph.D. dissertation, Harvard University, 1958), 1:257-313, and Adam Carse, *The Orchestra in the XVIIIth Century* (Cambridge: W. Heffer & Sons, 1940).

2. Michael Robinson, *Naples and Neapolitan Opera* (Oxford: Clarendon, 1972), p. 122.

3. So too does his only subsequent opera seria available to me: *La clemenza di Scipione* (London, 1778).

4. Hell, *Opernsinfonie*, p. 40. This passage translates as follows: "As main principle, it must be said first that the composer did not determine the instrumentarium for his work, but that he had to adjust, in instrumental as in vocal matters, to the possibilities of the theater at that time."

5. Carse, *Orchestra*, p. 34. One cannot determine from Carse's statistics (pp. 18-27) just how many flutists belonged to many of the orchestras he lists, for many of his eighteenth-century sources did not distinguish between flutists and oboists but counted them as a single group.

6. None of the other operas studied here was performed at Innsbruck. According to Walter Senn, in "Innsbrucker Hofmusik," *Österreichische Musikzeitschrift* 25 (1970):659-71, non-resident musicians were engaged to perform *Romolo ed Ersilia,* the court orchestra there having disbanded in 1748.

7. Carse, *Orchestra*, p. 34.

8. Further, the orchestral parts to *Carattaco* preserved in the British Library include parts for flutes and two different parts for oboes (Downes, "Johann Christian Bach," 1:265). At least four musicians must have played these instruments, as they did in *Orione*.

9. See, for example, *Ezio* 9; *Artaserse* 14; *Zenobia* 7; *Clelia* 12, 15; *Ruggiero* 11.

10. The English horns, their parts sounding a fifth lower than written, play only in the second movement of the sinfonia.

11. Spelled "tallies" in the British Library manuscript score of *Orione*, this instrument, probably an English horn or tenor oboe, sounds a fifth lower than written and appears in *Orione* 14.

12. A once popular member of the clarinet family with a pear-shaped bell, the "clarinetto d'amore" was pitched usually in the keys of A-flat or E, but sometimes in G or even B-flat (Oskar Kroll, *The Clarinet,* trans. Hilda Morris, ed. Anthony Baines [New York: Taplinger Publishing, 1968], pp. 111-12). Bach used the instrument in *Temistocle* 18 and the sinfonia to that opera but wrote its parts in D.

13. Handel may have used clarinets in *Tamerlano* (London, 1724) and *Riccardo primo* (London, 1727), but the evidence is ambiguous. See. R.B. Chatwin, "Handel and the Clarinet," *Galpin Society Journal* 3 (1950):3-8.

14. Cuthbert Girdlestone, *Jean-Phillipe Rameau: His Life and Work,* rev. and enl. ed. (New York: Dover, 1969), p. 294.

15. Ibid., p. 462. Carl Mennicke (*Hasse und die Brüder Graun als Symphoniker* [Leipzig: Breitkopf & Härtel, 1906], pp. 278-80) demurred, however, demonstrating that every note of these parts could be played on an eight-foot natural trumpet and concluding that Rameau intended the parts for clarino (trumpet) rather than the clarinet.

16. Friedrich Walter, *Geschichte des Theaters und der Musik am kurpfälzischen Hofe* (Leipzig: Breitkopf & Härtel, 1898), p. 224.

17. Carse, *Orchestra*, p. 36.

18. See, respectively, *Temistocle* 18 and *Orione* 14.

19. Hell, *Opernsinfonie*, pp. 51-52.

20. See p. 107, note c.

21. Hell, *Opernsinfonie,* p. 58. The passage translates as follows: "Evidently there were only two players for brass instruments, so that either only horns or only trumpets could be required."

22. Jommelli's *Temistocle* (1757), Hasse's *Artaserse* (1760), and Bach's *Catone in Utica* (1762).

23. Hasse's *Demofoonte* (1758) and *Achille in Sciro* (1759), and Bach's *Alessandro nell'Indie* (1762).

24. In each case—the sinfonia to *Armida abbandonata* and two arias in *Ifigenia in Tauride* (*Ifigenia* 6 and 15)—the instructions "Trombe e corni" appear before two staves, each of which carries only one part.

25. Unfortunately, few contemporary accounts of the constitution of the San Carlo orchestra survive. Basing his conclusions on records at San Carlo, Ulisse Prota-Giurleo (*La grand orchestra del R. Teatro San Carlo nel settecento* [Naples: By the author, 1927]) claimed that the orchestra, at least in 1742 and 1759, included four trumpet players, of whom some presumably played horn as well.

26. According to Carse's tabulations of the composition of eighteenth-century orchestras (Carse, *Orchestra*, pp. 18-27), the Dresden orchestra consistently included four or five oboists in addition to two or three flutists. No other orchestra included in the chart featured a larger total number of oboists and flutists.

     According to the same chart, most orchestras included two horns until the 1780s, when three or four horns became more common. The only orchestras Carse lists which already had a larger horn section in the 1750s and 1760s are those of Mannheim, Milan, and Stuttgart.

27. *Temistocle* 18.

28. *Semiramide* 12, *Didone* 14, and *Demofoonte* III 16.

29. Mannheim boasted two outstanding oboists: Friedrich Ramm (1744?-1811), who joined the orchestra in 1759 at the age of fourteen, and Ludwig August Lebrun (1746-90), who joined the orchestra in 1764. The principal bassoonist was Georg Wenzel Ritter (1748-1808), who joined the orchestra in 1764 and composed bassoon concertos and quartets (Walther, *Geschichtes des Theaters*, pp. 224-25).

30. *Olimpiade* 13; *Semiramide* 12, 16; *Didone* 14; and *Demofoonte* III 16.

31. The flutists of the Dresden orchestra, in particular, maintained a tradition of the highest caliber. In earlier times, the orchestra boasted such well-known virtuosi as Pierre Gabriel Buffardin (in the orchestra from 1715 to 1739) and Johann Joachim Quantz (in the orchestra from 1718 to 1741). In the days of the performances of Hasse's *Ezio, Re pastore,* and *Olimpiade,* the Dresden flutists were Wenzel Gottfried Dewerdeck, Francis Joseph Götzel, and Pietro Grassi Florio (Friedrich Wilhelm Marpurg, *Historisch-Kritische Beyträge zur Aufnahme der Musik* [Berlin: G.A. Lange, 1745-78], 2:476).

32. In his introductory sinfonias, Hasse used flutes according to a similar pattern. Of his five operas for Italy, only *Artaserse* opens with a sinfonia with flutes (and strings, oboes and horns). Of his Dresden and Vienna operas, on the other hand, all but one begin with the sound of flutes. (The exception, *Il trionfo di Clelia,* calls for English horns instead.)

33. Hell, *Opernsinfonie*, p. 59. This passage translates as follows: "In Rome the supply of trumpeters must have been plentiful. Evidently the aristocratic trumpeters remained longer at the disposal of the orchestra here. The scoring with trumpets *and* horns in the sinfonia is actually typical of works performed in Rome."

34. But it is important to note that this disparity arose on a regional level, not a city-by-city one. The flute parts Bach composed for Mannheim, for example, resemble those he wrote for London; the flute parts Hasse composed for Vienna resemble those he wrote for Dresden. As long as a composer remained north of the Alps, or in Italy, it seems he would not have had to modify his style of writing for these instruments.

35. Hasse usually expressed his intentions by verbal indications only, such as "Ob: ne' soli Rit."

36. In his opere serie, Bach did not employ the standard "classical" disposition of four pairs of woodwinds—flutes, oboes, clarinets, and bassoons—until 1774 in the overture to *Lucio Silla,* his second opera for Mannheim. (The first bars of this overture are reproduced in Downes, "Johann Christian Bach," 1:286-88.) As a point of comparison, Mozart did not write for this combination until 1778, four years later, when he composed the Symphony in D ("Paris," K. 297) and the ballet music for "Les petits riens" (K. Anh. 10), both for Paris.

37. Downes, for example, writes of *Orione,* "the orchestral writing is much more differentiated than we have found it before," Bach using his winds with a "new boldness" (Downes, "Johann Christian Bach," 2:231-34).

38. Downes, "Johann Christian Bach," 2:227.

39. Charles Sanford Terry, *Johann Christian Bach* (London: Oxford University Press, 1929), p. 68.

40. Charles Burney, *A General History of Music from the Earliest Ages to the Present Period,* 4 vols. (London: 1776-89), 4:482.

41. Ibid., 4:483.

42. *Clelia* 8. Hasse also combined flutes, bassoons, and horns with ripieno oboes in *Ruggiero* 14. In the other arias with independent parts for flutes and bassoons (*Olimpiade* 16 and *Achille* 23), he may have intended oboes to serve as ripienists and thus combined three pairs of woodwinds there as well.

43. See, for example, Donald Jay Grout, *A Short History of Opera,* 2d ed. (New York: Columbia University Press, 1965), p. 222.

44. The aria in question is "L'istesso tormento" from *Sofonisba;* here the woodwinds are not, however, joined by horns, as they always are in Bach's operas.

45. For a slightly later work, *Paride ed Elena* (Vienna, 1770), Gluck combined pairs of flutes, oboes, and bassoons, but only twice (for the overture and a dance). He rarely composed more than three parts for them, however, and never more than four.

46. Hell, *Opernsinfonie,* pp. 487-501.

47. Audrey Lynn Tolkoff, "The Stuttgart Operas of Niccolò Jommelli" (Ph.D. dissertation, Yale University, 1974), p. 66.

48. *Artaserse* 10 and "Non vi piacque, ingiusti Dei," a substitute aria Jommelli composed expressly for a 1765 revival of *Demofoonte* III.

49. *Pelope* 11; *Artaserse* 5, 17; *Demofoonte* III 11; and *Fetonte* 4, 7, 8. Three of these arias are located in *Fetonte,* until recently the only Jommelli opera available in modern edition. With its inclusion of flutes in arias, numerous choruses and ensembles (including five duets), and a programmatic overture, *Fetonte* hardly represents Jommelli's Stuttgart operas as a whole.

50. *Pelope* 13, and *Vologeso* 16.

51. According to Adam Carse (*Orchestra,* p. 27), two contemporary sources cast light on the constitution of the Stuttgart orchestra at this time: Marpurg's list of 1757 (Marpurg, *Historisch-Kritische Beyträge,* 3:65-67) and Burney's of 1772 (Charles Burney, *The Present State of Music in Germany, the Netherlands, and United Provinces,* 2d ed., corr. [London, 1775], 1:103). Neither Marpurg nor Burney mentions clarinettists, although it is conceivable that clarinet parts were played by oboists.

52. Marpurg lists three flutists and three oboists; Burney, two flutists and four oboists.

53. For his last four operas for Italy (1770-71), Jommelli composed flute parts for only one aria, *Achille* 4. This aria is likewise the shortest in the opera.

54. Like Hasse as well, Jommelli used trumpets also in the sinfonias he wrote for Italy. Only that of *Demofoonte* IV (Naples, 1770) makes no mention of the instrument.

Chapter 5

1. Rudolf Gerber, *Der Operntypus Johann Adolf Hasses und seine textichen Grundlagen,* (Leipzig: Kistner & Siegel, 1925), pp. 134-43.

2. Gerber maintains that the bassoon underwent a slight chronological development in Hasse's operas; he gives little supporting evidence, however (ibid., pp. 137-39).

3. Downes, for example, writes: "Hasse...made no change in his style of orchestration." Edward O. Downes, "The Operas of Johann Christian Bach as a Reflection of the Dominant Trends in *opera seria,* 1750-1780" (Ph.D. dissertation, Harvard University, 1958) 1:283. Millner, when describing the orchestration of Hasse's last opera, *Ruggiero,* states: "...his style simply does not change to any great extent between 1730 and 1771...oboes and flutes duplicate the melody" (Frederick Millner, review of *Johann Adolf Hasse: Ruggiero, ovvero L'eroica gratitudine* [Concentus musicus, Vol. 1], ed. Klaus Hortschansky, in *Music Review* 38 (August 1977):230.

4. Downes, "Johann Christian Bach," 1:284.

5. *Temistocle* 7 contains an extensive melodic part for solo bassoon; *Temistocle* 11, a similar part for oboe.

6. In *Ezio* 9, for example, Hasse limited oboe participation in the vocal sections to two five-note fragments in the middle of the second vocal section. Similarly, in *Ezio* 21, he introduced oboes into a vocal section but allowed them only to double the violins during a melisma. In several arias of *Il re pastore* and *Olimpiade,* on the other hand, oboes double violins through most of the A section (see *Re pastore* 2, 4, 7, 8, 10 and *Olimpiade* 3, 10, 11, 15). Only the occasionally low range of the violins seems to have brought about the few gaps in doubling.

7. In *Artaserse* 19 and *Zenobia* 7, for example, the oboes, which double the violins in the ritornellos, are silent throughout the first vocal section and accompany the voice only at the very end of the second vocal section.

8. Jean-Jacques Rousseau, *Dictionnaire de musique* (Paris: Chez la veuve Duchesne, 1768), p. 130. This passage translates as follows: "The oboe parts, which one extracts from the violin parts for a large orchestra, should not be copied exactly as they are in the original. But, besides the range which that instrument lacks in respect to the violin;... besides the agility which it lacks or which goes badly at certain speeds, the strength of the oboes should be reserved to mark better the principal notes and to give more accent to the music."

9. *Demofoonte* 1, 15; *Clelia* 4; *Siroe* 12, 17; *Romolo* 10.

10. *Ruggiero* 8.

11. The brief independent melodic duets for oboes in *Ruggiero* 17 are an exception.

12. "Tonic resolution phrase"—a phrase, sometimes an actual "second theme," beginning after a caesura on V/V and cadencing in the new key.

13. In other $\frac{3}{4}$ arias of *Ruggiero,* in fact, Hasse instructed oboes to double a similar scale fragment concluding an important phrase (see *Ruggiero* 4, 8, 11).

14. For the purpose of this chart, "independent harmonic support" is defined as pitches which, at least initially, are not sounded by the strings. This definition excludes passages such as those in figures 15a and b.

15. Further, the interpretation of these parts as fragmented lines emphasizing structure rests on rather ambiguous evidence (see above, p. 133, n.e.).

16. Of the six arias represented on the chart, two (*Demofoonte* 19 and *Achille* 22) are listed only because the oboes provide some degree of independent harmonic support. The parts are not fragmented.

17. Hasse seems to have appreciated the structural importance of this progression, for in later operas he continued to fortify it in similar fashion (see *Artaserse* 2; *Zenobia* 3; *Siroe* 3, 13; and *Ruggiero* 4, 8, 10).

    An additional harmonic context for which Hasse sometimes composed independent oboe parts is the progression $I - V_4^6 - I$ which occasionally concludes or follows the first phrase of the first vocal section and/or its repetition in the second vocal section (see *Re pastore* 2, *Demofoonte* 6, *Achille* 14, *Artaserse* 2, and *Ruggiero* 17).

18. All the operas which Jommelli and J.C. Bach composed for Italy in the earlier part of the 1755-72 period include such parts. These operas are Jommelli's *Creso* (Rome, 1757) and *Temistocle* (Naples, 1757) and Bach's *Artaserse* (Turin, 1761), *Catone in Utica* (Naples, 1761), and *Alessandro nell'Indie* (Naples, 1762).

19. One of the rare instances of such independent writing occurs in the aria "Se povero il ruscello," where oboes sustain the progression $I - IV_4^6 - I - IV_4^6$, the same context in which Hasse sometimes freed the oboes from their ties to the violins. (See above, n. 17.)

20. Rare exceptions are limited to (1) extensive independent melodic wind parts which often proceed in parallel thirds or sixths with the voice or alternate with it in brilliant roulades, and (2) an occasional chord, during which the voice either rests momentarily or sustains one note.

21. See, for instance, example 37.

22. Such exceptions average one or two per opera and are virtually confined to fast arias. In Jommelli's eleven extant operas of 1755-68, there are only twelve: *Artaserse* 3, 14; *Semiramide* 10; *Didone* 7, 8; *Demofoonte* III 1; *Enea* 1, 7, 8, 11; *Vologeso* 7; and *Fetonte* 7. After 1770, Jommelli granted winds to the B section of his modified da capo arias where the B section more closely resembles the character of the A section than it does in other types of arias.

23. The same two exceptions noted above for Jommelli (see above, n. 20) apply to Bach as well.

24. *Catone* 17.

25. *Artaserse* 9, 22, 25; *Catone* 7, 15.

26. *Carattaco* 2, 5, 8, 9, 14, 15, 20.

27. *Carattaco* 2 has parts for bassoon and pairs of clarinets and horns; *Carattaco* 5, pairs of oboes and horns; *Carattaco* 8, pairs of flutes and bassoons; and *Carattaco* 15, pairs of oboes and horns.

28. *Temistocle* 1, 2, 4, 5, 6, 7, 8, 9, 15, 18.

Chapter 6

1. Sometimes one horn accompanies two oboes, so that only three pitches sound simultaneously. When four instruments play, usually the horns double notes, either in unison or in octaves.

2. When given their own parts, bassoons rarely provide sustained harmonic support but instead supply a single bass line in the absence of the lower strings.

3. When all violins play the same part, two or more players of a ripieno woodwind—flutes or oboes—would likewise share one line.

4. Other instruments may join in, but such participation does not alter the basic trio character. A second pair of winds may double the first, perhaps in a different octave. Or when strings provide the bass, other strings—often the violas—may play along as well. In this latter case, the added instruments have an effect similar to that of the keyboard continuo in a trio sonata: they play extra notes or chords but remain in the background.

5. Exceptionally, in *Clelia* 14, Hasse assigned the top two lines to flute and oboe.

6. All of Hasse's flute parts for Italy merely double other lines, usually those of the violins and occasionally that of the voice.

7. In some arias, two horns supply the upper parts of the trio in the first ritornello and second vocal section (see *Artaserse* 4, *Romolo* 13, and *Ruggiero* 17). Whenever such passages appear in a new key—usually in the first vocal section or B section—oboes replace the horns.

8. In Jommelli's *Vologeso* 16, a one-bar solo passage for two oboes, bassoon, and two horns occurs several times. While there is no doubling, strictly speaking, horns and bassoon merely play the same note in two different octaves and in different rhythms, thus preserving the basic trio texture.

9. In his seven Stuttgart operas of the 1760s, Jommelli composed brief independent melodic ensemble passages in sixteen arias: *Olimpiade* 9; *Semiramide* 1; *Didone* 8, 12, 16; *Demofoonte* III 1, 2, 16; *Enea* 7, 12; *Vologeso* 4, 9, 16; and *Fetonte* 1, 4, 7. In the manuscripts, the word "soli" introduces such passages for oboes.

10. *Artaserse* 19, 20, 25; and *Catone* 7, 16.

11. Such parts appear in *Alessandro* 2, 5, 12, 15, 16, and 21.

12. Bach used these progressions as the basis of ensemble passages in *Alessandro* 2, 8, 10, 12, 15, 17, and 21.

13. See above, table 5.

14. *Ruggiero* 14.

15. Each pair may play one note of a triad. Or, oboes may play two notes, clarinets double the oboes, and flutes or bassoons provide a higher or lower pitch to complete the triad.

Bibliography

Secondary Literature

Abert, Anna Amalie. "Gluck." *Die Musik in Geschichte und Gegenwart,* 5:320-80.
———. "Opera in Italy and the Holy Roman Empire." *The New Oxford History of Music.* Vol. 7: *The Age of Enlightenment, 1745-1790.* London: Oxford University Press, 1973, pp. 1-199.
Abert, Hermann. *Niccolo Jommelli als Opernkomponist.* Halle: Max Niemeyer, 1908.
Aldrich, Putnam. *Rhythm in Seventeenth-Century Italian Monody.* New York: W.W. Norton, 1966.
Arcari, Paolo. *L'arte poetica di Pietro Metastasio.* Milan: Libreria Editrice Nazionale, 1902.
Barett-Ayres, Reginald. *Joseph Haydn and the String Quartet.* London: Barrie & Jenkins, 1974.
Bartha, Dénes, ed. *Joseph Haydn: Gesammelte Briefe und Aufzeichnungen.* Kassel: Bärenreiter, 1965.
Bauer, Wilhelm A. and Deutsch, Otto Erich, eds. *Mozart: Briefe und Aufzeichnungen.* 7 vols. Kassel: Bärenreiter, 1962.
Bloch, Henry. "Terradellas." *Die Musik in Geschichte und Gegenwart,* 13:243-46.
Blume, Friedrich. "Josef Haydns künstlerische Persönlichkeit in seinen Streichquartetten." *Jahrbuch der Musikbibliothek Peters* 38 (1931):24-48.
Bostian, R. Lee. "The Works of Rinaldo di Capua." Ph.D. dissertation, University of North Carolina, 1961.
Brook, Barry. "Sturm und Drang and the Romantic Period in Music." *Studies in Romanticism* 9 (1970):269-84.
Bukofzer, Manfred. *Music in the Baroque Era.* New York: W.W. Norton, 1947.
Burney, Charles. *A General History of Music from the Earliest Ages to the Present Period.* 4 vols. London, 1776-89.
———. *The Present State of Music in Germany, the Netherlands, and United Provinces.* 2 vols. 2d ed. London, 1775.
Burt, Nathaniel. "Opera in Arcadia." *Musical Quarterly* 41 (1955):145-70.
Caliri, Francesco. *Ritmi e stile.* Florence: Le Monnier, 1961.
Cantrell, Byron. "Tommaso Traetta and His Opera *Sofonisba.*" Ph.D. dissertation, University of California at Los Angeles, 1957.
Carse, Adam. *The Orchestra in the XVIIIth Century.* Cambridge: W. Heffer & Sons, 1940.
Chatwin, R.B. "Handel and the Clarinet." *Galpin Society Journal* 3 (1950):3-8.
Di Chiera, David. "The Life and Operas of Gian Francesco di Majo." Ph.D. dissertation, University of California at Los Angeles, 1962.
Dietz, Hanns-Bertold. "Feo." *The New Grove Dictionary of Music and Musicians.* London: Macmillan, 1980. 6:465-68.
Downes, Edward O.D. "The Neapolitan Tradition in Opera." *Report of the Eighth Congress of the International Musicological Society, New York, 1961.* Kassel: Bärenreiter, 1961, pp. 277-84.

_____. "The Operas of Johann Christian Bach as a Reflection of the Dominant Trends in *opera seria,* 1750-1780." 2 vols. Ph.D. dissertation, Harvard University, 1958.

Elwert, W. Theodor. *Italienische Metrik.* Munich: Max Huber, 1968.

Finscher, Ludwig. *Studien zur Geschichte des Streichquartetts.* Vol. 1: *Die Entstehung des klassischen Streichquartetts; Von den Vorformen zur Grundlegung durch Joseph Haydn.* Kassel: Bärenreiter, 1974.

Florimo, Francesco. *La scuola musicale di Napoli e i suoi conservatorii.* 4 vols. Naples: Vincenzo Morano, 1880-82.

Freeman, Robert. "Opera without Drama: Currents of Change in Italian Opera, 1675 to 1725, and the Roles Played Therein by Zeno, Caldara, and Others." Ph.D. dissertation, Princeton University, 1967.

Furstenau, Moritz. *Zur Geschichte der Musik und des Theaters am Hofe zu Dresden.* 2 vols. Dresden: Rudolf Kuntze, 1861-62.

Gallico, Claudio. "Rinaldo di Capua." *The New Grove Dictionary of Music and Musicians.* London: Macmillan, 1980. 16:42-43.

Geiringer, Karl. *Haydn: A Creative Life in Music.* Rev. ed. Berkeley: University of California Press, 1968.

Gerber, Rudolf. *Der Operntypus Johann Adolf Hasses und seine textichen Grundlagen.* Leipzig: Kistner & Siegel, 1925.

Girdlestone, Cuthbert. *Jean-Philippe Rameau: His Life and Work.* Rev. & enl. ed. New York: Dover, 1969.

Grout, Donald Jay. *A Short History of Opera.* 2d ed. New York: Columbia University Press, 1965.

Guarnerio, Pier Enea. *Manuale di versificazione italiana.* Milan: Villardi, 1893.

Hansell, Sven. "The Solo Cantatas, Motets and Antiphons of Johann Adolf Hasse." Ph.D. dissertation, University of Illinois, 1966.

Hansell, Sven and Hansell, Kathleen. Review of *Johann Adolf Hasse: Ruggiero, ovvero L'eroica gratitudine.* Edited by Klaus Hortschansky. *Journal of the American Musicological Society* 29 (1976):308-19.

Heartz, Daniel. "Critical Years in European Musical History: 1740-60." *Report of the Tenth Congress of the International Musicological Society, Ljubljana, 1967.* Kassel: Bärenreiter, 1980, pp. 160-68.

_____. "From Garrick to Gluck: The Reform of Theatre and Opera in the Mid-Eighteenth Century." *Proceedings of the Royal Musicological Society* (1967/68):111-27.

_____. "The Genesis of Mozart's *Idomeneo.*" *Musical Quarterly* 55 (1969):1-19.

_____. "Traetta." *The New Grove Dictionary of Music and Musicians.* London: Macmillan, 1980. 19:111-14.

Hell, Helmut. *Die neapolitanische Opernsinfonie in der ersten Hälfte des 18. Jahrhunderts. N. Porpora—L. Vinci—G.B. Pergolesi—L. Leo—N. Jommelli.* Münchner Veröffentlichungen zur Musikgeschichte, Vol. 19. Tutzing: Hans Schneider, 1971.

_____. "Pergolesi." *Die Musik in Geschichte und Gegenwart,* 10:1048-64.

Hill, John Walter. "Vivaldi's *Griselda.*" *Journal of the American Musicological Society* 31 (Spring, 1978):53-82.

Hinderberger, Adolf. *Die Motivik in Haydns Streichquartetten.* Turbenthal: Robert Furrers Erben, 1935.

Hortschansky, Klaus. Forward to *Johann Adolf Hasse: Ruggiero, ovvero L'eroica gratitudine.* Concentus musicus. Vol. 1. Cologne: Arno Volk, 1973.

Hucke, Helmut. "Die neapolitanische Tradition in der Oper." International Musicological Society. *Report of the Eighth Congress. New York City, 1961.* Kassel: Bärenreiter, 1961, pp. 253-77.

Jackson, Paul Joseph. "The Operas of David Pérez: Traditional and Progressive Features of the *Opera Seria* in the Middle of the Eighteenth Century." Ph.D. dissertation, Stanford University, 1967.

Köchel, Ludwig Ritter von. *Chronologisch-thematisches Verzeichnis sämtlicher Tonwerke Wolfgang Amadé Mozart.* 7th ed. Wiesbaden: Breitkopf und Härtel, 1965.

Kroll, Oskar. *The Clarinet.* Translated by Hilda Morris. Edited by Anthony Baines. New York: Taplinger Publishing, 1968.

Landon, H.C. Robbins. *Haydn: Chronicle and Works.* Vol. 2: *Haydn at Eszterháza 1766-1790.* Bloomington: University of Indiana Press, 1978.

_____. "La crise romantique dans la musique autrichienne vers 1770: Quelques précurseurs inconnus de la symphonie en sol mineur (KV 183) de Mozart." In *Les influences étrangères dans l'oeuvre de W.A. Mozart.* Edited by André Verchaly. Paris: n.p., 1956, pp. 27-47.

_____. *The Symphonies of Joseph Haydn.* New York: Macmillan, 1956.

Landon, H.C. Robbins, ed. *The Collected Correspondence and London Notebooks of Joseph Haydn.* London: Barrie & Rockliff, 1959.

Larsen, Jens Peter. *Die Haydn-Überlieferung.* Copenhagen: Einar Munksgaard, 1939.

Lawner, George. "Form and Drama in the Operas of Joseph Haydn." Ph.D. dissertation, University of Chicago, 1959.

Lehmann, Ursula. "Holzbauer." *Die Musik in Geschichte und Gegenwart,* 6:659-63.

Levi, Attilio. *Della versificazione.* Genoa: Apuania, 1931.

Lippman, Friedrich. "Der italienische Vers und der Musikalische Rhythmus: Zum Verhältnis von Vers und Musik in der italienischen Oper des 19. Jahrhunderts, mit einem Rückblick auf die 2. Hälfe des 18. Jahrhunderts." *Analecta musicologica* 12 (1973):253-369; 14 (1974):324-410; 15 (1975):298-333.

Lowinsky, Edward. "Mozart's Rhythm." In *The Creative World of Mozart.* Edited by Paul Henry Lang. New York: Norton, 1963, pp. 31-35.

McClymonds, Marita. "Jommelli." *The New Grove Dictionary of Music and Musicians.* London: Macmillan, 1980. 9:689-95.

_____. "Niccolò Jommelli: The Last Years." Ph.D. dissertation, University of California at Berkeley, 1978.

Marpurg, Friedrich Wilhelm. *Historisch-kritische Beyträge zur Aufnahme der Musik.* 5 vols. Berlin: G.A. Lange, 1754-78.

Meikle, Robert Burns. "Leonardo Vinci's *Artaserse:* An Edition with an Editorial and Critical Commentary." Ph.D. dissertation, Cornell University, 1970.

Metastasio, Pietro. *Tutte le opere di Pietro Metastasio.* Edited by Bruno Brunelli. Milan: Mondadori, 1943. Vol. 1.

Millner, Frederick. Review of *Johann Adolf Hasse: Ruggiero, ovvero L'eroica gratitudine.* Concentus Musicus, Vol. 1. Edited by Klaus Hortschansky. In *Music Review* 38 (August 1977): 230.

_____. *The Operas of Johann Adolf Hasse.* Ann Arbor: UMI Research Press, 1979.

Moe, Orin. "Texture in the String Quartets of Haydn to 1789." Ph.D. dissertation, University of California at Santa Barbara, 1970.

Mondolfi, Anna. "Lotti." *Die Musik in Geschichte und Gegenwart,* 8:1226-30.

Pagano, Roberta, and Bianchi, Lino. *Alessandro Scarlatti.* Turin: Radiotelevisione italiana, 1972.

Prota-Giurleo, Ulisse. *La grand orchestra del R. Teatro San Carlo nel settecento.* Naples: By the author, 1927.

Robinson, Michael. *Naples and Neapolitan Opera.* Oxford: Clarendon, 1972.

Rosen, Charles. *The Classical Style: Haydn, Mozart, Beethoven.* Rev. ed. London: Faber, 1976.

Rousseau, Jean-Jacques. *Dictionnaire de musique.* Paris: Chez la veuve Duchesne, 1768.

Rowell, Lewis E., Jr. "Four Operas of Antonio Vivaldi." Ph.D. dissertation, University of Rochester, 1959.

Sandberger, Adolf. "Zur Geschichte des Haydn'schen Streichquartetts." *Altbayerische Monatschrift* 2 (1900):41-64.

Sartori, Claudio. "Primo tentativo di catalogo unico dei libretti italiani a stampa fino all'anno 1800." Milan, 1968 et. seq.

Scholz-Michelitsch, Helga. "Wagenseil." *Die Musik in Geschichte und Gegenwart,* 14:68-74.

Senn, Walter. "Innsbrucker Hofmusik." *Österreichische Musikzeitschrift* 25 (1970):659-71.

Strohm, Reinhard. *Italienische Opernarien des frühen Settecento (1720-1730).* 2 vols. Analecta musicologica, Vol. 16. Cologne: Arno Volk, 1976.

Tedeschi, Giuliana. *Lingua, grammatica, stile.* Turin: G.B. Petrini, 1972.

Terry, Charles Sanford. *Johann Christian Bach.* London: Oxford University Press, 1929.

Tolkoff, Audrey Lynn. "The Stuttgart Operas of Niccolò Jommelli." Ph.D. dissertation, Yale University, 1974.

Walter, Friedrich. *Geschichte des Theaters und der Musik am Kurpfälzischen Hofe.* Leipzig: Breitkopf & Härtel, 1898.

Webster, James. "The Bass Part in Joseph Haydn's Early String Quartets and in Austrian Chamber Music, 1750-1780." Ph.D. dissertation, Princeton University, 1973.

_____. "The Chronology of Haydn's String Quartets." *Musical Quarterly* 61 (1975):17-46.

Weichlein, William J. "A Comparative Study of Five Settings of Metastasio's Libretto, *La Clemenza di Tito* (1734-1791)." Ph.D. dissertation, University of Michigan, 1956.

Westrup, J.A. "The Paradox of Eighteenth Century Music." In *Studies in Musicology: Essays in the History, Style, and Bibliography of Music in Memory of Glen Haydon.* Edited by James W. Pruett. Chapel Hill: University of North Carolina Press, 1969. pp. 118-32.

Wyzewa, Théodore de. "A propos du centenaire de la mort de Joseph Haydn." *Revue des deux mondes* 51 (1909):935-46.

Yorke-Long, Alan. *Music at Court: Four Eighteenth Century Studies.* London: Weidenfeld & Nicolson, 1954.

Critical Editions and Early Printed Scores

The following bibliography lists, in alphabetical order by composer, modern critical editions (both published and unpublished) and early printed scores. For each opera, the place and date of first performance is mentioned at the conclusion of the standard bibliographical entry.

Ariosti, Attilio. *Vespasiano.* London: By the author, n.d. (London, 1724.)

Arne, Thomas. *Artaxerxes.* London: John Johnson, n.d. (London, 1762.)

Bach, Johann Christian. *La clemenza di Scipione.* London: Welcker, [1778]; Reprint, Farnborough, England: Gregg International, 1972. (London, 1778.)

_____. *The Favorite Songs in the Opera Orione.* London: Welcker, 1763. (London, 1763.)

Gluck, Christoph Willibald. *Iphigénie en Tauride.* Ed., Gerhard Croll. Christoph Willibald Gluck: Sämtliche Werke, Ser. 1, Vol. 9. Kassel: Bärenreiter, 1973. (Paris, 1779.)

_____. *Orfeo ed Euridice.* Ed., Anna Amalie Abert and Ludwig Finscher. Christoph Willibald Gluck: Sämtliche Werke, Ser. 1, Vol. 1. Kassel: Bärenreiter, 1963. (Vienna, 1762.)

_____. *Paride ed Helena.* Ed., Rudolf Gerber. Christoph Willibald Gluck: Sämtliche Werke, Ser 1, Vol. 4. Kassel: Bärenreiter, 1954. (Vienna, 1770.)

_____. *Il re pastore.* Ed., László Somfai. Christoph Willibald Gluck: Sämtliche Werke, Ser. 3, Vol. 8. Kassel: Bärenreiter, 1968. (Vienna, 1756.)

_____. *Telemaco.* Ed., Karl Geiringer. Christoph Willibald Gluck: Sämtliche Werke, Ser. 1, Vol. 2. Kassel: Bärenreiter, 1972. (Vienna, 1765.)

Hasse, Johann Adolph. *Arminio.* Ed., Rudolf Gerber. Das Erbe deutscher Musik, Vol. 27. Mainz: B. Schott's Söhne, 1957. (Dresden, 1753.)

_____. *Ruggiero, ovvero L'eroica gratitudine.* Ed., Klaus Hortschansky. Concentus musicus, Vol. 1. Cologne: Arno Volk, 1973. (Milan, 1771.)

Haydn, Franz Joseph. *Armida.* Ed., Wilhelm Pfannkuch. Joseph Haydn Werke, Ser. 25, Vol. 12. Munich: G. Henle, 1965. (Eszterháza, 1784.)

Jommelli, Niccolò. *Fetonte.* Ed., Hermann Abert. Revised by Hans Joachim Moser. Denkmäler deutscher Tonkunst, Ser. 1, Vols. 32/33. Wiesbaden: Breitkopf & Härtel, 1958. (Stuttgart, 1768.)

_____. *Olimpiade.* Recueil des opéra[s] composés par Nicolas Jom[m]elli à la cour du Sérénissime duc de Wirtemberg. Stuttgart, 1783. (Stuttgart, 1761.)

Mozart, Wolfgang Amadeus. *Idomeneo, re di Creta.* Ed., Daniel Heartz. 2 vols. Wolfgang Amadeus Mozart: Neue Ausgabe sämtlicher Werke, Ser. 2, Vol. 52. Kassel: Bärenreiter, 1972. (Munich, 1781.)

_____. *Lucio Silla.* Wolfgang Amadeus Mozarts Sämtliche Werke, Ser. 5, No. 8. Leipzig: Breitkopf & Härtel; Reprint ed., Ann Arbor, MI: J.W. Edwards, 1955. (Milan, 1772.)

_____. *Mitridate, re di Ponto.* Ed., Luigi Tagliavini. Wolfgang Amadeus Mozart: Neue Ausgabe Sämtlicher Werke, Ser. 2. Vol. 54. Kassel: Bärenreiter, 1966. (Milan, 1770.)

_____. *Il re pastore.* Wolfgang Amadeus Mozarts Sämtliche Werke, Ser. 5, No. 10. Leipzig: Breitkopf & Härtel; Reprint ed., Ann Arbor, MI: J.W. Edwards, 1955. (Salzburg, 1775.)

Scarlatti, Alessandro. *Griselda.* Ed., Donald Jay Grout. The Operas of Alessandro Scarlatti, Vol. 3. Cambridge: Harvard University Press, 1975. (Rome, 1721.)

_____. *Marco Attilio Regolo.* Ed., Joscelyn Godwin. The Operas of Alessandro Scarlatti, Vol. 2. Cambridge: Harvard University Press, 1975. (Rome, 1719.)

Terradellas, Domingo. *La Merope.* Ed., Roberto Gerhard. Barcelona, Diputación provincial de Barcelona, 1951. (Rome, 1743.)

Traetta, Tommaso. *Antigone.* Ed., Aldo Rocchi. Florence, Maggio musicale fiorentino, 1962. (St. Petersburg, 1772.)

_____. *Sofonisba.* Ed., Byron Cantrell. In "Tommaso Traetta and His Opera *Sofonisba.*" Ph.D. dissertation, University of California at Los Angeles, 1957. (Mannheim, 1762.)

Vinci, Leonardo. *Artaserse.* Ed., Robert Burns Meikle. In "Leonardo Vinci's *Artaserse:* An Edition with an Editorial and Critical Commentary." Ph.D. dissertation, Cornell University, 1970. (Rome, 1730.)

Manuscript Scores

The following bibliography lists, in alphabetical order by composer, the manuscript sources consulted. Libraries and the cities in which they are located are represented by the RISM sigla. Autograph scores are indicated by underlined shelf numbers. Scores reproduced in *Italian Opera 1640-1770,* edited by Howard Mayer Brown and Eric Weimer (New York: Garland, 1978 et seq.) are indicated by *"Italian Opera"* and the appropriate volume number.

Bach, Johann Christian

Adriano in Siria (London, 1765)	P-La,	44-II-28 a 30
Artaserse (Turin, 1761)	GB-Lbm,	RM 22 a 18 (incomplete)
	P-La,	54-II-73 a 75
Alessandro nell'Indie	I-Mc,	Noseda B 34
(Naples, 1762)	P-La,	44-II-31 a 33
	US-Wc,	M1500. B14A5
Carattaco (London, 1767)	B-Bc,	2039 (*Italian Opera* 86)
Catone in Utica (Naples, 1761)	I-Nc,	6504
	P-La,	44-II-37 a 39

Orione (London, 1763)	GB-Lbm,	31717
Temistocle (Mannheim, 1772)	US-Wc,	M1500 .B14T3

Bernasconi, Andrea
La clemenza di Tito (Munich, 1768) — F-Pn, — 8348-50 (*Italian Opera* 88)

Bononcini, Antonio Maria
Griselda (Milan, 1718) — BRD-B, — 2185 (*Italian Opera* 21)

Caldara, Antonio
Olimpiade (Vienna, 1733) — A-Wn, — 17164 (*Italian Opera* 32)

Feo, Francesco
Andromaca (Rome, 1730) — GB-Lbm, — 24303 (*Italian Opera* 31)

Galuppi, Baldassare
Olimpiade (Milan, 1747) — I-Mc, — Noseda G99 (*Italian Opera* 41)

Gasparini, Francesco
Il Bajazet, second version (Reggio, 1719) — A-Wn, — 17251 (*Italian Opera* 24)

Giacomelli, Geminiano
Lucio Papirio Dittatore (Parma, 1729) — GB-Lam, — 71

Gluck, Christoph Willibald
Semiramide riconosciuta (Vienna, 1748) — A-Wn, — 17793 (*Italian Opera* 74)

Graun, Carl Heinrich
Artaserse (Berlin, 1743) — BRD-W, — Guelf. 81 (*Italian Opera* 40)

Hasse, Johann Adolf
Achille in Sciro (Naples, 1759) — I-Mc, / P-La, — *Part. Tr. ms. 166* / 46-IV-49 a 51

Artaserse, second version (Naples, 1760) — I-Mc, / P-La, — *Part. Tr. ms. 171* / 46-IV-55 and 46-V-1 e 2

Cleofide (Dresden, 1731) — B-Bc, — 2133

Demofoonte, second version (Naples, 1758) — I-Vc, — *Ospedaletto XIX 325* (Acts I and II only)
— P-La, — 46-IV-40 a 42
— US-Wc, — M1500 .H35D4

Ezio, second version (Dresden, 1755) — A-Wn, — 17292
— I-Mc, — *Part. Tr. ms. 173*
— US-Wc, — M1500 .H35E81

Nitteti (Venice, 1758)	BRD-Mbs, I-Vm,	195 IV-250-251
Olimpiade, first version (Dresden, 1756)	I-Mc,	*Part. Tr. ms. 153*
Il re pastore (Dresden, 1755)	I-Mc, US-Wc,	*Part. Tr. ms. 165* M1500 .H35R4
Romolo ed Ersilia (Innsbruck, 1765)	A-Wn, P-La,	17288 46-IV-43 a 45
Siroe, first version (Bologna, 1733)	A-Wn,	17256 (*Italian Opera* 33)
Siroe, second version (Warsaw, 1763)	I-Mc, US-Wc,	*Part. Tr. ms. 178* M1500 .H35S8
Il trionfo di Clelia (Vienna, 1762)	I-Mc, I-MOe,	*Part. Tr. ms. 158* (*Italian Opera* 83) F 545
Zenobia (Warsaw, 1761)	I-Mc,	*Part. Tr. ms. 163*
Holzbauer, Ignaz *Alessandro nell'Indie* (Milan, 1759)	I-Nc,	1784 (*Italian Opera* 79)
Jommelli, Niccolò *Achille in Sciro,* second version (Rome, 1771)	BRD-B,	11243
Armida abbandonata (Naples, 1770)	US-Wc,	M1500 .J72A4 (copy of B-Bc, K 2182)
Artaserse, second version (Stuttgart, 1756)	P-La, BRD-S1,	44-X-49 a 51 H.B. X 511 730
Creso (Rome, 1757)	US-Wc,	M1500 .J72C6
Demofoonte, second version (Milan, 1753)	I-Nc,	Rari 1.7.1
Demofoonte, third version (Stuttgart, 1764)	B-Bc, BRD-S1,	K 2186 <u>H.B. XVII 240 a/c</u> (*Italian Opera* 48)
Demofoonte, fourth version (Naples, 1770)	I-Mc,	Noseda H 54/I-III
Didone abbandonata, third version (Stuttgart, 1763)	A-Wn,	16488
Enea nel Lazio, second version (Stuttgart, 1766)	I-Nc,	Rari 7.7.25
Ezio, first version Bologna, 1741)	BRD-S1,	<u>H.B. XVII 244 a/c</u>

Ezio, fourth version (Lisbon 1772)	A-Wn,	Sm 9952
Ifigenia in Tauride (Naples, 1771)	US-Wc,	M1500 .J72I6
Pelope (Stuttgart, 1755)	I-Nc,	Rari 7.9.1/2
Semiramide riconosciuta, first version (Turin, 1741)	US-Wc,	M1500 .J72S4
Semiramide riconosciuta, third version (Stuttgart, 1762)	F-Pn,	D 6253/54
Temistocle, first version (Naples, 1757)	US-Wc	M1500 .J72T3
Vologeso (Stuttgart, 1766)	BRD-Sl,	H.B. XVIII 253 a/c

Latilla, Gaetano
Ezio (Naples, 1758)   US-Bh,   104

Leo, Leonardo

Andromaca (Naples, 1743)	DDR-LEm,	3860 (*Italian Opera* 39)
Demetrio (Naples, 1741)	I-Mc,	F 92
Demofoonte, second version (Naples, 1741)	GB-Lbm,	16043/44
Farnace (Naples, 1736)	A-Wn,	17715

Lotti, Antonio
Alessandro severo (Venice, 1716) DDR-Dlb, 2159 .F2 (*Italian Opera* 20)

Maio, Gian Francesco di

Adriano in Siria (Rome, 1769)	B-Bc,	2198 (*Italian Opera* 49)
Demofoonte (Rome, 1764)	F-Pn,	D 7257

Pergolesi, Giovanni Battista
Olimpiade (Rome, 1735)   B-BC,   2287 (*Italian Opera* 34)

Piccinni, Nicola
Catone in Utica (Mannheim, 1770)

            BRD-Mbs, 2424
            GB-Lbm   30792-4 (*Italian Opera* 50)

Porsile, Giuseppe
Spartaco (Vienna, 1726)   A-Wn,   18010 (*Italian Opera* 28)

Rinaldo di Capua
Vologeso (Rome, 1739)   US-NHu,   11 (*Italian Opera* 38)

Sarri, Domenico
Arsace (Naples, 1718)   I-Mc,   Noseda G 11 (*Italian Opera* 22)

Sarti, Giuseppe
    Didone abbandonata   DK-Kk,   689 P (*Italian Opera* 84)
    (Copenhagen, 1762)

Scarlatti, Alessandro
    Telemaco (Rome, 1718)   A-Wn,   16487 (*Italian Opera* 23)

Terradellas, Domingo
    Sesostri (Rome, 1751)   BRD-MUp,   4139 (*Italian Opera* 43)

Traetta, Tommaso
    Armida (Vienna, 1761)   A-Wn,   17861

    Ifigenia in Tauride (Vienna,   I-Fc,   Basevi 306 (*Italian Opera* 47)
    1763

    Siroe (Munich, 1767)   BRD-Mbs,   168

Vinci, Leonardo
    Catone in Utica (Rome, 1728)   BRD-B,   22376

    Didone abbandonata (Rome,   US-Cn,   Case VM 1500.V77d
    1726)   (*Italian Opera* 29)

Vivaldi, Antonio
    Griselda (Venice, 1735)   I-Tn,   Foà 36 (*Italian Opera* 35)

    Orlando, second version   I-Tn,   Giordano 39
    (Venice, 1727)

    Tito Manlio (Mantua, 1719)   I-Tn,   Foà 37

Wagenseil, Georg Christoph
    Ariodante (Venice, 1745)   A-Wn,   18019 (*Italian Opera* 73)

Index

ABB theme. *See also* Arias; Themes; and individual composers
—A section (first vocal), 11-12, 38: cadential phrase in, 31; duration, 30-*31, 33,* 37; instability, resolution of, 16; key, dominant, 16; sonata form in, 16; structure of, 15-16; text, setting, 17-18: and rhythm, 20, 23-24; and syllable and word accentuation, 18, *20-23,* 24; two-strophe, 15
—accompaniment, *61-62. See also* Wind ensembles, accompanimental; and Wind ensembles, independent melodic
—B section (second vocal): duration, 30, 37; instability, resolution of, 16; key, tonic, 16; text, setting, 17-18
—bass line in, *33-34;* Trommelbass, *42-43*
—cadence in, 18, 35: ascending bass line, expanded, *34-35;* duration, 32
—cadential phrase in, 18-19, 28, 31-32, *34-35*
—characteristics of, *30-32,* 33-34
—duration, 34, 37
—expansion of, 29-30, 33-*34, 36-37, 38-39, 42-*43
—formulas, 37; harmonic, 30, *31-33*
—Italian influence on, 41-42
—origins of, 18-19
—structure and purpose of, 18-20
—style change in, 36-37, 41-42
—text, 18, 19: setting of, 18, 20, 22; syllabication, and rhythm, *20-22;* word accentuation, and rhythm, *20-22*
Abert, Hermann, cited, 50
Accompaniment (*See also* Wind ensembles, accompanimental; Wind instrumentation); and bass line, rhythmic organization, 59-*60;* and melody, style change in, 25, 48, 54-55; and nonharmonic tones, use of, 59, 61-*62;* horns, use of, 70; motivic, rhythmic organization of, *58;* rhythm, organization of, 13, 61, 70, *73;* upper, and bass line, style change in, 55, 57-*58,* 59; woodwinds, use of, 70

Algarotti, Francesco, and opera seria reform, 25
Alignment, long-term, 61; short-term (vertical), *57-59*
Arias (*See also* under individual composers, works)
—A section (first vocal), 11-13: ABB theme, use of, 18-20, 27; alignment, vertical, and bass line, style change in, *57-58;* brevity of (ca. 1710-1730), 28; cadence in, *71-72;* instability and resolution, 16; omission of, 27; sonata form in, 16; structure, and text, 15-16; text, setting of, 17-18, 29; texture, style change in, *71-72;* wind ensemble, accompanimental, use of, 123-24, *125-29,* 130, 134-35, *136-40*
—accompaniment (*See also* Wind ensembles, accompanimental); and melody, relation of, 49; upper, and bass line, style change in, 57, *58-60*
—alignment, vertical, and bass line, style change in, *57-60*
—allegretto, 13
—allegro (fast) duple meter, 13, 28, *App. A-C:* rhythmic organization, melodic syncopation in, *55-56;* texture, 50; woodwinds, style change in, 96-97
—B section (second vocal): accompaniment, motivic, rhythmic organization of, *58;* modified da capo, 16-17, 27; text, setting, 16-18; wind ensemble, accompanimental, use of, 131, 135, 140
—bass line, style change in rhythmic organization, 55, 57
—cadences in, *71-72*
—cadential phrase in, 12, 18, 28
—caesura in, 19-20
—expansion of, size and harmonic, 27
—half da capo, 12, 27
—key, secondary, expanded, 27
—manuscript sources, 9-10
—melisma in, 17